DR. EDWARD BENES
PRESIDENT OF THE CZECHOSLOVAK REPUBLIC

in attempting a faithful sketch of the growth of Bohemian music from its origin to the present day.

At the very outset of my task I am confronted by a chain of difficulties. In the first place it is doubtful how far the mass of the British people has, even yet, come to connect the Republic of Czechoslovakia with Bohemia; while for long they definitely continued to connect Bohemia with Germany. For many years after the Great War the Czechs appeared to us as Germans seeking re-entrance among us under a fresh pseudonym; or, if they were accepted as identical with the Bohemians of old, they still seemed to us undesirable aliens; because the link between Bohemia and the Slavonic countries has never been clearly established in our minds.

Bohemia's past history with all that it signified for the rest of Europe remained long the sphere of specialists only. A 'Bohemian' conjured up for us the vision of a shaggy person of uncertain origin, endowed with an uncanny and ill-disciplined musical talent, leading the kind of life picturesquely described by Henri Murger in his famous novel *La Vie de Bohême*. Shakespeare, though he generously bestowed upon Bohemia the seaboard which, if it had existed in practical politics to-day, would have saved many Central European problems, hit her people a shrewd blow when he made the host of the Garter Inn, in *The Merry Wives of Windsor*, allude to a 'Bohemian-Tartar'. The term is there used to describe the strange appearance of Simple. But Tollet in a footnote to the play elucidates it thus: 'In Germany were several companies of vagabonds called Tartars and Zigens (Tsiganes); these were the same in Mezeray's opinion as those the French call Bohemians and the English gipsies.'

I am not sure that we have progressed far from this point of view. And yet, for all our ignorance, the history of Bohemia has occasionally converged with our own at interesting points of contact. In 1381, Richard II of England married Anne, sister of Wenceslaus, King of Bohemia. This was not the famous Wenceslaus (Vaclav I), saint and monarch, of whom we sing in our popular Christmas carol, but the fourth prince of that name to rule over Bohemia. There was a strong affinity between our Wycliff and Jan Hus. Again in 1641, that enlightened reformer Jan Amos Komensky (Comenius) visited England, and, under the auspices of the Long Parliament, proposed to found an academy on his own system of 'Pansophy'. The need for a universal

CHAPTER I

THERE is more than a grain of truth in the old proverb which says that every Czech is born, not indeed with a silver spoon in his mouth, but with a violin under his pillow. This saying may certainly be accepted as a time-honoured testimony to the innate musical proclivities of this nation which forms the western vanguard of the Slavonic race.

The history of the musical development of Bohemia, or as it is now called, Czechoslovakia, is very closely allied to her geographical position. Bohemia, a Slav country set for centuries like an island surrounded by assailant and erosive seas, passed through long periods of spiritual oppression during which at times her national individuality was in peril of total extinction. But her lot on the whole has been less cruel than that of the Slavonic countries situated further east, such as Serbia and Bulgaria, because she escaped the devastating sequels of the Ottoman conquest. The forces which surrounded Bohemia, pressing ever more heavily as the centuries went by upon her vitality, ignoring the very fact of her existence,[1] stifling her aspirations, silencing her speech and song, were, at the worst, Western forces; consequently not so wholly arrestive to culture as the domination of Turkey in Europe has invariably proved to be. In some paradoxical way the Czechs seem to have assimilated from their oppressors certain organized energies which, lacking to their sister races, have enabled them to put up a stouter and more persistent resistance against a long and determined effort to absorb them into the Germanic element.

In this book I deal with one of the forces which have saved the Czechs from falling into such racial apathy as would have ended in a fatally complete fusion with her rapacious neighbours.

The undying and passionate love of their mother-tongue and the songs which belong to it, has been a mystical food to the Czech soul, sustaining it through long periods of desolation. But because Czech music is so closely bound up with Czech history and geography it is difficult to understand it if we entirely ignore the past; I cannot avoid trenching a little on political vicissitudes

[1] 'The Austrian Government does not recognize the existence of a Czech question.' Prince Windischgraetz, President of the Council of Ministers, February 1894.

B   I

Smetana, and gave the London musical public the chance of hearing this very important work by the man who had devoted his life to the foundation of National Opera in Prague. We must never forget that Prague gave the breath of life—encouragement —to the young Mozart when his *Figaro* was produced there, and how he expressed eternal gratitude for the warmth of his reception, following the dispiriting and intriguing atmosphere of Vienna. Perhaps his *Don Giovanni* would never have proved the masterpiece it is but for the kindly warmth and enthusiasm that the Prague public lavished on its first performance there.

Chorally the Czechoslovaks have a fine tradition which they have built up for many years, with the result that their male-voice choirs are outstanding. We were fortunate in 1919 to hear the Prague and Moravian Teachers' Choirs when they first visited London for a Czechoslovak Festival in Queen's Hall, and set a standard hard to beat when they gave us the opportunity of hearing the choruses of Križkovsky and other native composers.

Her chapters on more recent composers such as Novák, Suk, Ostrčil, Vycpalek (whose interesting cantata *The Last Things of Man* I produced with the Liverpool Philharmonic Society in 1928), and Janáček (whose original *Slavonic Festival Mass* I introduced at the Norwich Musical Festival in the same year) will, I hope, draw attention to these less-known men. For both of these works Rosa Newmarch made *singable* English translations.

Of course Dvořák has always held his rightful place in our musical world, but I am not in agreement with those who regard his music in the light of a lesser Brahms. It is a pity that our musical public have taken his *New World* Symphony so much to heart as to neglect more or less his other symphonies. There is also the deeply interesting Violin Concerto so rarely performed, while the Violoncello Concerto is comparatively well known, and has been played by all the virtuosos. His chamber music is most lovely, full of beautiful themes, handled with a freshness of invention and outlook which stamp him as the greatest of Bohemian composers. is there extant a work more lovely than his choral masterpiece, the *Stabat Mater*? And why is that great dramatic cantata, *The Spectre's Bride*, so sadly neglected?

HENRY J. WOOD

Hove, 1942

INTRODUCTION

I know it was Mrs. Rosa Newmarch's wish that I should write this introduction, but having read her wonderfully interesting and comprehensive volume on the music of Czechoslovakia, anything I could say would be utterly redundant; and the only claim I can lay to my dear old friend's faith in any value such a preface would have is my long association with practically every Czech composer, so many of whose works I have introduced and conducted in the past forty-seven years, together with many other compositions of Slavonic origin.

It was fortunate indeed that Rosa Newmarch's last literary work should be devoted to Czechoslovak music, for I know of no one so well entitled and endowed with intimate knowledge of the peoples of that country. She had a deep affection for them all, and she herself had the right temperament to understand the characteristics of the people, and also the complete musical intuition which gave to her just that flair and authenticity for the task she has so charmingly and faithfully fulfilled within these pages.

I little thought, when in 1908 I persuaded her to write the Analytical Programme Notes for the Queen's Hall Symphony, Sunday, and Promenade Concerts, that I had opened a portal which led to a lifelong friendship, and a musical association which on so many occasions enabled me to gain insight into the vast array of Czechoslovak composers. She not only knew their language and literature, but was an intimate friend of the leading literary, musical, and political lights of the Bohemian firmament. For many years she had made long sojourns among them, entering into their everyday, care-free lives in such intimacy that their traditions and customs, their aspirations and line of thought, were as an open book to her: indeed her long association with the *people* developed into a very deep and lasting affection for the *arts* of Czechoslovakia.

I am positive that this work will have very far-reaching and helpful results in the interests of Czech music, as it draws attention to many composers with whom we are as yet only slightly acquainted.

I remember with pleasure that in 1906 I played at Queen's Hall the cycle of six symphonic poems, *My Fatherland*, by that it is worth while fighting for the freedom of a nation which gave the world the music of which she here writes with such admiration, love, and understanding, the present volume will contribute powerfully to this end.

EDWARD BENEŠ

CONTENTS

					PAGE
FOREWORD	.	.	.	.	v
INTRODUCTION	.	.	.	.	vii
CHAPTER					
I	.	.	.	.	1
II	.	.	.	.	10
III	.	.	.	.	19
IV	.	.	.	.	32
V	.	.	.	.	41
VI	.	.	.	.	54
VII	.	.	.	.	81
VIII	.	.	.	.	104
IX	.	.	.	.	125
X	.	.	.	.	152
XI	.	.	.	.	176
XII	.	.	.	.	195
XIII	.	.	.	.	211
XIV	.	.	.	.	228
INDEX	.	.	.	.	241

The Editor's thanks are due to those English and Czechoslovak friends who have kindly helped in the revision of the author's posthumous work.

FOREWORD

On the invitation of the publishers I have much pleasure in contributing a Foreword to this book. This first of all because it provides me with an opportunity of expressing in this way the thanks of the whole Czechoslovak nation for the splendid work which was performed by our never-to-be forgotten friend Rosa Newmarch in making our music known in England and elsewhere in the world. And secondly because I can here emphasize how highly we Czechoslovaks value music and culture generally, and how deeply conscious we are of the important part which is played by the exchange of cultural possessions in the political association between different peoples.

Hus, Komenský, Hollar, Smetana, Dvořák, Masaryk, Čapek—to mention only a few of the names which are already known to you in this country—were all workers in the cultural field. But their significance, and that of their works, is also political. Through their instrumentality the world was enriched by the contribution to common culture which has been made by our people. Through the genius expressed in their works our nation acquired universal respect. Their spiritual greatness helped to convince the world that the people which they represented had a right to an independent political existence.

From the Hussite chant 'You who are warriors of God', before the sonorous measures of which the German armies fell back in disorder five hundred years ago, there stretches an unbroken succession of musical works which, in addition to being on a high artistic level, have at the same time been a manifestation of the indomitable spirit of our nation. And on the other hand the fight which is to-day being conducted by the Czechoslovak people for the renewal of their political independence is at the same time a fight for the values of the human spirit, which received an eternal expression in the works of Smetana, Dvořák, Fibich, Suk, Janáček, and those other composers to whom in this book Rosa Newmarch has dedicated such penetrating studies.

In this, her posthumous work, which brings to a conclusion her fruitful and valuable labours, for which we Czechoslovaks shall never cease to be grateful, I see a contribution by our great friend to our struggle to-day. For if it is at all necessary to demonstrate

OXFORD UNIVERSITY PRESS
AMEN HOUSE, E.C.4
London   Edinburgh   Glasgow   New York
Toronto   Melbourne   Capetown   Bombay
Calcutta   Madras
HUMPHREY MILFORD
PUBLISHER TO THE UNIVERSITY

First published 1942
Reprinted - 1943

The Music of
CZECHOSLOVAKIA

ROSA NEWMARCH

OXFORD UNIVERSITY PRESS

LONDON   NEW YORK   TORONTO

BUST OF SMETANA

J. V. MYSLBEK

language and a league of nations were features of his teaching. The Irish rebellion and other impending troubles diverted the thoughts of Parliament and the scheme proved abortive. But Comenius during his sojourn among us awakened the interest and sympathy of no less a personage than John Milton.

Later on, when we come to consider the conditions of their social life in the eighteenth century, it will be easy to understand how the ideas of the Bohemians as a dispossessed and wandering people became implanted in those happier countries wherein so many of them took refuge. Meanwhile the tradition of the essential vagabondage of the race may be allowed to drop into the oblivion which is gradually swallowing up many national fables since the peoples of the world have intermixed so frankly and freely on the field, and in the camps and hospitals, during the Great War and in the present conflict.

The Bohemians, whose early literature was largely of a mystical and controversially religious type, and whose University, founded at Prague by Charles IV in 1348, attracted students from England as well as from the Continental countries, have been for centuries distinguished by a serious intelligence, and do not resemble the type depicted by gossip and prejudice. The part played by the Czechoslovak legions during the Great War of 1914–18, on various fronts—and more especially in Siberia—proved them to be a race of rare energy, organizing power, and intrepidity. They asked, and received, the help of the democratic nations in re-establishing their freedom; they asked that we should study their ideals and their culture, and decide if indeed they were worthy of friendship and moral support. But although the allied powers established the freedom of the Czechoslovak Republic[1] they did not, as events have shown, preserve its integrity. The work of emancipation, political and social, begun by President Masaryk, with all the *naïvetés* and deficiencies which stamp a young generation not yet completely educated for the democracy bestowed upon it, and the difficulty of a swift transformation of ideals into action, have, as evinced by the Munich Four-Power Agreement, been totally and shamefully ignored.

It was not mere coincidence that enabled the Czechs to use their freedom better than did any of the other newly-enfranchised peoples. Less versatile and experimentive than the Russians of

[1] On 21 July 1920, the British Government granted recognition of the newly established Czechoslovak Government.

the days before the last war; lacking the mystical qualities of the Serbs, but better organized mentally: the soundness of the Czechs has made itself felt in all our dealings with them, even when it meant the forfeit of territory rightfully won.

Is it now too late for music to be the telepathic link between ourselves and this nation whose self-determination we helped to assure? Undoubtedly music is the most direct expression of the Czech national temperament; a language which we can readily understand and which they know how to speak eloquently and forcibly to all who are interested to hear.

The very early history of Bohemian music is wrapped in obscurity. It seems probable that it progressed on similar lines to that of Russia, and that the primitive songs of both lands, incurring the disapproval of the first evangelizers on account of their pagan tendencies, were zealously suppressed. In Russia, on account of its vast area, these 'diabolical' songs found places of refuge in the extreme north such as were not available in smaller Bohemia, where traces of them are much rarer. So much so, that some authorities believe there was no singing among the Bohemians until after their conversion to Christianity. With the tenth century more authentic details about music are available. Adalbert, the second Bishop of Prague, canonized as St. Vojtech after his death in 997, is said to have composed the venerable 'Hospodine pomiluj ny' (*Kyrie eleison*), of which Ambros writes in his *Geschichte der Musik* that it was probably the oldest example of such sequentiae, introduced in the time of the first missionaries to the Slavs, SS. Cyril and Methodius. This plainchant melody in the form in which it was composed, or arranged, by Adalbert, was specially permitted to be sung at Mass by Pope John XV, A.D. 922. Apart from the liturgy, it was sung by the people in time of warfare, of drought, and at other grave crises in the national life. Another venerable and venerated tune is the *Hymn of St. Vaclav* (Wenceslaus) which may have originated as early as the eleventh century, although its author is usually said to be Arnestus, first Archbishop of Prague (1345–78). It takes the form of a *Kyrielle*, each verse, after invoking the intercession of St. Vaclav on behalf of his people, ending with the *Kyrie eleison*, which on the lips of the uneducated folk was pronounced Krles. Like the 'Hospodine pomiluj ny', this hymn became a famous ceremonial song, and in the fifteenth century it was adopted by the Catholics in opposition to the Hussite hymn, 'All ye who are Warriors of God'.

As early as the foundation of the bishopric of Prague, in 973, the need for attracting the new converts—and perhaps of consoling them for the loss of their primitive songs—by means of an impressive musical ritual, was clearly felt. The love of religious ceremonial, thus early implanted in the hearts of the Czechs, still abides with them, as may be seen at any of the great pilgrimages at which frequent musical services, religious processions, and the lusty singing of the old Gregorian hymns, seem to exercise a more powerful attraction than 'all the fun of the fair', carried on simultaneously in booths pitched just outside the church square.

The Cathedral of St. Vitus at Prague was the centre of musical activity during the eleventh and twelfth centuries. In the second half of the thirteenth century there are records of a new organ having been built for the Cathedral, and in 1259 provision was made for a choir of twelve boys ('bonifantes') and the singers with worn voices were weeded out and replaced by new ones.

Archbishop Arnestus was certainly a musician of capacity, and it was due to his influence that the art was included in the curriculum of the University founded in his day in Prague. The head of the Music School, Záviš (1379–1418), may be described as the Bohemian Tallis. It is claimed that he wrote at least one famous love-song and probably brought into vogue the dancing-songs which began to be popular about that time.

Until the close of the fourteenth century few details are to be learnt about secular music in Bohemia. Of instrumental music, it is recorded that when Břetislav I made his triumphal entrance into Prague he was welcomed by joyous bands of youths and maidens dancing to the sound of drums and pipes. At the coronation of Vaclav II (1297) eight instruments are enumerated as having been used on the occasion. Hostinsky gives their Latin names: *tympana, nabla, chori, tuba sambucique sonori, rota, figella,* and *lira.* Individual musicians remain anonymous, almost the only exception being Dobrata, who is mentioned as 'joculator' at the Court of Duke Vladislav I, early in the twelfth century. After a lifetime of faithful service he was rewarded by a grant of land at Vysoké Mýto.

Secular music, such as it was, must have been greatly influenced by the political relations of the state and coloured by the tastes which happened to prevail at Court. From the close of the Přemysl dynasty until the advent of John of Luxembourg brought French culture to the fore, German influence was paramount.

The education of the Crown Prince in Paris gave occasion for frequent communication between the two countries. The illustrious troubadour, Guillaume Machaut (1284–1377), for thirty years private secretary to John of Luxembourg, gave an impetus to the study of French music and verse at the Court of Bohemia.

Charles IV outdid all his predecessors in the patronage of music. In his day the Chapter of the Cathedral of St. Vitus maintained at least 150 choristers. The Passion Plays and the 'Laments of the Virgin Mary' gave the first impulse to dramatic music, for though the themes of the latter were borrowed from the Church, their treatment was in the popular style. Charles's love of the art extended to secular music. He liked to hear jocund trumpet-music on holidays, and was liberal and gracious to his court musicians.

The linguistic conflict between the Latin of the Western ritual and the Slavonic of the Eastern rite was a prominent feature of Bohemian church history. Latin was introduced by the priests of the Roman Church—German Catholics—who superseded the Graeco-Slavonic monks in 1096. St. Methodius, Archbishop of Moravia, was then dead, but the language into which he and his fellow missioner,[1] St. Cyril, had translated the Scriptures and liturgical books remained dear to his converts. The use of Latin was associated with the German interlopers; thus we see how many centuries old is this question of the rights of country and language in Bohemia.

An old legend of St. Procopius relates how his ghost, revisiting his own monastery of Sazava and finding the Germans—cuckoos then as since—snugly in possession, tells them roundly that it was not for their benefit that he had founded the institution. 'Ye are infamous Hungarians,[2] sprung from anywhere,' thus the irate apparition apostrophises the intruders—'delay not, get ye quickly back to Prague.' Procopius, knowing with whom he had to deal, had recourse also to physical persuasion and trounced the Germans so severely with a stout cudgel that they were glad to flee from this form of 'spirit-rapping' and leave the monastery to its rightful Slavonic owners.

---

[1] Two alphabets were invented by these missionaries: the *glagolithic*, and the *cyrillic*, which is still used in the Serbian and Orthodox Russian liturgies.

[2] 'Germans' or 'Hungarians' are interchangeable terms of opprobrium in the Czechoslovak legends and folk-songs, just as Germans and Tatars are confounded in the Russian popular literature.

To return to the safer ground of historical fact. The Czechs never entirely lost their invincible pride in their own language, and Charles IV—in some respects a good nationalist—restored, with the Pope's sanction, the Slavonic liturgy, so that for a while the citizens of Prague could hear the service bequeathed to them by their first apostles sung by Byzantine monks in the royal monastery of Emaus, while elsewhere the Ambrosian plainchant, introduced from Milan, was in general use.

Amid all this ecclesiastical pomp and activity, Záviš's rare examples of profane art must have struck a contrasting note.

The Hussite Wars (1419–68) turned men's minds from secular music. Love-songs, drinking- and dancing-songs, did not accord with the grim struggles of conscience which then absorbed the Bohemian people. Hus himself was quick to realize the great power of music as a propagandist force. In his time the Latin hymns were eagerly translated into the vernacular. Hymns which are practically fierce war-songs were composed, or adapted to fresh words, and collected in finely illuminated manuscripts by the Unity of the Bohemian Brethren, who exercised great influence in Moravia. Each religious party had its own hymns, which expressed its individual aspirations. The Utraquists, or Calixtines, represented the moderate followers of Hus; while the Táborites, or extreme reformers, who occupied the town of Tábor under the leadership of the famous warrior John Žižka, were in many respects the Tolstoyites of the fifteenth century. One of the oldest and most famous Hussite hymns, 'All ye, champions of th' Almighty', much sung by the fighting forces of Czechoslovakia during the Great War, is said to have been written by one of Žižka's soldiers, which would put the date of the composition somewhere about 1419.

From the last decade of the fifteenth century until the battle of the White Mountain[1] (1620) wrought ruin to the national life of Bohemia, music was more widely cultivated and less exclusively ecclesiastical than in Russia during the same period.

Imitating the example of their sovereign, Ferdinand I, who

[1] The desperate efforts of the Czechs to free themselves from Austria were completely defeated on this occasion. The leaders of the movement were executed; the nobility scattered; the towns implicated in the rising were crushed under punitive taxation; books in the Czech language were burnt wholesale. The Slavonic population dropped from 3,000,000 to 800,000. In 1790, the historian Pelcl believed that another half century would witness the extinction of the race.

founded the first Court Chapel in Bohemia, the nobles began to set up their own private bands, the most famous of which belonged to the powerful house of Rosenburg, or Rozmberk. This family possessed a superb music library, comprising works by Orlando di Lasso, Melchior Franck, Phillipe de Monte—representative in fact of all the medieval schools of European music. An independent music school was established in Prague in 1616, and already half a century earlier Brother Blahoslav (1523–71) had collected the songs and hymns of the Moravian 'Unity', and published his famous theoretical treatise, *Musica*. Native talent was encouraged by a prosperous *bourgeoisie*, who organized musical societies in the cities. Nor were the working classes excluded from this aesthetic activity. Musical education must have been fairly general if, as Hantich tells us in his brochure, *La Musique Tchèque*, the folk at this time found no difficulty in joining correctly in two-, three-, and four-part church music.

Among the Bohemian composers of the sixteenth century one of the most prominent was Johann Trajan Turnovský, parish priest of Netvor and Sepekov, some of whose works have been preserved in the manuscript song-book of Benešov, now in the library of the Prague Conservatoire. It is remarkable, as Dr. Branberger has pointed out, that Trajan makes use of the true male voice choir at a period when it was extremely rare. Women and boys took no part in medieval choral singing; the soprano and alto parts in the works of Palestrina were taken by *falsetti*; nevertheless three- and four-part choral works for soprano and alto, corresponding to our female voice choir, were rather the rule than the exception in the sixteenth century. It is therefore surprising to find how often Trajan wrote distinctively for male voices. Frequently he places his higher voices in the C alto clef, but keeps them low, moving in a narrow compass; but there are many instances in which he writes for his higher voices in the tenor clef, thus making a practice of what was an exceptional procedure at that time. It is evident that he must have been one of the earliest, if not the very first, of the sixteenth-century composers to use the true male chorus. How he came to write in this way remains a problem, but, says Dr. Branberger, it is certain that in this respect the Bohemian school takes precedence of its contemporaries.

Trajan was a great artist. His works, which were written to Bohemian words, will bear comparison with those of the masters of Italy and the Netherlands. 'He has a character of his own; his own style and original method of construction,' says Branberger. 'He combines his parts with great skill, sometimes in homophony, sometimes quite independently and in imitation. He does not shrink from audacious dissonances. . . . The sonority of his male choruses is fine. All is resonant and well developed. It is difficult to believe that Trajan was the first to make use of this style in Bohemia. Perhaps in practice it existed before his time although every trace of it is lost to us.'

Trajan's male choruses in five and six parts are short masterpieces. One or two of these have been sung at historical concerts in Prague,[1] and well justified the title bestowed upon the composer, 'the Palestrina of Bohemia'.

[1] Dr. Branberger in his article 'Der Männerchor in Böhmen im 16ten Jahrhunderte' cites in particular two choruses, 'The glad day now appears', and 'Praised be the Lord Jesus Christ'.

CHAPTER II

LET me now glance back once more to the fatal year, 1620, when the Battle of the White Mountain sealed the doom of Bohemian independence for three centuries to come. In other countries, at that period, modern music was beginning to emerge from the old polyphonic school. But just when Monteverde had shown in his *Arianna* how to express intensity of emotion in dramatic music and the outlook of the art was bright with new hopes and un-dreamed-of possibilities, Bohemia, so richly endowed with musical intelligence, lost her place among the nations and was reduced to the status of a German province.

Ferdinand II, a conscientious bigot, proceeded from religious persecution to the systematic stifling of all civil liberty and intellectual aspiration. Towns were deprived of their charters, law courts of their powers of jurisdiction, universities and schools of their national character.

By the end of the Thirty Years War (1618–48) the Bohemian peasantry had sunk into a species of serfdom under the heel of an alien aristocracy. Many of the nobles into whose possession the land passed under Austrian rule acquired their vast estates because of their notorious zeal in keeping down the indigenous population. In the second generation, after the new nobility had acquired hereditary rights, there may have been some relaxation of tyranny, but the account of the peasant risings which occurred from time to time prove that the oppression was often intolerable. The people lived in such extreme poverty that they were fortunate who could add some trade, or other honest occupation, to the cultivation of their impoverished plots of land. Amid all this wretchedness, there were certain ways whereby the children of the poorer classes might improve their circumstances. The one most in favour was to go into service in the 'great house' of the district, castle, or manor as the case might be, and to obtain the situation of groom, scullion, footman, or forester was the desire of most of the young village folk. It meant to them warmth, good clothing— even though it were a livery—and plenty of food. 'The Castle' employed a number of servants of both sexes who were indispensable to the life of pleasure led by the gentry of those days, which included balls, concerts, and hunting parties. The candidates for domestic service were chosen from the peasants on the recommendation of the bailiff or the clergy. But there was one thing that strongly influenced a young man's chances of being accepted in his lordship's household—a promise of musical talent. Among the foresters and huntsmen, the lad who could play a rousing 'call' upon the horn was more appreciated than an unmusical dependent with a knowledge of woodcraft. In some of the noble families teachers were employed to examine the huntsmen as to their capacity to supply the 'harmony' on hunting-horns and bugles that was such a characteristic feature of the chase in those days.[1] The fanfares were often in four or five parts, and besides these and the various 'calls', or signals, the horn music sometimes took a more extended form on special occasions. The tradition of excellent horn-playing has always lingered among the Czechs. The huntsmen were often repaid in kind for their lusty music, a hare or a chunk of venison being the reward of a cheery and well-sustained fanfare. In 1682, Count František A. Špork sent two of his dependents to study the horn in Paris where, under Louis XIII, it had been much cultivated as an adjunct to sport.

Nor was music neglected among the indoor servants. As in Russia at about the same period, the household domestics supplied the material for the master's private band. The three brothers Havelka in the service of Count Rudolf Chotek doubled their duties in this way; Augustine the cook was oboist and violinist, František the scullion was a clarinet player, and Wenceslaus the confectioner was also a clarinettist. Josef Overmeyer a violinist of some repute, a pupil of Kamel and Tartini, was a footman in the establishment of Prince Fürstenberg. Sometimes, as in the case of Joseph Haydn, who was engaged as director of the music to Count Morzin of Lukavice at a salary of about £20 a year, no second or more menial office was required of him. The system of patronage, repellent as it may be to a democratic generation, worked well in practice, at any rate in Bohemia and Moravia, where the nobles furnished many instances of kindness to young musicians, giving them opportunities not only for the cultivation of their art, but for their general intellectual progress. For what

---

[1] And not only of the chase. Lady Mary Wortley-Montagu in a letter written from Vienna in January 1717, says of the public balls: 'the music is good, if they had not that detestable habit of mixing hunting horns with it that almost deafen the company. But that noise is so agreeable here they never make a concert without them.'

was the alternative in those days? In eighteenth-century Bohemia, education in the rural schools was still very inadequate. In summer the children did not attend because they could be more useful on the land; in winter only those provided with boots and warm clothing would walk to the village schools. Yet even under adverse circumstances illiteracy has never been very rife in Bohemia. In the winter of 1787 in certain districts the school attendance rose to about sixty-two per cent of the able-bodied children. Poor as was the general teaching, music does not seem to have been neglected in these schools. Burney in his 'Tours'[1] bears witness to this fact. 'I crossed Bohemia from south to north,' he writes in 1772, 'and being very assiduous in my inquiries how the common people learned music, I found out at length that not only in every large town, but in all villages where there is a reading and writing school, children of both sexes are taught music. At Teuchenbrod, Janich, Czaslau, Bonischbrod, and other places, I visited these schools; and at Czaslau I caught them in the act. . . . I went into the school which was full of little children of both sexes, from six to ten or eleven years old, who were reading, writing, playing on violins, hautbois, bassoons, and other instruments. The organist (also the schoolmaster) had in a small room of his house four clavichords, with little boys practising on them all; his son of nine years old was a very good performer.'

'Many of those who learn music', continues Burney, 'go afterwards to the plough and to other laborious employments; and then their knowledge of music turns to no other account than to enable them to sing in their parish church, and as an innocent domestic recreation, which are, perhaps, among the best and most unexceptionable purposes that music can be applied to.'

What I have written in this volume with regard to the church singing and the folk-song meetings shows that the keen interest taken in these forms of recreation still remained amongst the Czechoslovaks a hundred and fifty years after Burney's visit.

The love of this art among the upper classes in Bohemia was not limited to listening to the playing of their dependents. Frequently they themselves took a more active part in the performance of music.

One of the most remarkable instances of the dissemination of

[1] *The Present State of Music in Germany, the Netherlands, and United Provinces*, by Charles Burney, Mus.D., F.R.S. Vol. ii.

musical talent throughout every division of Bohemian society is that of Christopher Harant of Polžic[1] (1564–1621), a nobleman who was not only an excellent painter, but a literary man and a composer. Harant has left a book entitled: *A Journey from the Kingdom of Bohemia to Venice, and thence to the Holy Land, and the Land of Judea, and still further to Egypt; visiting later Mount Horeb, Sinai and St. Catherine in the Desert of Arabia* (1608). In this volume appears a Motet in six parts, *Qui confidunt*, which proves this Bohemian humanist and poet to have been also a great master of vocal polyphony, to whom all the technique of the Netherlands school was child's play. This Motet was composed in Jerusalem, in 1598, and Harant was incited to the work by a little company of pious monks who were also accomplished musicians. The traveller relates how they used to assemble on a balcony and sing 'various beautiful motets and compositions in four or five parts'. It would be interesting to know what they sang under the clear evening sky of Palestine. Works of the older school of Josquin des Prés, or John of Limburg? The comparatively new compositions of Palestrina and his contemporaries? Or, since communication with the Holy Land extended to all Europe, some of Tallis's *Cantiones Sacrae*, or a lovely motet by Taverner or Shepherd? Or were there among the company other composers as apt and capable as Christopher Harant of Polžic, so that they were able to make their own music in every sense of the word?

There is no doubt that a systematic search of private collections in Czechoslovakia might reveal some musical treasures of this epoch by native artists other than Harant.

In spite of the formation of the *Collegium Musicum*, in 1616, organized musical life in Prague did not make rapid progress. After the catastrophe of the White Mountain, four years later, the concerts of the college were never again given in public. It was not until the eighteenth century that musical institutions became an important factor in the social life of Prague. Three citizens, whose names deserve to be recorded in every history of Czech music, approached the Austrian Vice-Regent with a petition to enable them to found an Academy of Music: George Adalbert Kalivoda, Philip Franz Kreutzberger, and Jan Živný. Of these, two were professional musicians: Živný being esteemed as a horn-

---

[1] For some account of Christopher Harant of Polžic, see *Musikgeschichtliches aus Böhmen*, by Dr. Johann Branberger, of the Ministry of Education and Public Enlightenment in the Czechoslovak Republic.

player, while Kalivoda was a composer and lutenist, probably one of those who gathered around the celebrated amateur lute-player, Count Logi. The petition was favourably received subject to a suitable patron being found to lend official countenance to the project. Baron Hartig, a distinguished amateur, was suggested for the position.

While Count Logi was famed far afield as one of the finest lutenists of his day, Baron Hartig and his friend Anton von Adlersfeld were excellent pianists, or rather harpsichord players. The musical life of these three aristocrats seems to have been full and stimulating. After the example of the Italians, the Academy of Music in Prague (1715) was not a teaching institution, but a society somewhat on the lines of our own Academy of Ancient Music, established in 1710 by such influential amateurs as the Earl of Abercorn and professionals of the standing of Dr. Pepusch and Geminiani. A German musician, Gottfried Heinrich Stoltzel (1690–1749), who on his return from Italy in 1715 broke his journey in Prague, was so well satisfied with life there that he remained three years. We are indebted to him for some account of the weekly meetings of the Prague Academy.[1] Let us picture the scene. A noble music-room in Hartig's house, 'the room of the iron doors' (what an ideally quiet atmosphere it implies!), where the most gifted musicians in Prague, amateur and professional, met for a musical symposium. Here Logi would spend hours, 'or even whole days', playing the lute, or listening to Baron Hartig, who had 'a skilled artistic and delicate touch', and possessed a collection of the best instruments of the period. Usually the proceedings opened with an overture; a series of concertos interspersed with songs and instrumental solos followed, then the concert would wind up with 'a strong symphony'. Thus we learn from Stoltzel that in 1715, full forty years before Haydn's first symphonic essay was given to the world while he was in the service of the Bohemian nobleman Count Morzyn,[2] the form was being cultivated in this musical circle. It is more than probable that the 'strong symphonies' mentioned by Stoltzel were the work of Johann Friedrich Fasch (1688–1768), Haydn's predecessor as director of Count Morzyn's band. Fasch was undoubtedly one of the first pre-Haydn symphonists.

[1] From Johann Mattheson's *Ehren-Pforte*, Hamburg, 1740.
[2] I allude to what is commonly regarded as Haydn's First Symphony in D major, the 'Lukavec' (1759).

Stoltzel further describes Hartig as 'Kenner, Könner und Gönner der Musik' (Patron, Performer, and Pundit of Music), and says that a performance of a Mass by Lotti which this amateur organized in the Jesuit Church, in the Old Town of Prague, was the finest music he ever heard in his life. We get a thumbnail sketch of the Herr Baron seated in the body of the church with the score before him, in order that 'the power of harmony should not merely enter in at his ears, but that his eyes might follow the movements of the notes'.

Admirable as was the activity of laymen, rich and poor, in the service of music, the Church was still the most powerful and stead-fast friend of the art. The monasteries were wealthy and their dignitaries among the best patrons of musical talent. The occasions for the use of music were frequent: numerous outdoor processions on Sundays and festivals, pompous services in churches and cathedrals, and pilgrimages. Every large church had its appointed number of singers which was increased on special occasions. In 1679, when the Emperor attended service in the Cathedral of St. Vitus, Prague, the choir consisted of 200 singers, divided into four separate bodies, who sang a *Te Deum* with such superb effect as to win the favourable opinion of all the foreigners taking part in the ceremony. In 1715, at the consecration of the Column of the Holy Trinity, which was erected in the Mala Strana to commemorate the passing of an epidemic of the plague in 1713, 200 singers and musicians took part in the ceremony. Again, at the canonization of St. John Nepomuk (1729), the music in the Cathedral of St. Vitus was shared between two choirs each numbering 150 choristers, and fifty-six choirs and singing societies joined in the procession after the service. The monasteries vied with each other on such occasions as Christmas, Shrove Tuesday, Eastertide, or the Festivals of St. Wenceslaus and St. John Nepomuk. The seminarists in the communities got up performances of so-called oratorios and even operas.

Music at the Courts of the Prince-Bishops of Austria received unstinted appreciation, more especially at Salzburg and Olomouc, then the cultural centre of Moravia. The Prince-Bishop of Olomouc, Karl Lichtenstein-Kastelkorn (1664–94), collected much valuable musical material at his residential castle at Kroměřiž, where he maintained an orchestra, the leader of which was Jacob Handl-Gallus. One of the members of the orchestra was Heinrich Franz Biber 'Kammerdiener', violinist and composer, who passed into the service of the Bishop of Salzburg in 1673. He was succeeded at Olomouc by the Slav, Paul Weiwanovsky, one of the 'field-trumpeters' at the Bishop's Court. By the end of the seventeenth century the 'field-trumpeter' had given place to a musician whose knowledge of notation and superior instrumental technique removed him far from the original type. His development brought about a parallel evolution in musical form in the Entrada, the outcome of the medieval fanfare, gradually adapted to the accompaniment of a dance-measure at indoor festivals. There is plenty of documentary evidence that the Prince-Bishops cultivated secular—and particularly ballet—music at their Courts. In a letter from Karl Lichtenstein to Cunibert von Weuzelsberg in Vienna, requesting him to look for some ballets suitable for the Olomouc orchestra, he says it comprised ten to twelve fiddles, eight trumpets and seven clarinets, or, as they were then called, clarions. The clarinet is said to have been invented by Denner in 1690.

The archives at Kroměřiž contain one or two letters from Jacobus Stainer, the famous violin-maker, naming prices for instruments supplied to the Lichtenstein orchestra; two 'violins di braccio' cost twenty-six thalers apiece, and for 'ein extraordinari schen (schön) and gueten *Viola de gamba*' twenty thalers was the sum asked.

But great as was the musical activity of the churches and monasteries, the pilgrimages probably did still more to popularize the art. They were truly democratic in their tendencies. As the people flocked to the place of pilgrimage they were frequently joined at various stages by musicians of repute. The gatherings led to the composition of a class of work known as the 'figured Masses', which were so planned that a great number of singers taking part in the music should have a chance of distinguishing themselves as soloists. 'How proud and blest', says Hulka, 'were the parents who could boast a "solo boy" among their children! The whole congregation gazed on the proud mother of such a wonder-child and she for the time being forgot in her joy all the trouble and care that awaited her outside the church-doors.'

Such pilgrimages are still undertaken. I witnessed in 1919 the annual festival of SS. Cyril and Methodius, the first evangelizers of the Slavs, which is celebrated in June, when not less than 50,000 peasants made their way to the great convent church at Velehrad, in Moravia. All day and all night the roads in the vicinity were vocal with the songs and hymns of the pilgrims. Each village marched under its own banner and under the guidance of its own priest, and was accompanied by a portion at any rate of the local church choir. The quality of the music was not, I imagine, what it was in the eighteenth century. Now and then a fine Gregorian hymn tune attracted attention amid much that was of indifferent order. Occasionally the foot-weary pilgrims were braced by a vigorous accompaniment from a cornet, or a fife, which somewhat detracted from the reverential spirit in which the whole thing was undertaken. The night before the festival of 1919 was one of fitful storms, and moonless. In the little town of Uherské Hradiště, two or three miles from the goal of pilgrimage, the constant tramp of feet—though many walked bare-foot for economy's sake—made sleep impossible. An interesting tune quickly drew me to my window and it was a strange and touching sight to see these village contingents in their picturesque costumes, doggedly covering the last stage of their journey, constantly revealed by flares of summer lightning. The next morning was fine, and this great mass of people in their white, green, and crimson dresses, moving about in the open space in front of the church seemed like a field of midsummer flowers gently swaying in the wind. It was easy to realize how important a part these occasions had played in the aesthetic as well as the religious development of the Czechoslovaks from medieval times down to the present day.

The practice of music being so widespread and, on the whole, so advantageous to its adepts, it is not surprising that parents encouraged the least show of talent in their children. Dablač (1785) states that candidates for ordination were not acceptable unless they had a fair musical knowledge. Boys who were once accepted as choristers might be considered as fully provided for. František Benda, Černohorsky, Gluck, Zelenka, Brixi, Mysliveček, Tůma, John Chrysostom, John George Baptist Neruda, are a few among the more or less distinguished musicians who owed their early training to the monastic schools of Bohemia. To-day, on the woodwork of old choir-stalls and organs, some record is often to be found of the once famous choristers who figured there as soloists.

Native talent, even as early as the seventeenth and eighteenth centuries, found itself confronted with some rivalry. In 1627, Ferdinand II granted to the Jews the privilege of studying music, and they were not slow to take advantage of it. In the earlier half

c

of the eighteenth century the blind Jew, Loebel, a pupil of František Benda, had a band which was in demand for dance-music. But their activities spread to other departments, and, in 1641, the Archbishop of Prague thought it necessary to forbid the engagement of Jews to assist in the Sunday and Saints' day services. The order seems to have been disregarded, because, ten years later, the organists and musicians of Prague again petitioned the Archbishop to restrain Jews from playing in churches, not, curiously enough, on theological grounds, but because they 'had no notion of music, were rough and unskilled performers, and could not keep time'. But they found plenty of work at weddings and other festivities. Six members of the Jewish Guild of Players of Prague were engaged for the Carnival at Dresden in 1695. How different this spirit of tolerance to the fierce hatred and persecution displayed by the Germans in the twentieth century!

CHAPTER III

In spite of the widespread musical culture which astonished travellers to Bohemia in the eighteenth century, Prague was fast losing its position of musical ascendancy. For with wealth, patronage, and power vested, almost exclusively, in Teutonic hands, and the shifting of the seat of government to Vienna, the nobles, who as patrons had helped to make Prague the centre of music in Europe, followed the Court to the Austrian capital. They preferred prosperity to the inevitable poverty which they would incur by remaining in Prague: there was little thought of patriotism. Consequently, in the words of a Czech historian, 'almost all the musical sources which welled up from the soil of Bohemia sped by the shortest course to join the main stream of the world's music'. The artistic strength of Bohemia, instead of being husbanded at home, was absorbed by other countries. The world, then as now, made little distinction between Bohemians and gipsies. The best chance of success lay in sinking nationality and accepting universal citizenship.

The search for Czech talent scattered throughout Europe under names which, chameleon-like, took the etymological colouring of the land in which the exiled chanced to have settled, begins with the eighteenth century. The impulse given to the various branches of musical art in many European centres by these Bohemian emigrants is an interesting field of study in which there still remains room for research. It would be inappropriate in a simple outline of Bohemian musical history, written by a foreigner, to go far into this work of investigation, recognition, and restitution. This must be the task of Czechoslovak writers themselves. It is possible, however, to do justice to some of these half-forgotten exiles whose fine work for their art tends to prove that Bohemia's privation was the world's gain. We must not expect to find among the eighteenth-century Bohemians luminaries of the first magnitude. They can show a solid array of musical talent and industry, great executive ability, pedagogic gifts of the highest order, and occasional flashes of inspiration which, under happier conditions, might have developed into something potent. Burney, who is disposed to belittle the effects of universal musical education among the Bohemians because, at that time, it had not produced a composer of outstanding fame, ignores the *mass enjoyment* which was the most profitable result of giving every inhabitant a chance of becoming a proficient musician. But in summing up his impressions he is shrewd enough to see that political oppression undoubtedly influenced the situation. 'In many parts of Bohemia', he says, 'the Gothic power over vassals still subsists, and these people have seldom any ambition to excel in music . . . now and then, indeed, a man of genius among them becomes an admirable musician, whether he will or not; but when that happens, he generally runs away and settles in some other country where he can enjoy the fruits of his talent.'

No one nowadays is in a position to share Burney's enthusiasm for Stamitz, whom he points out as a typical example of Bohemian genius. 'Brought up in the common school', writes the historian, 'among children of common talents, who lived and died unnoticed, he, like another Shakespeare, broke through all difficulties and discouragements; and, as the eye of one pervaded all nature, the other without quitting nature pushed out further than any one had done before him; his genius was truly original, bold, and nervous; invention, fire, and contrast, in the quick movements; a tender, graceful, and insinuating melody in the slow; together with the ingenuity and richness of the accompaniments, characterize his productions; all replete with great effects, produced by an enthusiasm of genius, refined, but not repressed by cultivation.'

The now forgotten subject of this fervent eulogy was probably Jan Wenzl (Wenceslaus) Stamitz (1717–61), the most renowned of a musical family who hailed from Německý Brod, where the father was village schoolmaster and cantor of the church. A gifted violinist, he entered the service of the Elector of Mannheim in 1745. He was a prolific composer, and probably the most talented of Haydn's predecessors both in symphony and chamber music. A good deal of his music, including concertos, sonatas, and symphonies, was published in Paris, where his son Karel (1746–1801) settled in 1770, and was famous for his skill on the viola and viola d'amore. Karel visited London in 1778, and produced an opera of his own in St. Petersburg some ten years later. Jan Stamitz left forty-five symphonies, but Karel surpassed his father, bringing his own figure up to seventy.[1]

The Bendas furnished an example of a whole family absorbed in this way into the ranks of German musicians. They might be called the Bach family of Bohemia.

[1] See Riemann.

Jan Jiří Benda, who combined the occupation of weaver and local musician in the villages of Staré and Nové Benátky, had four sons and one daughter who all distinguished themselves in the musical profession and, at least in two instances, passed on their talent to a third generation. František, the eldest of Jan Jiří's boys (1709–86), founded a school of violin playing, and succeeded Graun as orchestral leader to Frederick the Great, ending his days at Potsdam in 1786. Two of his sons followed in his footsteps: Friedrich Wilhelm Heinrich (1754–1814) was a member of the Court band and a composer of operas, oratorios, and instrumental works; Carl Hermann Heinrich was esteemed an excellent violinist.

The weaver's second son Johann (1713–52) joined František in Berlin and became also a member of Frederick the Great's orchestra. Joseph, the youngest (1724–1804), was a violinist in the service of Frederich Wilhelm II, and lived in Berlin, where his son Ernst (1747–85) was also occupied with music and helped to institute the amateur concerts in the Prussian capital. Anna Franziska (1726–80), whose married name was Hattasch, was a well-known singer in her day.

But the flower of the family was the third son, Jiří, or George (1722–95), who by the invention of the modern melodrama made a European reputation. There exists an admirable monograph on this composer by Karel Hůlka[1] which furnishes many interesting details about the musical life of Bohemia in the eighteenth century.

Under the conditions of social existence described in the preceding pages, it is not surprising to find a man in the position of Jan Jiří Benda not merely rejoicing that his boys should learn the rudiments of music, but looking to it as a supplementary source of livelihood. František, thanks to a good soprano voice, was taken early into the choir of the Benedictine Church of St. Michael, in Prague. Jiří, in his early years, remained at home and accompanied his father as assistant fiddler at rustic festivals.

Among the tales of his childhood which Jiří Benda liked to relate in later years is one which humorously and pathetically illustrates the privations and occasional joys of his precarious vocation. Father and son were engaged to play at a village wedding. They were stationed near the door of the room leading into the kitchen, and all the well-laden and succulent dishes for the

---

[1] *Jiří Benda, Studie o starším Českém Hudebníku*, by Karel Hůlka, published by Mojmír Urbánek, Prague, 1903.

marriage feast were carried in under the nose of the hungry little fiddler. It was hardly within the limits of a human boy's endurance. Nevertheless he fiddled away bravely until a huge joint of roast pork, armour-plated in brown crackling and swimming in a sea of savoury gravy, was borne past, leaving delectable odours in its wake. Jiří's whole empty inward being was set in piteous commotion. His bow scraped the strings mechanically, his eyes followed the dish greedily. Suddenly, overcome with hunger and yearning, down he dropped in a dead faint. Help was forthcoming, and with returning consciousness he was heard to murmur in weak but passionate tones the two words: *roast pork, roast pork*. The kind-hearted hosts supplied a liberal portion and Jiří was soon fiddling with renewed energy.

In 1740, František, who had gone to Berlin, sent for his younger brother, and Jiří remained there several years as second violin in the royal band. According to official documents, he was appointed Kapellmeister to the Duke of Gotha in 1750. His duties included the supervision of the music in church and at the Court Theatre. In addition he had some leisure for composition and had already made his first essays in Berlin. During the next fifteen years he wrote a good many church works, his Six Sonatas for Cembalo with accompaniment for string quartet, and the Clavier Concertos, which were played both at Court and among his own circle of friends. During this time he gave serious consideration to dramatic music. More especially he pondered the question of Italian music which completely dominated the public taste. In the Italian music which he had heard and studied on his own account he found much that was superficial; much that seemed to set aside all that he had acquired in his solid German musical education. On the other hand ambition spurred him on to win dramatic fame. How could he penetrate the secrets of Italian opera without studying it in the land of its origin? Had not Johann Adolf Hasse a generation earlier gone to Naples and Venice, and returned to Dresden the most popular composer of his day? And then there was the example of his compatriot Mysliveček who was actually in Italy at that time and, having grasped the basis of Italian music, had won a glorious name at a stroke. With equal chances he, Benda, might also be known to posterity with Hasse 'il Sassone', and Mysliveček 'il Divino Boemo'. He pondered his dream and made persistent efforts to secure its realization. Benda had an ardent and persevering temperament and the episode of the roast pork more or less repeated itself in his maturity. He succeeded in getting what he wanted from his good-natured patron and master, Duke Frederick of Gotha, and in September 1767 received the money for his journey and left the Ducal Chapel, in the care of his leader, Schieck.

Benda's first stage was Munich. He had friends at the Kurfürst's Court who procured him entrance to the concerts at Nymphenberg and introduced him to the Kurfürst who asked to hear some of his sonatas and concertos, and showed his appreciation by presenting the composer with a gold watch. From Munich Benda went to Venice, where he sought the acquaintance of Adolf Hasse who had then resigned his post in Dresden and settled permanently in Venice. In Gotha, as we have seen, Benda, while longing to assimilate the secrets of Italian success, was not among the uncritical enthusiasts of Italian opera. Soon after his arrival in Venice he went with his friend Rust, the musical director at Dessau, to hear an opera by Galuppi. Accustomed to the fuller sonority of orchestration and the richer harmony of the German school, Benda was disgusted with the 'tinkling tones' of the Venice orchestra and left the theatre after the first act of the opera. Afterwards, although he could not reconcile himself to all the tricks of the operatic trade, he became more acclimatized to the Italian style, confessed that his first clear impressions of the possibilities of dramatic art came to him in the Italian opera houses, and assiduously attended every performance which came his way. On his journey to Rome he composed a church cantata which he dispatched to Gotha in time for the Duke's birthday festival, a work which shows he had already acquired something of the Italian style.

When Benda returned to take up his work in Gotha he was honoured by the new title of Kapelldirector instead of Kapellmeister as before. His patron, Duke Frederick III, died in 1772.

A chain of unexpected events now led to Benda's opportunity of doing something great and new for dramatic art. In 1774 the Duke of Weimar's castle, including the theatre, was destroyed by fire. The actors suddenly found themselves without occupation and the Duchess of Weimar wrote to the Duke of Gotha asking his assistance for the homeless company. An invitation to the ducal theatre at Gotha was gladly accepted. Among the company was Johann Christian Brandes and his wife. The musical conductor Anton Schweitzer, who had already been introduced to

Benda in Venice, now appeared upon the scene as a possible rival
to the Kapelldirector. The newcomer had been busy in Weimar
setting to music Brandes's text for *Ariadne on Naxos*, but he laid
it aside for a libretto—*Alceste*, by a greater man, the court poet
Wieland. The music written for *Ariadne* he remodelled for
Alceste, and he had moreover the incentive of pitting himself in
Gotha against a musician of such repute as Benda. *Alceste*, a
Singspiel, or play interspersed with songs, was produced with
immense success at Weimar and held its place on the German
stage for at least half a century.

The reception accorded to *Alceste* aroused Benda's envy and
just then Brandes came forward with the discarded libretto of
Ariadne on Naxos. Benda was pleased with the text, but he felt
that he must handle it in a new form in order to attract the
attention of the musical world. He had in mind also the fact that
though Frau Brandes might not be a great vocalist, her declamation and dramatic sense were of a high order. In striving to use
the talents of this actress for musical ends he evolved the form of
melodrama. It is true that Rousseau's *Pygmalion*, which was not
produced in Paris till a year after the first performance of *Ariadne*
in Gotha (1774), has been claimed by some historians as the
earliest essay in melodrama. But it is doubtful whether Benda
was aware of Rousseau's work while planning his own, and as
regards musical worth *Ariadne* ranks far above *Pygmalion* for its
veristic and moving expression of human passion. The despair
of the deserted heroine and the raging of the storm on the rocky
coasts of the island offered many indications for descriptive music,
as it was then understood. The melodrama, or duodrama, as it
was called by its composer, is not a play interspersed with songs
like the Singspiel, but consists of declamation linked to music
which endeavours to express the sentiments suggested by the
words. The novelty of its form and the seriousness of the music
did not immediately appeal to those who constituted themselves
guardians of the public taste. Benda was reproached for using the
orchestra as the medium of emotional expression instead of the
vocal music. The attempt at tone-painting was resented by some
critics, and the faults of the work were magnified by Schweitzer's
adherents, who had plenty to say about the 'unholy alliance'
between speech and music, the interruption of the dramatic
action by orchestral interludes, and the endless flow of music
which was aimlessly and vaguely picturesque. Nevertheless its

fame spread outside Gotha, and by 1787 several editions of the work had appeared. Reichardt, one of the most enlightened critics of the period, wrote enthusiastically about *Ariadne on Naxos* after the Berlin production in 1782. He went to the theatre already somewhat biased by adverse criticism, but was immediately impressed by the beauty of the overture. 'And so it was to the end of the piece,' he says. 'I began by being touched by an indescribable emotion, tossed here and there on surges of feeling, and as it were under a spell . . . it is certain that Benda's genius attained its aim marvellously well; that his music fitted every human emotion and swept away all my doubts.' Writing in the *Musikalische Almanach* after Benda's death in 1796, Reichardt pays this fine tribute to the composer: 'In truth such genial music was never before heard on our German stage. The public is now aware of the unprecedented success attained by *Ariadne on Naxos* throughout Germany, from Berlin to Mannheim and from Vienna to Hamburg.' Judged from a modern standpoint, Benda's *Ariadne on Naxos* is a germinative work; but greater in its powers of suggestion than in actual accomplishment. The opening theme which holds a prospect of broad development—a movement *grave e largo* in the style of a Lulli overture—hardly carries out its promise, and declines to a mere *levée de rideau*. The work, however, undoubtedly opened up a new path in dramatic music; a path which led to such varied achievements as the grave-digging scene in *Fidelio*, some pages of *Egmont*, the incantation scene in *Der Freischütz*, and, in more recent years, to Humperdinck's *Die Königskinder* and Strauss's *Enoch Arden*. It is but just to remember that the pioneer intellect which opened the way was a Slav intellect put out to service with a German princeling.

The success of *Ariadne* induced Benda to follow it up with a second melodrama *Medea*, to a text by Gotter. Except for the introduction (*Grave e maestoso*), which is somewhat more elaborate than the prelude to *Ariadne*, the work is not so strong as its predecessor. Its fate was sealed when Cherubini's masterpiece on the same subject with its atmosphere of glowing passion took the operatic stage by storm. Benda projected a third dramatic work based on Shakespeare's *Romeo and Juliet* (1778), but about this time he fell into disfavour at the Court of Gotha and, resigning his post, migrated to Hamburg, where, in a freer *bourgeois* atmosphere, a popular and national opera had long been flourishing in a way that was hardly possible in the restricted environment of a Court theatre. Benda shortly retired to the village of Kostritz, in Thuringia, where he died in 1795.

While many Bohemian musicians were swallowed up by Germany, a few made their mark in other lands, notably Josef Mysliveček (1737–81), who took up his abode in Italy. Here his operas enjoyed extraordinary popularity. Naples was the scene of his most brilliant triumphs, and the people would hardly suffer him to visit any other centres. The fascinating but wayward singer Cattarina Gabrielli preferred his songs to those of any of his contemporaries, and Mozart recommended Mysliveček's sonatas to the attention of his sister.[1] It is interesting to know that his oratorio *Abraham and Isaac* passed for a long time as the work of Haydn; but whether it contains any of the marked Slavicisms which abound in the music of the Croatian composer I am unable to say. The name of Mysliveček did not trip lightly from the tongues of the Italians, who re-christened him Venatorini or 'Il divino Boemo'.

The name appears very frequently in the correspondence of the Mozart family. Leopold Mozart seems to have met the Bohemian musician for the first time at Bologna, in 1770, and to have formed a friendship which lasted for the rest of Mysliveček's life. Wolfgang and his mother both speak of the Slav composer as the most enthusiastic admirer and loyal friend of the young genius. There is a pathetic account of their visit in 1777 to the popular opera writer, then in the Herzogspital at Munich, a victim of the results of his wild and dissolute existence. He was a man of singular charm and generous disposition, but a Bohemian in the most undesirable sense of the word. He early discerned the great gifts of Mozart, and thought very highly of his sister Anna. 'Mysliveček kisses Nannerl's virtuoso hands,' wrote Leopold Mozart to his wife from Milan in 1773.

Mysliveček's invention was as fertile as that of most eighteenth-century composers. His first great operatic success, *Il Bellerofonte*, was produced at Parma in 1764, after which he poured forth a continuous stream of operas, oratorios, symphonies, and other works. He returned from Munich to Naples for the first perfor-

---

[1] 'I know what Mysliveček's sonatas are like for I played them in Munich. They are quite easy and sound well. My advice is that my sister, whom I most humbly greet, should play them with much expression, gusto, and fire, and learn them by heart. For they are sonatas which must please everybody, easy to memorize and effective when played with the necessary precision.'

mance of his *Olimpiade* (1778), which created a *furore*. But his health was broken and he died in Rome, on 4 February 1781, at the comparatively early age of forty-four.

The close of the seventeenth century saw the birth of Bohuslav Černohorský (1684–1740), whose church music was extolled by all his contemporaries. It is now difficult to judge of the quality of his creative gift, for nearly all his manuscripts were destroyed in a fire which took place at the Minorite Convent, at Prague, in 1753.[1] Černohorský, who was a friar of this order, migrated early in life to Italy where he became choirmaster at the Santo in Padua, and afterwards organist at Assisi. He was a great teacher and, as his surviving works bear witness, one of the most skilled contrapuntists of his time. While living at Assisi, Tartini went to him for instruction. In Italy he was known as 'Il Padre Boemo'. In middle life he made his way back to Prague and was appointed musical director at the famous Tyn Church, and afterwards organist at St. Jacob's in that city. At this time Gluck, who was eighteen years of age, came to Prague to study under this cele- brated master. In order to enjoy this privilege he underwent many privations, earning a precarious living by singing in choirs and playing the violin at rustic festivals. Černohorský died in 1742.

One of Černohorský's most interesting pupils was Jan Zach (1699–1773), a very fine organist. He held appointments at the Cathedral of St. Vitus and at St. Martin's Church in Prague, and then, like most of his contemporaries, left his native land and settled in Mainz. A strange and mystical personality, he ended his days in a madhouse. In his exile he did not forget the peculiar quality of his own folk music. Reminiscences of the popular songs linger in his compositions. The influence of this fluent and unaffected popular melody upon the works of Haydn, Mozart, and Beethoven is evident. This melodic charm is one of the elements of Slavonic music—considered apart from the orient- alism that crept into Russian music and gave it a colour which is absent from the music of the Western Slavs. Zach was fond of chromatic modulations; he uses the chord of the diminished

---

[1] Among the rare examples of his music in print is a Choral-fugue with string orchestra, *Laudatur Jesus Christus* (in the National Museum, Prague). Three compositions for organ may be found in Otto Schmid's collection of *Organ Works by the Old Bohemian Composers* (Schlesinger, Berlin).

seventh and the augmented second frequently. 'A preference for chromatic, and often exotic, themes is particularly characteristic of Zach,' says Dr. Branberger. He left a beautiful *Solemn Requiem* in E minor.

Another pupil of Černohorský was František Tůma (1704–74), who went to Vienna in order to study under that highly respectable and erudite musician Johann Joseph Fux and remained there in the service of the dowager Empress Elizabeth. He was a devout-minded man, and a solid and accomplished musician. His *a capella* Masses show a mastery of the old polyphonic style.[1] In the orchestral accompaniments to other Masses he follows the procedure of his master in dividing his strings and in the use of trombones. At that time this instrument was frequently employed in church works and only fell out of fashion for a time late in the eighteenth century.[2] Tůma spent many of his later years in religious communities and died in the monastery of the Brothers of Charity in Vienna.

Jan Dyzmas Zelenka (1678–1745), a fellow pupil of Tůma's under Černohorský, was engaged for a time in the service of Baron Hartig, mentioned in a previous chapter. He afterwards settled in Dresden. He had also the advantage of a visit to Italy where he received instruction from Lotti. But though something of a cosmopolitan he did not wholly sever his art from his native land. In 1723 he wrote the music for a Latin play, *The Melodrama of Saint Wenceslaus*, and also a Motet to Czech words, a very unusual proceeding at that period, when the language was as much in disfavour as the nation itself.

An emigrant of considerable repute was František Habermann (1706–83), who studied in Italy, travelled in Spain and France, and held posts in Paris and Florence. Dr. Branberger says of this composer:

'he was a great master of counterpoint and a remarkable teacher. His works are almost all lost. This is a pity, especially as regards the Masses which were dedicated to Bohemian patrons and printed. When Handel visited Italy for the second time (1728–9) he probably knew Habermann's compositions, some of which have been found copied and sketched in score

---

[1] Some of these, edited by Schmid, are published by Breitkopf and Härtel.

[2] Beethoven's Equali for Four Trombones date from 1812.

among Handel's originals. These are the *Gloria in Excelsis Deo* and the *Kyrie* of which Chrysander in his *Life of Handel*[1] tells us that Handel used the theme from the introduction to the *Gloria* for choruses in *Hercules* and *Agrippina*. The theme of the Fugue in the *Kyrie* is to be found in the *Allegro* of Handel's Seventh Pianoforte Suite. According to Chrysander the writing in Handel's manuscript copy probably dates from 1740–50. It is interesting that Habermann so often composed only the *Kyrie* and *Gloria*, the development of which he carried a long way and divided into many sections. This is the new form of Mass, resembling perhaps Bach's so-called short Masses which consist also of the *Kyrie* and *Gloria*. To-day I know of two such works of Habermann, in D major and A minor. In the former the *Kyrie* is preceded by a long and very finished instrumental prelude, which is remarkable as an unusual peculiarity. Handel also wrote Overtures to his Church music (the so-called Chandos Anthems). These overtures have verve and humour: they are not at all churchy in style and seem rather to have been taken from the symphonies. The instrumentation with two oboes and two horns also reminds us of the first symphonies. Habermann's music reveals in many respects the happy playful period of the Viennese classical composers, and favours a secular character, but in the fugues he shows himself an accomplished master, especially in the double-fugue of the D major *Kyrie*.'

Charles Czerny (1791–1857), though born at Vienna, was of Czech blood. As a composer he showed that combination of loquacity and industry peculiar to many of his compatriots at that date. Among his thousand works nothing is remembered but his Practical Pianoforte School, yet undoubtedly he exercised great influence upon the technique of pianoforte playing.

Even greater in this respect were the services of Jean Dussek (1761–1812), who hailed from Čáslav in Bohemia, the Slavonic form of his name being Jan Ladislav Dušek. For a time Dussek studied with Philipp Emanuel Bach at Hamburg. A renowned virtuoso on the organ, the pianoforte and the then-fashionable harmonica, he settled in Paris until the rising tide of revolution made it expedient for this favourite of Marie Antoinette to withdraw to England. He remained with us twelve years, greatly honoured as a pianist and teacher. Having failed in the music

[1] Vol. I, pp. 178–9.

business, which he unwisely added to his artistic occupations, Dussek left England, deeply in debt, and returned to Bohemia. Prince Louis Ferdinand of Prussia then adopted the musician, rather as a friend than as a servitor. The Prince's death at the battle of Saalfeld in 1806 called forth from Dussek one of the most sincere tributes ever offered from protégé to protector—his *Harmonic Elegy*. This work, together with *The Invocation*, *The Farewell*, and some of the slow movements from his sonatas—all for pianoforte—are practically the only works which have survived the changes of style and pianistic methods that have succeeded each other since Dussek's day. Vaclav Jan Tomašek (1775–1850), once the autocrat of musical life in Prague, says of Dussek's playing: 'His fingers were like a company of ten singers, endowed with equal executive powers, and able to produce with the utmost perfection whatever their director could require.' The same authority tells us that Dussek introduced the innovation of placing his pianoforte sideways on the platform, a custom which other virtuosi were quick to follow, 'though they may have no very interesting profile to exhibit'.

Jan Ladislav Dussek must not be confounded with his namesake Franz Dušek (Dussek), a native of Chotěboř, who lived between 1736–99, and was noted in Prague as a pioneer of poetic feeling and an excellent interpreter of Bach. This Dušek was an intimate friend of Mozart from his Salzburg days.

Wenzel Pichl (1741–1805), born near Tabor, accompanied the Archduke Ferdinand to Milan as Court composer. He must have taken his duties seriously, for he wrote nearly seven hundred works—symphonies, concertos, masses, and operas poured from his pen with fatal facility. Nevertheless, as he received pressing invitations to become Director of the Imperial Court Chapel at St. Petersburg—probably in succession to Paesiello or Galuppi—we may assume that he was a composer of considerable repute.

Another distinguished exile who exercised some influence on the art in general was Anton Josef Reicha (1770–1836), a native of Prague, who was a good all-round musician at eighteen, and played second flute in the private band of Maximilian of Austria. While living in Vienna he frequented an interesting circle which included Beethoven and Haydn. In 1808 he settled in Paris, and had the satisfaction of seeing three of his operas staged there: *Cagliostro* (1810), *Natalie* (1816), and *Sappho* (1822). In 1818 Reicha succeeded Méhul as Professor of Counterpoint at the

Conservatoire. He composed a good deal of chamber music for unusual combinations of wind and strings; the capacities of the former were well understood by him, and in encouraging the study of wind instruments he followed a national tradition, for Bohemia has been particularly rich in wind virtuosi: the oboists Flaška, Fiala, and the two Červenkas; the flautist Sedláček; Wenceslas Batka, Čejka, and later Kopras, bassoonists; Fridlovský, the clarinettist; Palsa, Mokowecký, and Janatka, horn players —all these helped to raise the standard of orchestral-playing at home and abroad.

In spite of this almost general exodus of native talent there have always been fine examples of patriotic self-sacrifice among Czech musicians. Such was Victor Brixi, the famous organist of Poděbrady, who declined the post of Court Musician to Francis I because he would not leave the land of his birth. Mention must also be made of František Brixi (1732–71), of whom the late Professor Sacchetti, in his *History of Music*, says: 'His sacred works, especially his Masses, are distinguished for their admirable declamation, attaining here and there to real dramatic pathos. . . . Each part in his polyphonic compositions has its own individual interest, and his modulations are simple, natural, and, at the same time, original.'

Later on we see Smetana choosing to limit his energies to national opera rather than win a wider reputation by adopting a more cosmopolitan style. Some day it will be an historian's task to restore to the various Slav races of Central Europe the plumes plucked from them and insolently worn in the caps of their oppressors. Sir Henry Hadow has already done this act of justice for Haydn; but almost as much remains to be accomplished in the aesthetic as in the political sphere.

CHAPTER IV

THREE provinces speaking two dialects, but united in a supreme aspiration for national independence, make up the country called, collectively, Czechoslovakia. The most westerly province, Bohemia proper, is the home of the Czechs, and its capital is the ancient city of Praha (Prague), the proud citadel which has held ever inviolate the ideals of a race struggling continually against the strangle-hold of pan-Germanism. In Slovakia—the eastern division—dwells an innumerous, tragic peasantry, whose homes lie at the foot of the Tatra (Carpathian) Mountains. It is a folk richly endowed with the artistic sense. Wedged between the two is the old duchy of Moravia, which has also contributed its portion to the general treasury of Bohemian literature and music.

The geographical distribution of the three provinces has exercised a strong influence upon the popular music. In the west, that is to say, in old Bohemia, proximity to Germany has helped to modify the characteristic Slavonic features of the primitive folk-songs. On the other hand, the songs of the Slovak peasantry, confined within narrower local boundaries and remote from currents of cosmopolitan culture, have retained most of their archaic peculiarities. The two musical tendencies—eastern and western—dwell side by side in a certain harmony of patriotic sentiment, but each clings to its own tonal and rhythmic system. Now and again we come upon a song common to both ends of the Republic, and then we have an opportunity of comparing the Czech with the Slovak variant and noting the difference in treatment. This variation in racial music is not confined to Czechoslovakia. Scandinavian folk-song offers a similar phenomenon. The melodies of Sweden and Denmark, the lands that lie nearest to Western civilization, although not wanting in charm, are tamer and more conventionalized than those of Norway, which produced a Grieg, or those of Finland, which boasts a Sibelius. And the same judgement would, I think, result from setting fifty Great Russian folk-songs side by side with an equal number of Polish melodies. Nearer home we have a further example in the difference of colour which distinguishes an English from a Celtic folk-song. There is no question that the less sophisticated songs hold the greater attraction for musicians, since the chief interest and value of folk-music lies for the present generation in its germinal and suggestive possibilities, depending on the scales of which it is constructed and the elasticity of its rhythm; in other words, upon the degree of elemental vitality and originality which the tourniquets of convention still permit to course in its veins.

The songs of old Bohemia—Czech songs—are, generally speaking, more pleasing than striking, for their modal and rhythmic angles have been gradually ground away by friction with the rock of German *Kultur*; nor have they been able to escape altogether from its prescriptions, nor from some echo of ultra-German sentimentality. But gems—a trifle too polished for folk-songs— are certainly to be found among collections of Czech popular music, and many beautiful and touching examples of folk poetry have found their appropriate musical settings.

In contrast to Western Bohemia, a large proportion of the Slovak folk-tunes are tetrachordal, producing results that arrest and stimulate the ear trained exclusively to the use of the ordinary diatonic scales—if indeed such ears still exist. The folk-song collectors of the earlier part of the last century paid scant attention to the modal construction of the tunes they harvested, consequently the early results of their salvage give us a very imperfect idea of how songs sounded when sung by the peasants. The last quarter of a century has witnessed great improvements in Bohemia, as in Russia, in the methods of studying and writing down the tunes; more respect has been paid to the folk spirit, and a fuller recognition of the complex psychology of the songs has led to many changes in the manner of harmonizing them. Anonymous songs, which are—or have been—adapted so as to become the expression of collective sentiment, must necessarily lose something of their primitive emotionalism and inimitable charm when they pass to paper through the hands of an individual, even though he be a Balakirev or a Milan Lichard. Those who know the difference between polite folk-song performances heard at some city festival or ethnographical congress, and the singing of a little crowd, say, of Russian peasants in the village street on a summer evening, are prepared to accept the assurance that only among the folk who have lived under the frown of the Carpathians, and the still darker shadow of Hungarian rule, can we hope to recapture all the shy, essential beauty of the songs of Slovakia. And not the beauty only, but the intimate character of the songs is apt to evaporate in a more sophisticated execution of

D

them: the queer, sometimes brutal humour, the note of cruel suffering; the something that corresponds to the acrid odours of labour which hang about the clothes of the peasantry. The quality of the peasants' voices in Russia is frequently hideous, but they make you thrill to their sincerity.

Even in this small easternmost province of Bohemia there are two distinct racial types: the White Slovak, the mountaineer, who has the strong, dark, melancholy, mystical nature of the High-lander; and the Red Slovak, or dalesman, prosperous and conse-quently gayer, colour-loving, quicker perhaps of intellect than his brother of the hills, and certainly more easily moved to passion. Experts who know the country and the people intimately can readily trace this contrast of temperament in the popular music of Slovakia.

The chief musical characteristics of the Slovak songs, besides the basis of the ancient modes, may be briefly summarized. Their rhythm is invariably binary. Milan Lichard, in an interest-ing and instructive article[1] on the subject, says that triple time is unknown in the genuine folk melodies, and when it occurs it may be taken to indicate that the tune is of foreign origin, or that it has been wrongly noted down. The oldest type of song is con-structed on very simple themes. Later on, when a knowledge of music, and especially of Church music, became more widespread, themes of the songs assumed a more developed form, with a rhythmic symmetry that suggests the work of a skilled hand. Examples of most of the Church modes are to be found in the songs of this period.

'One note one syllable' is the rule with the setting of the Slovak songs. In this respect it is interesting to compare them with the popular melodies of the Serbs, in which many notes are sung to one syllable, sometimes curiously delaying the singer in the midst of an arresting statement, and imparting an Oriental and rhap-sodic character to the music. But the Serbian folk-music, for historical and ethnographical reasons, is not a little coloured by Turkish and other un-European elements, while that of Bohemia has been modified by quite other influences. As I have already pointed out, it was inevitable that close intercourse with Germany should have its effect upon the Czech arts. In the case of the Slovaks the alien element entered by way of Hungary. The so-

[1] *Slovak Popular Melodies* by Milan Lichard. Reprinted from *Racial Problems in Hungary*, by R. Seton-Watson. (Constable & Co.)

called 'Magyar' scale, which Liszt took from gipsy sources and made fatally popular, and the distorted rhythms and sensational emotionalism of the Tsigane musicians, have left their traces on many virile and simple Moravian and Slovak melodies. There are few countries of Central Europe whose music is free from a certain number of gipsy tunes and gipsy devices. This exotic element penetrates chiefly through urban centres where gipsy bands play and sing in the public gardens, captivating the ears of the *blasé* townsman and the half-educated amateur. How often newly-returned tourists from Russia have expiated on the fascinating folk-music they had heard there, and produced pieces which proved on examination to be just those ditties sung by the gipsy musicians in the restaurants on the Islands at Petrograd, or at the Sokolniky Park near Moscow. Personally I confess to a sneaking liking for some of these tunes—especially the lively ones —in spite of their cheap passion and frank vulgarity. Their dash and glitter, their violent rhythms and insolent themes come as a relief after a weary day of hard work or social boredom. But although a dust of cayenne pepper is a good stimulant to a jaded palate, too liberal a mixture of this Hungarian *paprika* with the wholesome potage of the Slovak folk-music is apt to produce something degenerate.

There is one remarkable disparity between the method of performance of the Russian and Czechoslovak songs. Among the great Russian peasantry solo-singing was the exception rather than the rule. A few rune-singers who sang the ancient epics, the 'long-drawn songs' called *bylina*, lingered until modern times in the extreme north (on the borders of Finland). Such a bard was Paraska, whom Jean Sibelius remembered hearing in boyhood, when she was of untold age and had accumulated a repertory that could outlast a Wagner trilogy. In 1915–16 another ancient beldame astonished society in the Russian capitals by her singing of the *bylina*. But such instances are rare. Part-singing, with all its democratic significance, has always flourished among the Russian peasantry. The spirit of co-operation, as displayed by their admirable *artels*, or mutual aid societies, extended to their highest forms of recreation—dancing and singing. Even in the days of serfdom the landowner encouraged these amusements, and peasants would often go up to 'the great house' on a summer evening to entertain their master's family, and would be repaid for their performances by refreshments. But in Bohemia and

Slovakia political interference gradually extinguished choral singing, and though of recent years there has been a great revival of it among the students and townspeople, the majority of the folksongs seem at one time to have been sung as solos.

The poetic basis of popular song is much the same in every country: patriotism, love and courtship, revelry, the procession of the seasons, Nature in its varying aspects—these are the subjects common to all folk-songs; but their emotional character is influenced by the history of each individual country. The Czechoslovak songs are much concerned with Nature, and with the fate of suffering Bohemia. Here is an example which bewails the vanished splendours of Nitra, the ancient capital of the so-called 'Great Moravian Empire':[1]

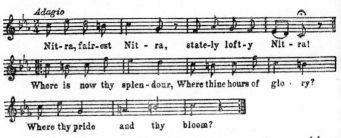

Other verses tell how Svatopluk held his court there, and how Methodius, the first evangelist to the Slavs, tarried within its venerable walls. The following is a song of a less tragic and more homely character. Like many folk-song texts, the actual words are inconsistent; the tree is called a fir, but its fruits are 'walnuts':

[1] Including Bohemia, extending right down to the Adriatic ('Bohemia by the Sea'). This was before the Magyar invasion of Hungary, which separated the Slavs and subjugated the Slovaks.

The most popular of hero-songs is that relating to the robber, Janošík, the Robin Hood of Bohemian popular literature. Janošík, with his band of followers, lived in the fastnesses of the Carpathians, and revenged himself on society for the death of his father, a true and straight man, who was cruelly beaten to death because he could no longer work. Throughout Slovakia the name of this popular hero is famous, and his deeds are recounted in many legends. He was a robber who took from the rich to give to the poor.

Heigh, mountain woods, Woodland vales, Path that skirts the moun-tain! Fa-ther was a straight man, I must be a rob-ber, True and straight my fa-ther, I must be a rob-ber.

In the summer of 1919 I enjoyed the rather uncommon privilege, for a stranger, of hearing an informal 'sing-song' by members of the Sokol at Uherské Hradiště, Moravia. The Sokols, or gymnastic associations of the Czechs, were one of the beneficial outgrowths of the national movement of the 'forties. They were founded by Dr. Miroslav Tyrš, a patriot-philosopher who believed that 'the smaller the nation, the greater need to pay attention to its healthy growth'. The word Sokol means Falcon, a symbol of swift, untiring, fearless energy. The Sokol Unions, formed with the chief idea of giving to every young Czech a chance to develop his physical and intellectual powers in a gracious harmony, incidentally were the means of keeping alive the patriotic sentiments of the people. They bring all classes together in a wholesome and friendly democratic spirit. Their influence counted for much in the ultimate victory of the race. Physically they prepare fine material for the great struggle of arms in which the nation has more than once been involved in these recent years; morally 'they take interest in popular education, fight corrupt literature and coarse entertainments, oppose reactionary tendencies in politics, agitate for equal rights' (Dr. J. L. Fisher). The

Sokols would not be Czech in spirit if they did not include singing among the healthful recreations which they stimulate. The unions extend in a network throughout the country and all have their informal musical evenings.

Through the kindness of a schoolmaster in the typical little Moravian town, I was invited one evening to the restaurant of the Sokol where the singers usually met once or twice a week after business hours. During the War of 1914–18 these meetings had been abandoned, and the singers were consequently out of practice. It was their first reunion since the signing of the armistice. For this reason perhaps they fought rather shy of letting me hear their impromptu performance. Their leader, the veterinary surgeon of the district, declined to sing at first, partly because he did not like being taken unawares 'by a musical critic', and partly, I think, because he thought the songs were not always quite 'ladylike'. Fortunately when I was personally introduced to him—with extreme care and tactfulness—by my host, he was apparently soon satisfied that I was neither critical nor ladylike. So, having passed muster, I was invited with great cordiality to take my place at the end of a long table, the 'vet' being opposite to me and the singers ranged down each side of the board. About ten men of varied ages—and outward seeming all of the *bourgeoisie*, not of the peasantry—were assembled. But by degrees others dropped in until the number was certainly doubled. One or two wives also looked in to keep me in countenance, but they did not sit at the singers' table. When we were each supplied with a glass of some chosen beverage—some of the Moravian wines are quite conducive to convivial song—the 'vet' started the first number, the familiar and dearly loved 'Boleraz, boleraz'. Tears were in the eyes and voice of the leader when he afterwards went on to give the first verse of a hopelessly sad soldier song, 'Kamaradi moji' (*My comrades*): 'Comrades, do not leave me here, Bury me under the green lime tree.' Fearing that the songs were all going to be in this decorous and solemn vein, I presently ventured to inquire: Had they no drinking-songs? No dancing-songs? The 'vet's' eyes twinkled like two merry stars on a frosty night. He raised his glass to me from the far end of the table and broke into a popular Slovak tune. This was followed by several others in the same jovial mood. Then by my special request, they struck up a rollicking dance-song, with its haunting tune and absurd, untranslatable jingle of a text. The voices were of pleasant quality, not trained voices such as we heard in London from the Teachers' Choirs at the Czechoslovak Musical Festival in 1919; but the unaccompanied singing, which was nearly always in unison, was in excellent tune. Although the entertainment was quite casual there was an underlying feeling of love and respect for the songs. Glasses were filled and refilled fairly often as the evening went on, but the singing never degenerated into rowdyism—it was always vocal. It would be difficult to give any idea of the intense verve and contrasting melancholy combined in the leader's interpretations. His protean personality dominated the whole company. A typical Slovak, clean-shaven, with handsome well-cut features and a mobile mouth, his moods changed in a flash, and the play of his expressive features rendered the meaning of the songs perfectly intelligible, even when the rapid enunciation, coupled with the use of local idioms, made it very difficult for a foreigner to follow the texts. His memory for words and music never failed for an instant. Without him, the singing of the townsmen might perhaps have flagged into tameness; but I realized that in his vocation he must have mixed daily among farmers and peasants, caught up the true spirit of the folk-music, and shared in many a festivity. Now and again in the dancing-songs he gave a wild yell —like the sudden shout given to hearten the dancers in the quick Scottish reel; but he managed this so skilfully that it hardly seemed to break the continuity of the tune he was singing. The yell is, I am told, a feature of the Slovak dances and is emitted in a moment of great excitement, when the lads snatch up their partners like children, toss them up and set them down again in the twinkling of an eye.

After an ebullient phase we returned to a more sentimental vein. When I had listened for two hours I was obliged to go on elsewhere. By way of farewell my friends wound up with the ever-popular 'Dobrú noc, má míla' (*Good night, my dearie*); but I heard that the sitting was prolonged for hours after I had said good-bye. A Slovak and his songs are not lightly parted.

Of the melodic versions of the songs mentioned in this chapter the first three are from a collection published by a circle of students who call themselves The Idol Worshippers. Most of those which I heard at Uherské Hradiště I found afterwards in a very interesting collection of two-hundred Slovak songs, given to me by the gifted Moravian musician, Jan Kunc, who edited it. In his preface to the second edition (1918), he says that the publication of yet another song-book needs no justification, since, thanks to the great love of singing among the masses, each new collection quickly passes into several editions. Some idea of the vast treasury of national song which exists in Czechoslovakia may be gathered from Kunc's remark that he found himself faced by a difficult problem of selection, having 7,000 songs at his disposal and space for only 200. And these, we must bear in mind, are exclusively Slovak songs; those of the Wallachians, the Těšín (Teschen) Silesians, and the Hanacks being classed by him separately. Naturally there exist a good many variants of songs which are habitually sung from memory, and in Kunc's collection these are preserved in smaller notation. Fresh songs are continually being added to existing collections. In the song-book in question at least thirty out of the two hundred appear in print for the first time.

Of the musical value of the folk-songs we may judge by the profound influence which they have exercised upon the work of the modern Bohemian composers—Smetana, Dvořák, Fibich, Novák, Suk, Kovařovic, and Janáček. This fact will stand out more and more clearly as this book proceeds.

To the spiritual value of the folk-songs and their enduring power to act as a stimulus upon the national consciousness so often threatened with extinction, we have frequent testimony in the history of the country. Music played its part in the Hussite Wars, in the long struggle to maintain the existence of the Czech language, and, in more recent times, who can doubt that the unanimity and determination with which the Czechoslovak legionaries fought for their freedom, and ours, on almost every front owed much to the continual incentive of the folk-songs? In France, in Italy, in Russia, the old songs of Bohemia, Moravia, and Slovakia were sung in the camp and the field, just as 'the Chalicers' sang them in the streets of Winchester as they took their hard way from Archangel to France. Whatsoever may be lacking to the needs of these intrepid soldiers, the regimental choirs feed their comrades with the music they have learnt as soon as they could lisp. The fullest commissariat would not satisfy the nature of this folk unless it was salted with song.

CHAPTER V

BOHEMIA, though fully awake since the tenth century to the interest of Church music, realized the secular side of the art very slowly. Zdeněk Nejedlý fixes upon the year 1786 as marking a new departure in Czech musical history. It was the same year in which Mozart's *Figaro* cast such a spell upon Prague that the composer himself wrote about this time to Gottfried von Jacquin: 'nothing is played, sung, or whistled here but my *Figaro*'. As by magic the city of ecclesiastical music was transformed into 'Mozart's Prague'. The modern spirit of that period as exemplified in Mozart, found in fact a more assured and cordial welcome in the Bohemian capital than in Vienna. If the Bohemians had cause to be thankful for this regenerative breath of secular music, Mozart on his side was deeply grateful for the warmth of his reception in Prague, coming at a moment when the atmosphere of Vienna was poisoned for him by intrigue. So chilled was he by the neglect of the Court and influential circles, and by the public craze for such composers as Martin and Dittersdorf, that he contemplated taking refuge in England. At this moment the Bohemians welcomed him and took him *con amore* to their warm and enthusiastic hearts. As all the world knows, he showed his gratitude by setting to work to compose 'something really good for Prague'; that 'something' being *Don Giovanni*, which was first performed there on 29 October 1787.

Not the least interesting part of a sojourn in Prague is due to the teeming memories of Mozart evoked by the sight of the old German Theatre, the house in the triangular Coal Market—the ancient hostelry of 'The Three Lions', where the composer and his wife stayed in 1787, and the Villa Bertramka in the suburb of Kosiře, formerly the house of his friends, František and Josefa Dušek, where the composer often took refuge from the noise of the city. 'A ray of sunshine falling on an old grey ruined wall', is Prochazka's happy, but aesthetically inaccurate, description of Mozart's presence in eighteenth-century Prague, for at the time of Mozart's first visit Prague was by no means a city of grey ruin. Through the seventeenth and eighteenth centuries architects such as the Milanese Marini, Kilian Dientzenhofer, Johann Lukas von Hildebrandt, and Fischer von Erlach had been working to turn the Bohemian capital into 'a supreme architectural delight', as Sacheverell Sitwell says in his delightful book on German Baroque Art. The Tower of the Charles Bridge, the Priory of the Knights of Malta, the lovely Belvedere built for Ferdinand I by a pupil of Jacob Sansovino; later buildings, such as the Kinsky and Nostic Palaces, due to Dientzenhofer, and the Palace of Count Glam-Gallas, designed by Fischer von Erlach; the Church of St. Nicholas and a great number of smaller Baroque buildings, some of them built from the plans of Hildebrandt, made Prague a fitting birthplace for the imperishable masterpiece *Don Giovanni*.

The Mozart cult lasted from 1786 until far into the nineteenth century, and, preached by such blind devotees as Tomašek, Vitašek, and Dionys (Divis) Weber, finally became a doubtful blessing because it closed the musical life of the city to the progressive ideas which had sprung up meanwhile in other centres; particularly those which had resulted from Beethoven's emancipation of the art.

The apathy of musical thought and activity which fell upon Prague early in the nineteenth century was partly owing to the unprogressive attitude of Venceslav Tomašek, whose account of Dušek at the piano I quoted in an earlier chapter. Born at Skutec in 1775, where his father was a weaver and the owner of a small drapery business, Tomašek came to the capital as a youth to study law, but fell so completely a victim to the enchantment of Mozart's *Don Giovanni* that, after hearing it, he abandoned his first purpose and determined to become a musician. Lacking the means to obtain tuition, he taught himself harmony and counterpoint, and became an efficient pianist. Eventually he opened a flourishing pianoforte school in Prague.

His church compositions, including Masses (two of which are Requiems) and a four-part *Te Deum*, were much admired by his contemporaries. His opera *Seraphina*—the only one which he permitted to be staged—appears to have been a weak effort; yet his settings of such ballads as Burger's *Leonora* and Goethe's *Erlkönig* prove that he was not devoid of dramatic instinct. His pianoforte pieces, the *Eclogues*, *Rhapsodies*, and *Dithyrambi*, are interesting as efforts to escape from classical tradition, and, in their titles at any rate, foreshadow the piano music of a later day. They may not inconceivably have had some influence upon Schumann and his immediate followers. In recent years an attempt to revive some of them has been made by Czech pianists.

But apart from this branch of his art Tomašek remained obstinately conservative, encased like a fly in amber in the first enthusiasms of his youth; and although his particular incrustation had the perfume and golden transparency of the Mozartian tradition, it hindered him from becoming the helpful leader of a progressive school. For Tomašek was as much an autocrat in the musical life of Prague as Dr. Samuel Johnson in the literary world of London. Hanslick, who had been his pupil before he left his native town to settle in Vienna, says of Tomašek that 'the older he grew, the firmer he sat, the centre of an admiring circle. It was considered a sign of insanity for an artist to leave Prague without having made himself known to Tomašek.' Wagner, during his visit in 1832, did not forget to do so.

Though he lived until 1850, and must therefore have been cognisant of the romantic movement, and even known Weber personally while the composer of *Der Freischütz* was Director of the State Opera in Prague, Tomašek never budged from his entrenchments. He heard Beethoven play and was impressed by his fire and audacity as a pianist, though his criticism is qualified by disapproval; but it is doubtful whether Beethoven as the composer of the nine symphonies and the later pianoforte sonatas, had any message for him at all. Undoubtedly, however, as a pedagogue Tomašek accomplished a useful work, for he was a great advocate for thoroughness in every detail of his art, and from his school some excellent pianists and teachers passed out into the world. Among these were Alexander Dreyschock (1818–69), a once famous virtuoso who was Professor of the Pianoforte at St. Petersburg Conservatoire; Jules Schulhoff (1825–98), who took Paris by storm in the 'forties of last century; William Kuhe (1823–1912), who came to England on a concert tour with the tenor Pischek and remained here, being appointed to a professorship at the Royal Academy of Music in 1886; and among critics, that brilliant and acrid reactionary, Eduard Hanslick (born in Prague, 1825, died 1904).

Quite as reactionary as Tomašek was Dionys (Divis) Weber (1776–1842), first Director of the Prague Conservatoire and a pupil of Abbé Vogler, to whom even more appropriately than to his master we might apply the last lines of Browning's poem:

> . . . My resting place is found,
> The C major of this life, so now I will try to sleep.

Dionys Weber slumbered many years in his directorate, avoiding as far as possible any startling psychic modulations. It must be accounted to his credit, however, that when Wagner came to Prague at nineteen, with an untried Symphony in C in his portfolio, Weber gave him a chance of hearing how it sounded, which was of the greatest importance to the young composer. The orchestra of the Conservatoire was requisitioned for the purpose and this—if we may trust the opinion of Spontini—was unusually good for a pupils' orchestra. It was probably on this occasion that the Director told Wagner that he regarded Beethoven's 'Eroica' Symphony as 'an utter abortion', an opinion which, after all, he shared with many of his contemporaries in Germany. History does not record his opinion of Wagner's work; but he probably approved of its Mozartian tendencies.

The last member of the powerful triumvirate which fought the rising tide of modernism in Prague was Jan August Vitašek (1771–1839), first Principal of the Organ School. He was of more importance as a composer than Dionys Weber, and the critics of the time speak of his Masses and Requiems as having breadth and a certain loftiness of style. He succeeded Kozeluh as music master to the family of Count Bedrich Nostic and was eventually appointed Musical Director to the cathedral of St. Vitus. Although not of progressive tendencies he was genuinely serviceable to the musical life of Prague and refused to leave it for a post in Vienna offered to him by Salieri. Vitašek was the centre of a group of intelligent young men, pupils and disciples, one of whom, F. M. Knize (1784–1840), the choirmaster of St. Haztal, Prague, was somewhat of a pioneer in the national movement and published two books of Czech songs. Josef Krejči (1822–81), successively Director of the Organ School and the Conservatoire, was a strong reactionary. Josef Proksch (1794–1864) set up a Pianoforte School in Prague which rivalled that of Tomašek. He enjoys the distinction of having been both the friend and teacher of Smetana. The fame of Ignaz Moscheles (1794–1870) reached beyond Bohemia. After a course at the Conservatoire under Dionys Weber, he went to Vienna and continued his studies with Albrechtsberger and Salieri. Although probably the most distinguished pianist of the period preceding Chopin and Liszt, he exercised no influence on musical progress in Bohemia.

At this time Moravia could point to two or three gifted musicians who cultivated the folk element. Bohumír Rieger (1764–

1855), Ludvik, Knight of Dietrich (1804–58), who wrote the song 'Moravo, Moravicko mila', and F. B. Kott (1808–84), whose operas *Žižka's Oak* (1840) and *Dalibor* (1846) deal with national subjects.

Although the old classicism lingered in Prague after the close of the eighteenth century, the dawn of a new period was at hand. Two important institutions were founded at the beginning of the nineteenth century: the Union of Musical Artists for the Support of Widows and Orphans (1803), and the Society for the Improvement of Musical Art in Bohemia. The first of the organizations gave to Prague a more regular concert activity and a permanent orchestra; the second, founded by an influential section of the old Czech nobility, with Count Jan Nostic as President, opened its music school in 1811, and this institution, following perhaps the example of Paris, soon adopted the name of Conservatoire. In addition to these, were the Society for the Encouragement of Church Music (1827), developing into the Organ School, which amalgamated with the Conservatoire in 1880, and the Cecilia Society started by Anton Apt in 1840. One result of the activity was the gradual cessation of the polite serfdom of the musicians employed in various capacities by the aristocracy. The professional musician became a free man, although perhaps he paid for his liberty by new forms of material anxiety.

The rise of a national party in politics and literature was bound to affect the arts, and by the middle of the nineteenth century great changes had taken place in the aspirations and ideals of the Czechs.

Meanwhile, although the most influential musical party in Prague, under the dictatorship of Tomašek, ignored most of the music composed after the death of Mozart, the presence of Carl Maria von Weber as Chief Conductor at the State Theatre from 1813 to 1816 effected some changes in the musical apathy that had befallen the life of the city.

Before Weber came to Prague at the urgent request of the Director, Carl Liebich, the opera under Venceslav Muller had greatly degenerated The whole work of organization had to be begun anew. Weber threw himself heart and soul into the task of regeneration, and succeeded in raising the standard of performance to the highest level. But outside the opera house the atmosphere was far from sympathetic to this representative of the new romantic tendency in music. Long wars had exhausted the wealth of the aristocracy, the friction between the State policy and the national sentiment was becoming every day more acute, and the public was growing cold and indifferent when Weber came to the rescue of the opera in Prague. During his direction he produced works by Spohr, Méhul, Cherubini, and even Beethoven's *Fidelio*. His own operas—this was several years before the appearance of *Der Freischutz*—never awoke much enthusiasm. It is not surprising that his letters reflect his discouragement and spiritual isolation during the years of his activity in Prague, culminating in the bitter observation made to his brother Gottfried in 1815, that the place, infatuated by the past, seemed to him 'like a lunatic asylum'.

Twenty years later Romanticism took a firm hold upon Bohemia. It appeared in the first instance to flow more freely through literary than musical channels, and came with patriotic poetry on the one hand and Byronism on the other. Hynek Macha with his romantic poem *Maj (May)* was the herald of its arrival, and after his premature death the movement was carried on by the poets Halek and Jan Neruda, who blended with a passionate love of their unhappy country a knowledge and appreciation of a wider world culture. In music, the romantic impulse came from a group of young men who were mostly law students at the Prague University. In what the subtle connexion between music and the law actually consists the psychologists may some day reveal to us; in the meantime this movement in Prague inevitably reminds us of the part played by the School of Jurisprudence in the development of Russian music. Serov, Stassov, Tchaikovsky all passed the early years of manhood in the law school.

One of the first romantics in classical Prague was J. B. Kittl (1809–65), a pupil of Tomašek. As far as his own creative work was concerned Kittl merely exchanged the older classical traditions of his master's school for the cult of Mendelssohn, in whose style he wrote several overtures, symphonies, and some chamber music, including a septet, besides a few unsuccessful German operas. But as Director of the Conservatoire (1843–65) he introduced a freer spirit into that somewhat hidebound institution.

His fellow student of law, August Ambros (1816–76) was a bolder progressive spirit. He was not a professional musician, for he held a professorship at the University and a post in the Austrian Civil Service; but he had critical acumen and considerable literary ability joined to a love of the art. His *History of*

Music, written in German, although carried no further than the seventeenth century, is a valuable work of its kind. Berlioz, while touring in Germany in the 'forties, read an intelligent and sympathetic article upon his *King Lear* written by Ambros. This induced him to visit Prague for the sake of the small circle of his admirers there. His concerts, although bitterly opposed by the conservative element, were a triumph for Ambros and his party. Venceslav Veit (1806–64) might make cheap sport of Berlioz and parody his *Symphonie Fantastique* under the title of 'Episode in the Life of a Tailor', but the public, which had begun to think more clearly for itself than in Weber's day, signified its desire to repudiate the direction of such leaders by flocking in a healthy reaction to hear something unaccustomed. Berlioz's visit opened the way for other artists who each had something fresh to offer 'Mozart's Prague' which had been too long Tomašek's Prague. Liszt followed Berlioz, and gladly returned more than once. During the following decade Wagner's operas became established in the repertory. Prague became once more the hospitable centre of musical appreciation which she has since remained.

Thus we see that a strong universal and secular current flowed through the Bohemian capital from about 1840 onwards, but it carried with it mainly the cosmopolitan—and particularly the German—elements of society. There was nothing in all this that answered to the patriotic aspirations of a naturally musical race, rapidly re-awakening to national consciousness and longing for intimate self-expression in art and literature, just as Russia before Glinka's coming yearned and groped her way towards a national music. The arts of the Slavonic peoples have never approached to maturity through such gradual, steady, and spacious ascents as characterize the cultural development of happier and more prosperous races. Rather have their arts been at the mercy of stormy tides of political and social vicissitude; now marooned in remote places of refuge—the shores of Onega, the mountain slopes of Slovakia—out of touch with the main stream of intellectual progress; and, in the case of music, clinging passionately to the narrow plank of folk-song as offering a certain degree of familiar security. So, *Prague* might worship Mozart, acclaim Berlioz, be fascinated by Liszt, and pay due tribute to Wagner, but *Bohemia* hungered for music that should be moulded 'a little nearer to her heart's desire'. With the renaissance of the Czech spirit in literature, with the collection of the treasures of an ancient folk-lore by

Kollar and others, and the general movement to the folk for relief from the oppressive weight of Teutonic culture, there arose a new tendency in music—a tendency with separatist aims and a clear, if somewhat intolerant, policy.

It seems both unnecessary and ungenerous to drag into the light and dissect all the weaknesses, faults, and failures of that natural impulse. In theory its first representatives made—almost inevitably—the fundamental error of looking upon the national and the folk interests as one and the same thing; in practice they made the mistake of imitating rather than assimilating the folk-song material; the process of assimilation being a matter of time, while imitation appealed to the impatience of a growing nation. They showed, too, a certain degree of aggressiveness which, although not admirable in itself, is often the sole method of safe-guarding the infancy of a new ideal. The immediate result was a sharp division between the specialist musicians and the disciples of the folk-song cult, leaving the activities of the latter too exclusively in the hands of enthusiastic but inexperienced amateurs. It was a repetition of what occurred in Russia when a series of half-competent composers of the calibre of Paskievich and Verstovsky sought to build up national music on a folk-song basis. These dipped their fingers into the plastic material and created a sub-stance which perhaps served to awaken a craving for better things; but they forgot that only by mixing with the folk-song ingredients the leaven of inspiration could the result be a satisfactory musical sustenance for the multitude.

The urgent desire for song which possessed the entire Czech people no doubt gave the first impetus to the national movement which for some years progressed side by side with the cosmopolitan tendency without mingling with it. The practical problem for the rising generation of composers was the satisfaction of the ever-increasing needs of the masses. One of the earliest musicians to respond to this demand was Jan Jakub Ryba (1755–1815). He published two good collections of folk-songs under German titles, but with Czech words: *Zwolf Böhmische Lieder* (1800) and *Neue Böhmische Lieder* (1808); and also *Louka* (1807) and *Dobra Betulinka*, settings of Czech verses by one of the earliest national poets—Puchmajer. Ryba's *Funeral Songs* and *Song-book for the Young*, for use in Czech schools, supplied two practical require-ments. Josef Chmelensky brought out his *Venec* (a Garland of Czech Songs) between 1835–9. Macháček also published two collections of National Songs with the assistance of other musicians. The preservation of the genuine article was a good work, but the mere imitation of them became a matter of habit and led eventually to the prevalence of sentimental melody and a kind of music which had no great artistic value.[1]

The folk-song influence did not, however, even in the days preceding Smetana, invariably tend to an inferior standard of composition. A. F. Tovacovsky (1825–74), who founded a Slovak Choral Union in Vienna in 1862, made some clever arrangements of Slovak songs which became popular with vocalists. Pavel Križkovsky carried the artistic treatment of the folk-songs still further. It is in fact claimed for him by some thoughtful writers that he was the generator of the Czech National School and left far deeper traces of his influence upon the artistic life of his people than any other of Smetana's forerunners.

Križkovsky, whose baptismal name was Karel—although he was generally known by his monastic name of Paul—was born in Bohemian Silesia, 9 January 1820. He came of a family of poor but talented musicians and the uncle who brought him up was anxious that he should follow some more lucrative occupation. Accordingly the boy was forbidden even to talk of music. Nevertheless at the risk of severe punishment he managed to learn something by playing on his uncle's clarinet when the latter was out of the house. He also hung about the choir of the village church at Neplachovice until his uncle was persuaded to let him join the choir school. One day he was taken to the town of Opava a few miles from his home, where he had the good luck to hear High Mass in the Church of St. Mary. The following Sunday he was missing from his parish church, and every week the same story was repeated. He would tramp to Opava and stand at the choir door gazing wistfully at the singers as they filed in. He became known to some of the choirmen, and one kind soul begged permission to bring him in and let him sit besides the sopranos in the choir. Of course it was not intended that he should sing, but when the leading boy went astray in his solo, Križkovsky took up the part and sang it through correctly to the end, much to the astonishment of the choirmaster. To this exploit he owed a place in the foundation of the choir school. After his voice broke he entered on a long struggle with poverty, but succeeded after many

[1] *Strucny Prehled Dejin České Hudby* (A short general view of Czech Musical History) by Dr. Jaromir Borecky.

E

interruptions in taking a degree (Doctor of Philosophy) at Brno, the capital of Moravia. Here he entered the Augustinian Community of St. Thomas in 1845. He finished his novitiate and became a professor in the following year. The Professor of Divinity in the Community was F. Sušil, a famous collector of the Moravian folk-tunes, and it was due to intercourse with him that Križkovsky became fully conscious of his nationality and began to study and love the folk-music as the utterance of his own people. It was in this spirit that he began to arrange some of the popular tunes for four-part male-voice choir. Sušil saw with joy that the work which, at his request, such accomplished musicians as Rieger had attempted with only partial success, was carried out by this young man with unfailing tact and sympathy. Rieger was at that time Director of the music at the monastery church and was very helpful to Križkovsky in his general musical studies. Eventually he turned over the direction of the choir to his pupil, who kept the post until 1872. Križkovsky also spent six months in Prague in order to extend his knowledge of music old and new.

He was, therefore, well equipped on the technical side of his art when he approached the folk-music and, entering deeply into its spirit and traditions, composed in 1860 that touching and beautiful male-voice chorus *Utonula*,[1] which was received with enthusiasm in Prague and subsequently found its way into the repertory of every choral society in Bohemia. Had he written only this one work his country might have been proud of him, but he followed it up by other compositions for the same combination of voices: *Divca* (Lassie), at once tender and impassioned and charmingly harmonized; and *Dar za Lasku* (*The Love-gift*). In these choral songs we feel that while the material is redolent of the folk-music the treatment of it is masterly. Smetana's observation that it was not until he heard Križkovsky's choruses that he really understood the full significance of the Czech folk-melody sets these works in the light of a revelation.

In later years he composed many more part-songs and choruses: *Prosba Odvedeneho* (*The Recruit's Prayer*), *Zaloba* (*The Plaint*), *Zatoc se* (*Turn around*) for solo quartet and chorus, the words from a folk-song; *Zahrada Bozi* (*God's Garden*) and *Modlitba Sv. Cyrilla na sotnach* (*Prayer of St. Cyril on his Deathbed*); a funeral

[1] *Utonula* ('The Drowned Maiden') was first heard in England during the visit of the Moravian and Prague Male-Voice Choirs in May–June 1919.

song with accompaniment for trombones; a humorous chorus *Vyprask* (*Threshing*) in the polyphonic style; and a good many solo songs, some arrangements and some original. His Cantata in honour of SS. Cyril and Methodius, *Two Stars from the East*, composed for the Millenary Anniversary of the first coming of these Evangelizers to Moravia, is perhaps his most ambitious effort in sacred music. Unfortunately many of Križkovsky's works have been lost. Comparatively few were printed and he had no system of numbering them. In his excessive modesty he never thought of posterity. His choral works were dedicated to various societies to which he gave the manuscripts to be copied —and saw them no more.

Križkovsky was a pillar of the musical life of Brno, where he conducted some memorable performances of sacred music. Several leading musicians of the present day were in his choir and owe their early education to him: Jan Vojaček, at one time conductor at the Vienna Opera, and the gifted operatic composer, Leoš Janáček. He was benevolent to the poor and a warm supporter of every national enterprise. A paralytic stroke put an end to his active career in 1883, and he retired to his old Community of the Austin Friars, Brno, where he died in 1885.

Križkovsky was the first Czech composer whose knowledge of music as an art combined with profound insight into the spirit of the folk-songs enabled him to fuse the two elements in a satisfactory way. He was therefore the true precursor of Smetana, although his inspiration was less copious and the circumstances of his life not at all favourable to a full development on the secular, dramatic, and universal sides of his art.

While the development of choral music made rapid progress in Bohemia, especially after the institution of the Society called 'Hlahol' (*Tone*) in 1861, national opera made scarcely any advance. Every condition of the social life tended to impede this hot-house blossom of musical art, which finds it difficult to flourish in any country without the help of state protection or capitalist enterprise. At the State Theatre in Prague at the close of the eighteenth, and well into the nineteenth, century, representations in Czech were discouraged in every possible way. It was not unusual for the curtain to be summarily lowered in the midst of a Czech play if the 'Direction' considered that it lasted too long, or was in any other way objectionable to the authorities. On Sundays—the great theatre-going day in the week for the people—Czech pieces were altogether banned. At the State 'Bouda' (1786),[1] and the theatre organized by Tyl in the refectory of the Theatine Monastery, in the Mala Strana (1834–6), the vernacular was tolerated and plays with songs were given. The music of these *Singspiele* was furnished by choirmasters such as Volanek[2] or Trava; but all this was as remote from national opera as were the comedies with musical interludes which amused the Russians at a somewhat earlier period.

In 1823, a German opera, *The Swiss Family* by Weigl, was produced in Czech. It was an amateurish affair intended to attract theatre-goers at Christmastide. The one singer in the caste who could claim to be an operatic artist, Katerina Kometova, had an immense reception, and the promoters of the scheme were so elated that they determined to follow up this success with an opera composed by a Czech to a Czech libretto. The moving spirit of the production of *The Swiss Family* was František Škroup (1801–62), a young lawyer who had gained some slight experience both as a conductor and operatic singer. Light-heartedly he undertook the task of writing a national opera, and, having secured the cooperation of Chmelensky as librettist, *Dratenik (The Tinker)* was completed by the festival of Candlemas, 1826. It was the first native opera produced in Bohemia and its reception surpassed in enthusiasm anything that its authors could have hoped for it. When we come to turn the pages of this two-act opera in the light of unbiased criticism,[3] we are forced to acknowledge that it was the hunger of the public for a native-made opera rather than the merits of the work itself which ensured its success. The music, from the overture in early Moravian style to the last page in which the National Hymn of the Czechs, from a later work, was afterwards incorporated, is fluent, brisk, and melodious with very little attempt at dramatic characterization, and very superficial as regards the reflection of the folk element. The tears and ecstasies of the audience were doubtless a subjective manifestation; they could hardly have been called forth by this pleasantly uninspired and rather superficial music.

[1] The word 'Bouda' signifies literally a booth or shanty.

[2] Volanek composed an opera, *The Masquerade in the Seraglio*. Trava supplied the music for one or two *Singspiele* such as *The Boisterous Peasant*, &c.

[3] A reprint of the work, with its old-fashioned semi-German typography, was issued by the Umelecka Beseda (Society of Arts), Prague, in 1913.

Škroup attempted a more ambitious subject a few years later in *The Marriage of Libuše* (1834), and proved that he certainly had not the epic touch. He drops too easily from the national style to the idiom of the Italian opera with which he was familiar. The inconsistencies of his style are such as we find in nearly all the early attempts to create a national art by the mere *imitation of folk-song*. The claim made on Škroup's behalf that because he wrote the first opera in the vernacular he founded a school of National Opera is hardly valid. But certain Czech critics, in their anxiety to give all the honour to Smetana, which is his due, have wasted energy in heaping contempt upon Škroup's modest essays. Between the production of *Dratenik* and Smetana's first appearance on the scene—an interval of some thirty years—it is only possible to point to one example of Czech opera—Macour's *Žižka's Oak* (1847).

After spending the years from 1827–57 as chief conductor at the State Theatre in Prague, Škroup moved to Rotterdam, where he died in 1862. In addition to the works already mentioned, he composed *Oldrich and Božena*, several quite forgotten German operas, *Die Geisterbraut*, *Drahomira*, &c., and music for a farcical play *Fidlovacka* (1834), which contains the song 'Kde domov můj' ('Where is my home') which has been adopted as the Czech national anthem. For this tune—dear from its familiarity rather than its national aroma—and for his courage in braving many hindrances opposed to native opera, the Czechoslovak people will always hold in honour the name of František Škroup.

CHAPTER VI

DURING the years in which Škroup was preparing *Dratenik* for an expectant, but undiscriminating public, an event took place which was to have a supreme influence on the future history of Czech music. In the picturesque town of Litomysl, situated in the heart of Bohemia on the borders of the province of Moravia, Bedřich Smetana was born on 2 March 1824. His father František Smetana, the manager of a brewery belonging to Count Waldstein, was an energetic business man, fond of music as a recreation; good-tempered, but with an underlying streak of harshness. Married three times, he had already seven daughters—five by his second wife and two by his third marriage with Barbara Luik— so that the arrival of the first boy Bedřich, was the occasion of great rejoicing.

The boy's musical education began early under a local musician, Antonin Chmelík, and at five he was able to take part in a quartet played in honour of his father's birthday. He made his first public appearance as a pianist at the age of six, when on 4 October 1830 he played an arrangement of the overture to Auber's *La Muette de Portici*, at a concert to celebrate the name-day of the Emperor Francis I. Amid deafening applause Count Waldenstein's secretary lifted the little boy up in his arms that the audience might get a better view of him. About this age he composed a valse and a gallop. Litomysl was proud of its wonder-child.

In 1831 his father moved to Jindrichuv-Hradec where he became brewer to Count Czernin. This place, once the seat of the great family of Rosemberk, lies south of Litomysl, and in coaching days was one of the halting-places between Prague and Vienna. It is a beautiful town, full of fine old houses dating from the most prosperous and oppressive period of the Austrian régime. The scenery is typical of Southern Bohemia; rolling uplands, long stretches of forest land, with here and there one of 'Bohemia's pools like silver bowls agleam' lying almost flush with its setting of rich greensward. Here Bedřich attended an elementary school and afterwards the Gymnasium. He continued his musical education under the guidance of the local organist, Ikavec. At fourteen he was sent to school with his brother at Jihlava, although shortly afterwards he was moved to Nemecky-

Brod to continue his studies. Meanwhile his father had acquired a small property at Ruzkova Lhotice, where the boy spent his holidays in surroundings which he afterwards depicted in his serenely beautiful symphonic poem, *In the Fields and Forests of Bohemia*.

At this time his artistic life was narrow and all that he heard of the wider musical world of Prague allured him irresistibly. His father finally gave way to his persistent entreaties and Bedřich was permitted to continue his schooling at the Gymnasium in the capital, where he arrived in 1839. A shy and rustic youth, he was looked down upon by his more sophisticated fellow-students, the majority of whom were the sons of the prosperous German burgher class. Here, as in all the schools he attended, it was inevitable that his education should be wholly German, so that a quarter of a century later this ardent patriot, and master of declamation as far as the vernacular was concerned, felt himself obliged to apologize for the faults he made in writing his own language.

Prague, dreaming by the waters of Vltava of a great free past; brooded over by the Hrad, stern and silent above its bowers of foliage; its rows of dark, deserted windows lit up only by the flames of sunset, must have appealed to all that was patriotic and romantic in the young student. He had gone there at a moment when a new life was beginning to pulse in the hopeless old city. Josef Jungman, the Director of the Gymnasium which Smetana attended, was the compiler of an epoch-making book, the great Dictionary of the Czech language; Palacky's *History of the Czech Nation* had aroused interest; the authenticity of the manuscript of Kraluv Dvur, that famous collection of historical and lyrical poems, was a burning question for discussion among the Czechs, as was the origin of the Kalevala to the Finns about the same time. Though the realization of freedom and a new republic with Masaryk as its leading spirit was still a remote prospect, Bohemia was no longer 'a fen of stagnant waters'. Hope stirred there, if only as an intellectual movement.

In Prague Smetana laid in a store of impressions to be reflected in his music in years to come. He formed a quartet among his friends for which he wrote a String Quartet and composed a few polkas. He frequented such concerts as he could afford, but neglected the practical object of his life in Prague—his Gymnasium classes. As a result his father decided to take him away from the city of temptation and place him under the care of his cousin, Professor J. F. Smetana, as a boarder in the school of the Premonstratensians at Plzen. But his musical talents were quickly discovered by his teachers and one of them at least, Father Beer, could not resist exploiting them in society, so that the youth of sixteen, who played Liszt and Thalberg with such remarkable virtuosity, was soon in demand as a social asset and spent much time in social music-making.

Although he knew very little of the technical side of his art, and his compositions were not much better than improvisations, his ideals, even at this time, soared above mere dilettantism and revealed the true artist that was in him.

We have written proofs of the loftiness of his young ambitions and the frankness of his self-criticism. In his diary which he kept at Plzen, he says that he desires to be 'a Mozart in composition and a Liszt in technique'. On the manuscript of an overture composed in 1842 he wrote a few years later: 'Composed at Plzen in the darkness of the most complete ignorance of all musical science and only saved from destruction by fire thanks to the intercession of the owner, who was anxious to keep this effusion as a curiosity of its kind.' The owner was Katherine Otilie Kollar, his future wife. They had met in childhood at Jindrichuv-Hradec, and later on, the Kollars, then established at Plzen, had opened their doors to the young student. Their daughter was then in Prague studying music with Josef Proksch, but the young people saw each other during her holidays, and the romantic first love which this graceful and intelligent girl awoke in Smetana expressed itself in a little cycle of piano pieces which were the first really individual compositions of Smetana.

He finished his course at the Gymnasium in 1843, but without scholastic honours, and his cousin the Professor, convinced that Bedřich was only fit for a musical career, persuaded his father to let him follow what the youth himself calls 'my life and my salvation'. But the elder Smetana had other intentions. It was one thing to have a distinguished local amateur in the family, and quite another to see his eldest son struggling along in the worst paid of professions instead of becoming a brewer like his brother Anton. Moreover, František Smetana had fallen upon adverse times, and having been obliged to part with his property at Ruzkova Lhotice, was barely keeping the wolf from the door by means of a small brewery at Obristvi. If Bedřich was set upon going to

Prague, let him take twenty golden florins—the only patrimony he was ever likely to get—and manage his own affairs. Thus equipped, the young man of nineteen sought the capital with the idea of becoming a pianist. Thanks to the recommendation of Katherine Kollar, Josef Proksch undertook to give him lessons on credit, and after a short time Kittl, then Director of the Prague Conservatoire, procured for Smetana the post of music master in the family of Count Leopold Thun, with board, lodging, and a salary of 300 florins a year. He remained four years in this capacity, living with the Thuns sometimes in their beautiful, romantic, melancholy palace in the Mala Strana at Prague, and some part of the year at one of their summer residences—Ronsperg, or the estate of Bon Repos, near Nové Benatky, the district whence came Jiři Benda in the previous century. This country home of the Thuns lay to the north-east of Bohemia, and so the circle of his intimacy with all the varied aspects of his native country was completed; a very important factor in his future development, for in the majority of his works we are aware of the wonderful knowledge and sympathy which interpenetrate their musical fabric.

It was probably during the quiet summer months spent at Bon Repos that Smetana, in the light of the more disciplined training acquired during his winter courses of work with Proksch, began to find himself as a creative musician. His thoughts turned from virtuosity to composition. It was here that the idea of the Bagatelles and Impromptus came to him: a cycle of music poems which should evoke the image of the beloved and express his fresh and youthful passion. The pieces, naïvely labelled *Innocence*, *Idylle*, *Longing*, *Love*, &c., are not great music, but they are sincerely felt—the music of real life, which makes us understand the love story of Smetana and Katherine Kollar; the charm and inocuous coquetry of the girl, the tenderness, warmth, and impatience of the earnest and unsullied youth. Their value in a study of Smetana's music lies, however, chiefly in their demonstration of his particular cast of thought and emotion. They are the first outcome of a sufficiency of technical knowledge to use his medium freely, and he flies at once to musical portraiture, to autobiography, to an art that gives clear expression to that which belongs to his own spiritual life. In short this early work contains the germ of his whole art. The substance of the mature Smetana, the Smetana of the Symphonic Poems *My Fatherland*, and the

Quartet 'From my Life', of Smetana the individualist, the 'programme' composer, the disciple of Berlioz and Liszt, is inchoate in this cycle of simple love-poems.

As he felt the basis of his musical science become more sure Smetana longed for freedom and a larger artistic life. He was also impatient to make a home to which he could take his betrothed. At this time the fortunes of Katherine Kollar were better than his own, for she had a fair number of pupils among the aristocratic families of Prague, and when Bedřich decided to give up his post in the Thun household she was engaged in his place. He soon found himself in great poverty. No position as conductor or organist offered itself, a concert tour proved a financial failure, and his project of opening a music school was impossible of realization without capital. It was at this juncture that he turned to Liszt—the good Samaritan of the musical world. In a long letter written in May 1848, he lays before the generous master all the wounds inflicted upon him by the blows of adversity, explains his hope of making a living out of a school on the lines of that of Proksch, and asks for a loan of 400 florins. 'I have no security to offer but myself and my word', he writes, 'but that I hold sacred and therefore more sure than a hundred guarantees.' Liszt in reply accepted the dedication of the young man's *Six Characteristic Pieces for Piano*, Op. 1, and must have slipped something besides goodwill and kindly appreciation between the pages of his letter, for the School was started successfully, and on 27 August 1849 Smetana married Katherine Kollar.

These were years of political unrest. The Revolution of 1848, which brought about the abdication of the aged Emperor Ferdinand I, and seemed for a time likely to set up a federal Austria and give a reasonable autonomy to the Bohemian people, was not without influence upon Smetana, who composed a March for the Students' Legion during the stormy days of June, and a *Solemn Overture*, Op. 4, which was conducted by Škroup at one of the concerts on Žofin Island in April 1849. Undoubtedly he was at heart a liberal and a patriot. But the force of circumstances which bent even the stubborn wills of the Czech people seems to have driven Smetana into a strange position, for we find him in 1850 appointed Director of Music to the old Emperor, who after his abdication resided in the Hradčany at Prague. It is difficult to imagine the future lyric poet of Bohemia's beauties, joys, and afflictions in the capacity of Court-musician to a Habsburg. The connexion did not last long. Smetana composed a Triumphal Symphony in E major, based upon Haydn's Austrian National Hymn, for the marriage of the new Emperor Francis Joseph I who began his reign with constitutional promises that proved abortive. The very genesis of this work is touched with irony: an epithalamium for a Habsburg prince written by a Czech musician on an Austrian National Hymn composed by a Croatian. Smetana's ardent patriotism glowed through the flimsy veil of obsequious language in which the dedication was couched. His work was set aside by some Court official and this was the first of a long series of rebuffs suffered for Bohemia's sake. His chief comfort during the next few years was the appreciation of his work shown by Liszt, Clara Schumann, and one or two others. Liszt visited Prague in 1849 and 1856; Smetana was at Weimar in 1849 and 1857, and they met at Buda-Pest in 1865. His music-school kept him from starvation, but it was impossible to make headway against the tides of oppression and prejudice, and Smetana eventually succumbed to the temptation which denuded Bohemia of so many of her best men, and accepted the post of musical director at Gothenburg in Sweden, offered to him through the recommendation of the pianist, A. D. Dreyschock. The position brought him a fairly liberal salary and opportunities for free musical activity.

Smetana remained five years at Gothenburg where he inspired genuine respect as a musician and was liked as a man. He conducted the orchestra and choral society of the *Harmoniska Sallskapet*, gave lessons (Christine Nilsson is said to have been among his pupils), and contributed generally to raise the standard of taste in his temporary home. In a letter written to Liszt he speaks of his own compositions, the symphonic poems *Richard III*, Op. 11, and *Wallenstein's Camp*, Op. 14. He is Liszt's wholehearted admirer, and perhaps at this period of his life inclined to pay him that form of homage said to be the sincerest flattery.

Smetana composed *Richard III* with a clear programme in his mind. Writing to J. Srb when over twenty years had elapsed since the first performance of the work, he says: 'As to the explanation: whoever knows Shakespeare's *Richard III* can re-evoke for himself just as he pleases the whole tragedy while listening to the music. All I can say is that with the first bar I introduced my own presentment of Richard in a musical form. This, the principal theme (it appears in the basses), dominates the entire compo-

sition, varied in different ways. Before the *Finale* I have endeavoured to give a musical picture of Richard's dreadful dream
in his tent before the battle, when the spectres of all his victims
pass before him in the night and announce his defeat on the
morrow. The conclusion describes Richard's fall. The middle
section of the Poem depicts Richard's triumph as a King and afterwards his gradual deterioration.'

Wallenstein's Camp, 'music for the introduction to Schiller's
tragedy-drama', as Proksch calls it, was composed at Gothenburg
in 1858–9 and produced for the first time, together with *Richard III*,
at Žofin, Prague, in 1862. Here the scene of the play takes him on
to his native soil, to that very Plzen where he had scraped through
the Gymnasium classes, been fêted as an amateur pianist, and
met his first love. The motley crowd gathered under Wallenstein's command contained as we know various Slavonic elements
which might have given Smetana an opportunity of introducing
some national colour had he been disposed to take it. The fact
that he made no use of indigenous melody shows that he was not
much concerned at that period of his career with the creation of
'a national idiom'. Comparison of *Wallenstein's Camp* (1859)
with the camp orgies in the Symphonic Poem *Sarka* (1875) shows
the evolution of his methods in this respect, for though he uses no
actual folk material in the later work, yet an unmistakable national
feeling pervades its atmosphere.

The Symphonic Poem *Hakon Jarl*, Op. 16, also dates from
Smetana's sojourn in Gothenburg, where it was completed in
1861, and, like his other early compositions, was first produced in
Prague in 1864. The idea of the work was suggested by Oelen-
schlager's now-forgotten tragedy which tells how the mighty
pagan hero, Hakon Jarl, is finally overthrown by the rightful heir
to the throne of Norway, Olaf Trygvason. Hakon Jarl, usurper
and tyrant though he was, stands out as a fine epic figure, who, in
Smetana's estimation, dwarfs the Christian hero, Olaf. We feel
that the composer's sympathies were with the powerful chieftain
and his warriors; while, as a Czech, he is drawn towards a race
which is struggling for its freedom. It was the contrast between
the Christian and heathen components which interested him
musically, and he produced a vigorous work, although the influence of Liszt detracts something from its originality. The supernatural element in Hakon Jarl is a pale copy of the Witches'
Scene in Shakespeare's *Macbeth*, for which Smetana had written

piano music in 1859. It is characteristic of the man's modesty and delicate conscientiousness that he did not use his position as musical director to produce any of these three symphonic poems in Gothenburg.

The last years of Smetana's life in Sweden were shadowed by the illness of his wife Katherine. The climate of the North did not agree with her, and she retired to Bohemia without him. She did not live to reach home, but died at Dresden on 15 April 1859. We know so little about the inner life of these two since the realization of their love-dream in 1849, that we can only surmise that their conjugal life was peaceful. And since marriages, like countries, may be the happier for having no histories, that Smetana married again in the following year need not be taken as a proof that he was inconstant, or that his first marriage was not a success. The event is amply accounted for by the fact that he was a widower at thirty-six, and moreover a widower in exile. His second wife, Barbara Ferdinandi, was a Bohemian, so devoted to her country that after a few months in Gothenburg she began to pine, and Smetana resolved, partly on this account, to resign his post and turn his face homewards. But apart from domestic matters the supreme hour of decision had already struck for him. In Gothenburg he was a person of importance, and free from worldly cares. He was beginning, too, to be known in cosmopolitan circles. But with the prospect of happier times in Bohemia, the choice now lay between the hope of universal fame and the reviving interests of his country. Possibly some prescience warned him that in Bohemia bitter disappointment and endless conflicts awaited him. He was not the man to shrink from what he had come to regard as his mission; namely, the endowment of the Czech people with a series of musical works that should reflect the whole national genius shown in the mirror of a strong and clear personality.

The improvement in the social and political conditions of the Czechs in the early 'sixties awoke a responsive thrill in the artistic life of the country. The long-cherished project to erect a National Theatre in Prague now seemed within sight of fulfilment. This was indeed a remarkable advance when we consider that up to this time the German theatre and language had continued to overshadow all native talent and to hinder productions in the Czech language.

In 1862 the Bohemian Diet secured a site and built the Provisional Theatre at a cost of 106,000 florins. From all over the country people gave financial support, so that the money was raised by public subscription; a truly remarkable effort which only goes to prove once again the universal love of music among the Czech people. Ill-luck, however, attended the efforts of the Czechs to provide a worthy home for the performance of native opera and drama. When sufficient funds had been collected to replace the Provisional Theatre by a permanent one, the new building was destroyed by fire soon after its inauguration in 1881. In an incredibly short time the nation made good its loss, and the present National Theatre (Národní Divadlo) now stands on the bank of Vltava as much a witness to the courage and determination of the race as to its aesthetic gifts. But this is to anticipate events by some twenty years.

When Smetana returned to Prague from Sweden, the social atmosphere, although renewed by hopes of greater liberty, was still somewhat fusty with lingering intrigue, and the disloyalty inevitable among a people who had lived for centuries a grinding existence between the upper and nether millstones of political oppression and arrogant, or at best unsympathetic, patronage. In Bohemia, as in other annexed and embittered countries, society harboured some servile natures even as late as the 'sixties of last century, and also—which was excusable under the circumstances —some chauvinistic patriots who saw the country's good only from the narrowest cultural point of view. There was, however, a heroic spirit in action, and Smetana lived to foster it. From the moment of his return to Prague his activities were unceasing. He became conductor of the new choral society 'Hlahol', and of the concerts of the Academy Reading Club (*Akademicky Čtenarsky Spolek*); took part in founding *Umělecka Beseda* (the Society of Arts); organized chamber music; conducted Berlioz's 'Romeo and Juliet' at the Shakespearian Tercentenary Festival in 1864, and, soon after the subscription concerts of the Artistic Union had come into existence, directed at one of them the first performance in Prague of Liszt's 'St. Elizabeth'. He acted as musical critic for *Národní Listy* from 1864–5, and fought the battle of modern music as opposed to Italian opera, and also the abuse of the engagement of 'star' artists. His courage and candour made him many enemies.

For the members of 'Hlahol' he composed some of his finest

choral works: *The Three Riders* (*Trí jezdeí*), 1862, *The Renegade*
(*Odrodilec*), 1863, and *The Peasant* (*Rolnická*), one of the most
popular of his male-voice choruses; a Czech Song (*Česká Píseň*),
a cantata for mixed voices; the *Solemn Chorus* (*Slavnostni Sbor*)
and *Song of the Sea* (*Píseň na moři*) date from the 'seventies;
The Dower (*Věno*), *Prayer* (*Modlitba*), and *Our Song* (*Naše písen*)
were his last choral works written for men's voices only; besides
these he wrote the 'Three Choruses for Women's Voices' to
words by Sladek. Even the earliest group of these compositions
shows a masterly use of vocal colour, and a careful treatment of
the text, which promises much for his later operatic achievements.
All have kept their places in the repertories of the leading choral
societies in Bohemia, although the improvement in choral technique during the last quarter of a century has led composers to
outdo these comparatively simple unaccompanied choruses by
complexity of treatment.

In January 1862, with the assistance of the Artistic Union and
'Hlahol', Smetana gave a concert in the hall on Žofin Island.
Henceforth it became his deliberate intention to launch himself
on the full stream of musical life in Prague. His purpose was
clear: to act for Czech art in the double capacity of creator and
organizer and to remove once and for all from his nation the
reproach that it could only produce executant musicians. He had
wisely advised that the building of a great National Opera House
should be postponed until a really fine monument could be
erected. But the Provisional Theatre was now an accomplished
fact, and 'the creation of a true Czech opera became a question of
national honour'. The first of Smetana's patriotic operas, *The
Brandenburgers in Bohemia* ('Braniboři v Čechach') was produced
in January 1866. Through his friend and former pupil, Prochazka,
he procured his libretto from Karel Sabina and completed the
three-act opera as early as 1863. Various untoward events with-
held its production. Count Jan Harrach had offered a prize of
600 florins for the best Czech historical opera; but though the
judges included men of intelligence, such as Ambros and Kittl,
they were slow to discern the merits of Smetana's score. When
the public was at last given the opportunity of judging for itself it
did so with no uncertain voice. Smetana writes in his journal:
'First night of *The Brandenburgers*. Crowded house. I was recalled nine times. Conducted myself.' And again: 'Second
night of *The Brandenburgers*. The house packed and still greater

success.' In the following March he was awarded the Harrach prize.

From almost every point of view the libretto of *Braniboři* leaves much to be desired. It contains some gross historical errors which are not redeemed by any lofty, imaginative literary qualities. The period of the opera is that disastrous time following the death of Přemysl Otokar II (1192–1230), one of Bohemia's strongest kings, who died leaving his heir, a minor, to the mercies of Otho of Brandenburg, and his country a prey to a horde of German mercenaries and greedy settlers. The ravages of this alien incursion united the Bohemian nobles with the folk for the time being, and Otho was compelled to order the intruders to leave the country within three days. This historical material answered to the feelings of the hour which witnessed Smetana's return to Prague, and the scenes in which the populace demand the expulsion of the Brandenburgers, and shout in triumph at the news of their speedy departure, gave him the opportunity for which he was seeking to body forth the folk-spirit in music drama.

Both Smetana and the public for which he composed it outgrew *The Brandenburgers*, although it is still occasionally restored as an act of piety to the repertory of the National Opera (Národní Divadlo). But to the student it has a certain value because it contains the germ of all Smetana's art; in its delineation of character, its often forcible dramatic feeling, its lyric flow and national tendency. Smetana, who had studied Berlioz, Liszt, and Wagner to some purpose, did not of course approach the question of national opera from the simple standpoint of the folk-song. Still less was he attracted to Meyerbeer's school of dramatic music; to the constant preoccupation with 'effects', and the artificiality of opera characteristic of the first half of the nineteenth century; days when, for example, Rubini, for the convenience of the public, always took his high C punctually at 12.45 p.m.; when, in Nejedlý's forcible words, 'Falsehood had become lord of the whole artistic world, and desolation had fallen upon the holy places.'

From the outset, Smetana's nature inclined to naturalism in music, to a more or less concrete programme, and to a perfectly free and progressive form which he adapted to each case as it arose. The first of his national operas resembles in its dramatic outlines Moussorgsky's *Boris Godounov*: a prince in his minority, a ruthless guardian, a host of avaricious Teutons swarming into Bohemia, form the counterpart of the Poles striving to overrun

Western Russia in *Boris*, and a whole people rising in protest, swaying to and fro in their agony, and forming the chief protagonist of the drama. Unfortunately there was no great poet like Poushkin to inspire Sabina and give him the basis for a strong libretto. The literary material of *The Brandenburgers* is too flimsy to take the dye of national colour satisfactorily. Nor was Smetana free to approach his task in the same spirit of detachment and defiant independence which possessed the Russian composer when he took up the subject of Boris Godounov. In the first place the Bohemian composer did not develop in that dauntless isolation which kept Moussorgsky out of the main currents of musical life. Smetana had looked upon a much larger world of music and was naturally influenced by his more universal outlook. Then, again, he was captive to the exigencies of his time and could not afford to wait indefinitely to be understood by his countrymen.

On the appearance of *The Brandenburgers* his enemies assailed Smetana as a Wagnerian and a traitor to the folk spirit. Smetana undoubtedly shared Wagner's conviction that opera must be built upon drama, not upon the mere welding together of lyric numbers, whether or not they be based on folk melodies. He had studied Wagner's works and saw in his reforms the salvation of opera. In his own words: 'Meyerbeer's Grand Opera would have been the ruin of music drama, if Wagner had not in the end insisted upon a return from artificiality to naturalness and veracity.' The epithet 'Wagnerian' intended to be a badge of shame, forced upon Smetana by those who misunderstood his efforts, fitted him probably far better than appears in *The Brandenburgers*, for though he was anxious 'to get rid of all the old lumber' he was obliged for various reasons to make several concessions to public taste in this work. Therefore in studying this opera as the starting point of Smetana's dramatic works we must bear in mind that it was written at a period of artistic ferment when, as yet, the principles of national opera were not quite firmly fixed in Smetana's mind. One thing it shows clearly enough: that the composer in confronting the problem of nationality in music left the naïve ideals of Škroup far behind him, and aimed at a work based on dramatic realism, having at the same time a direct connexion with the life of the people.

If Smetana approached Wagner on the question of methods, he had quite different ideals in the matter of dramatic material. His choice of subjects from history, or everyday life, was dictated by

F

temperament, and the innate Slavonic leanings towards realism. Myth did not appeal to him. Only one of his nine operas deals with mythical characters,[1] and it is the work which with the greatest semblance of truth may be called Wagnerian. This preoccupation with reality necessitated the development of a very different style from that employed in *The Nibelungen Ring*. The principles of his art had to be patiently and independently built up. For Smetana, as for all masters of dramatic music, the requirements of declamation were the first point of consideration. Again we may compare him with Moussorgsky in his desire to bring musical declamation into closer relationship with speech. One of his chief difficulties was that at that period Czech prosody was in a much less settled condition than in the case of the Russian language. Dobrovsky (1753–1829), the great Bohemian philologist, had invented a system of accentuated prosody; later on, Jungman taught that poetry should be ruled by quantity, and the adoption of this unpractical idea as applied to the Czech language led to the neglect of the correct accent and gave rise to the most careless methods of pronouncing. Consequently Smetana found complete disorder in the sphere that was most important to him as a dramatic composer. None could say with authority how Czech words should be declaimed. Working at first by intuition, Smetana gradually evolved a system that entitled him to be regarded as the founder of Czech musical declamation. We see evidences of it in *The Brandenburgers*, and in much greater perfection in the works which followed. There remained, however, another task for him to face. The democratic type of Czech art demanded that the music should not be merely Czech, but redolent of the folk. Smetana, however, did not see the solution of this problem in the representation of the people through the folk-songs. Although in his first opera he gives a folk-scene on great lines which may be compared with the choral scenes in *Boris Godounov*, he shows just how far the folk element may penetrate the substance of modern opera, and observes a just proportion between modernity, nationality, and the folk-song element.

While waiting for the production of *The Brandenburgers* Smetana wrote his second opera, *The Bartered Bride*, by the Overture to which he won universal recognition. Sabina, who had not shown much skill or originality in the libretto of an historical

[1] *Dalibor*.

opera, retrieved his reputation in this picture from rural life. Composed between 1863–6, and produced at the Provisional Theatre in the year of its completion, *The Bartered Bride* is not perhaps a gem of the first order, but is nevertheless a perfectly cut and coloured stone of its kind—say a Bohemian garnet. In 1895 a German company performed the work at Drury Lane and it was revived some years later at Covent Garden. In neither case did it carry away the audience as it does in Bohemia, or even, before 1914, in south Germany. In America, where it was given at the Metropolitan Opera House, New York, in 1909, and also in Chicago, the enthusiasm it awakened was much warmer. But in America we may reckon with a much larger emigrant Czech element. For us it still awaits a performance by native artists who can give us the true spirit of the work: a production in which the scenery and dresses are really Czech, and not Tyrolean, with possibly a sprinkling of Neapolitan costumes among the chorus.

There have been several later representations of the opera, notably that given at Sadlers Wells in 1933, in which much of the true spirit of the work was recaptured, and the details of scenery and costume were duly respected. The writer of this book was responsible for the translation of the text from the original Czech.[1] She took nearly two years over the task and saw many performances of the opera in Czechoslovakia during this period. But we still lack an authoritative performance in its own language, for who truly knew what Russian opera was like until the Beecham productions by a native company in 1913 and 1914?

From beginning to end *The Bartered Bride* sparkles with fun and spirited action. For what it is—and it has no pretensions to be more than brilliant musical comedy—the work is perfect in its consistency, in the wonderful confluence of words and music and deft use of national colour. The framework is slight, but it is admirably articulated, and all its elements, literary and musical, are woven into a seamless tissue. As William Ritter picturesquely describes it, over the frail web of the plot 'the music lies like sparkling hoar frost on a network of branches'.

The opera in its present form is the result of a good deal of repolishing, but it has retained its spontaneity and lyrical flow. It was first performed as an operetta in two Acts with spoken

[1] *The Bartered Bride*, English edition published by Boosey and Hawkes, London, 1933.

dialogue; later on, when the composer expected a performance at the Opéra-Comique in Paris, he added the drinking chorus for male voices in Act I, and a new national dance in Act II, besides Mařenka's solo ('This dream of love'), which was a distinct gain, because at first humour preponderated a little too much over sentiment for the perfect balance of the comedy. In 1869, the work was definitely divided into three Acts, the Polka and Furiant being then interpolated. Finally, the most important change of all was made before the opera was performed in Leningrad, when the spoken dialogue was replaced by recitative. For this purpose Smetana had to evolve a style of flexible and realistic declamation far removed from the weighty utterances of Wagnerian heroes. Some of the characters in *The Bartered Bride* are loquacious to a degree which approaches patter. I am not sure that Smetana was the first composer to make one of his characters stammer in music, but he has been very successful with the stuttering phrases for the inarticulate Vašek, without, however, overdoing the joke.

The Overture lifts us off our feet with its madcap vivacity, and is a delightful picture of rustic festivity, enlivened by the hum of the peasants' chatter, and gay with many-coloured embroideries, rainbows of floating ribbon, and flower-garlands with which even the men in Moravia do not disdain to deck their hats. Although in painting Josef Manes had faithfully and brilliantly depicted the life of the people, there had been hitherto nothing like this in Bohemian music. Nor has it been surpassed in exuberant vitality and humour by any later work. As a rule Smetana did not precede his operas by an elaborate introduction (the Overture to *Libuše* was written with a special aim in view), but it seems as though he was striving to emulate Mozart in the scope and brilliance of the Prelude to *The Bartered Bride*. It is linked to the opera by the use of some of the chief motives heard in the course of the action: the festal theme of the marriage contract; the motive associated with Jeník's bargain; Mařenka's lament; and the lively opening chorus. The dances form an exhilarating feature of the opera, they fall into place quite naturally, being to this people as spontaneous an expression of joy as song itself.

From the time when this comic opera in its finished form was given at the Provisional Theatre in September 1870, the Czechs were not merely enraptured, but obsessed, by it. The spectacle of the public surfeiting on one particular composition and ignoring all the rest of the composer's works is not peculiar to Bohemia.

The serious operas that followed *The Bartered Bride* were often completely misunderstood by the public for which they were written, and the critics of the time, with the exception of Prochazka, were not equal to expounding the aims which Smetana sought to embody in them. Twenty years later Hostinksy, Nejedly, and a few other writers, set Smetana in a clearer light before his compatriots; while thanks to the devoted efforts of Kovařovic as conductor of the Národní Divadlo the whole series of his dramatic works was put before them time after time in the most painstaking and convincing interpretations. Smetana was too serious an artist to be lulled into complacency by the outburst of enthusiasm evoked by his first comic opera. He resented the efforts of public opinion to restrain his creative enterprise, and this drove him to belittle the music of *The Bartered Bride*, declaring that it had cost him no effort to compose. On a public occasion, in 1882, he displayed his not unnatural irritation with the craze for this early work when he asserted that: '*The Bartered Bride* is merely child's play. I composed it without ambition, just tossed it off, as it were, because after *The Brandenburgers* I was called a Wagnerian who could write nothing light, or in the national style. Therefore I had recourse immediately to Sabina for a libretto and wrote the thing after my own heart in those days, *straight off the reel in a way that beat even Offenbach himself hollow*.' We must allow for a certain degree of pique in this statement, for it is evident that Smetana thought the music worth a good deal of revision. But it explains why he did not follow up this success with a whole series of light operas which might have established himself and his colleague Sabina in a flourishing Gilbert and Sullivan partnership, the joy of Prague and a still more copious source of imitation for Vienna, which had echoed *The Bartered Bride* in many popular works.

By the autumn of 1866 Smetana was absorbed in *Dalibor*, which was finished by Christmas and produced for the first time on the occasion of the laying of the foundation stone of the permanent National Theatre (Národní Divadlo), Prague, on 16 May 1868. The actual performance took place in the Theatre of the New Town. *Dalibor* is based on a legend which is symbolic both of the temperament and the national destiny of the Czechs. The opera takes its title from the half-legendary hero, Dalibor, who is constantly at war with the Burgrave of Ploskovice; for the Burgrave has captured the knight's dearest friend, the minstrel Zdeněk, whose music voices all the joys and sorrows of the race, and put him to death by impalement. At the moment when the action of the opera begins Dalibor has taken the town of Ploskovice and revenged Zdeněk by killing the Burgrave. He has renounced all his possessions in order to live nearer to the heart of his suffering people. He is the type of liberator, fearless leader, and loyal friend, dear to the Czechs. He is not afraid to defy even the king himself in defence of the peasants' rights. Therefore he is seized and brought to trial, and condemned to perpetual imprisonment in one of the towers of the Hradcany.[1] But since, alas, a love-story must be dragged into opera as a concession to public taste, the compiler of the libretto, Joseph Wenzig, makes Milada, the Burgrave's sister, fall in love with Dalibor at the very time when she appears as his accuser. Disguised as a boy she succeeds in following him to prison. Dalibor has all the Czech passion for music, and asks his jailer to smuggle a fiddle into his dungeon. Milada brings it with his food, and also a rope ladder. Wonderful music issues from the tower, and even when the prisoner is deprived of his instrument, the voice of melody is not extinguished, because the spirit of Zdeněk visits his friend at night and plays the airs of long ago. Meanwhile Dalibor's followers are preparing an insurrection in his favour. The king discovers this and hastily gives orders that Dalibor is to be beheaded within the fortress walls. The sentence is to be carried out on the very same night on which Milada has planned the captive's escape. While she is awaiting his signal at the foot of the tower she hears the tolling of the bell as he is led to the scaffold. In the original version Dalibor is executed and Milada dies at the head of the party of rescue. But this tragic ending was altered for the performance of the work in Vienna, probably by order of the censor, and Dalibor was permitted to escape in time to receive the last embraces of the dying woman.

The actual history of Dalibor, incrusted with legends and fanciful details, is of little importance beside the symbolism of the tale. The hero is the personification of the national soul; the wraith of Zdeněk who visits his friend in the darkest hours of his affliction is the spirit of hope speaking, through the medium of music, a message of consolation and confidence heralding the dawn of a new day. This opera which, after the liberation of 1919, was revered as a kind of fulfilled gospel to the Czechs, met with

[1] The Daliborka Tower is shown to every tourist visiting Prague.

such a cold reception on its first appearance that it almost broke the composer's spirit. Various musical factions fell upon him with hostile comments, the most senseless and bitterest of criticisms being the reiterated accusation of Wagnerism. A conflict not unmixed with political rancour raged round *Dalibor*. In connexion with his first national opera I have already shown that Smetana was a progressive and wide-minded musician who could not, and did not, ignore all that Wagner had done for music drama. But his whole heart was set upon endowing his country with operas as Slavonic in inspiration as Wagner's were Germanic in spirit. 'What should I have to do with Wagnerism?' he cries in exasperation. 'I have quite enough to do with Smetanism, and I only want my style to be sincere.' We may absolve *Dalibor* from containing any conscious imitation of Wagnerian methods. If Smetana's enemies had not been blinded by prejudice, and anxious to hurl at him the stone with the sharpest edge to it, they might have found a more potent source of suggestion in Beethoven's *Fidelio*. There is no doubt that Wenzig had this opera in mind when he planned the libretto of *Dalibor*: Milada and Leonora are akin: the disguise, the duping of the old jailer, the prison scene—these are only the more salient points of resemblance. It is not improbable that Smetana himself had a hand in this dramatic analogy. But musically, also, he owes much to Beethoven's symphonies, where Wagner also found the germ of his leading motives. In the style and elaboration of his thematic material, in what has been described as his 'monothematism', the Czech composer aims at a clear, definite subject, making it the kernel of his whole work and using its variants for psychological suggestion. In his operas Smetana makes use of comparatively few leading themes. The entire structure of *Dalibor* may be said to be based on one motive with variants that characterize the changing actions and moods of the chief protagonists and an infinite variety of lesser members which serve to link the musical imagery into a whole. Consequently the work is wonderfully unified in style. There is none of the patchwork we find in such an opera for instance as Tchaikovsky's *Oprichnik*, where themes of Russian or Italian complexion jostle each other on every page. The theme of *Dalibor* seems to have been noted down by the composer as early as 1863. It appears in the opera soon after the opening fanfare, and in this form, *largo maestoso*, probably represents the destiny, rather than the personality, of Dalibor, and is always treated by the orchestra, rather than by an individual voice or instrument. A modified form of it, in F major, depicts Dalibor the proud knight and intrepid hero. Out of this theme grows the melody associated with Dalibor's murdered friend Zdeněk. It is of a softer type and more suited to its eventual use as a violin solo when the spirit of Zdeněk appears to Dalibor in the dungeon. It is impossible to follow in detail the many interesting mutations of the fundamental theme. The motive of deliverance—another derivative—appears as a brilliant little fanfare in G major. The leading theme reappears with tragic intensity at the close of the opera. We hear it first in a heroic mood in the major, then in a plaintive minor tonality until finally, gathering strength, it returns in an augmented form and blazes forth the intimation that although the good knight Dalibor has been foully done to death, his fame will live for ever on the lips and in the hearts of the people.

William Ritter thinks that Smetana's power reached its zenith in *Dalibor*. He has for this work an almost undiscriminating quality of praise which finds its echo in the hearts of the whole Czech nation. Admitting that the libretto is not a great success, he says of the opera as a whole: 'It contains immortal pages, parts even, which are of such splendour that the entire drama is transfigured by them. *Dalibor* is the first work of Smetana's which we heard: it won us over to him . . . *and that on our way back from Bayreuth.*' I quote this unqualified eulogy the more willingly that I cannot altogether endorse it. *Dalibor* seems to me a work of considerable, almost feminine, charm, and many weaknesses. The scene in the dungeon when the spirit of Zdeněk appears to the sleeping knight and consoles him with paradisal music played on his violin, is a direct challenge to the composer's inspiration. We are worked up to this musical climax and reach it in a condition of emotional expectancy, and whether we rest satisfied with the strains of the melody (*Andante amoroso*) is perhaps a purely subjective matter, but personally it leaves me disappointed. M. Ritter finds it 'celestial'; I find it tender, charged with mild elegiac feeling; such a lament Dalibor might have sung from earth for his dead friend; but it is not what we have been led to expect, since it comes from heaven to earth. Zdeněk as an artist has learnt no new ecstasy, caught no divine afflatus from his translation to another world. The orchestration of the opera as a whole, so highly praised by almost all writers upon Smetana, left me wondering at its frequent lapses into poverty of resource and apparently wilful neglect of the means at his disposal. The Bohemian composers, it is true, have not favoured that polychromatic exuberance of instrumentation so successfully cultivated by the Eastern Slavs. It is not necessary —is indeed hardly suitable—to clothe their simpler, more organized, and self-expressive thematic material in such oriental splendour. The melodic expression, the cast of thought of the Czechoslovaks is far removed from those Asiatic influences of which there are still abundant traces in the music of the Russians. But although we must not expect from the Czechs those orchestral coruscations to which the school of Rimsky-Korsakov has, perhaps too completely, accustomed us, yet Smetana, Dvořák, and their followers have, generally speaking, used the orchestra with considerable individuality. Remembering the vigour and certainty with which Smetana has coloured his musical ideas in his cycle of Symphonic Poems 'Ma Vlast' (*My Fatherland*), and the sense of climax displayed in the full and majestic effects in certain pages of *Libuše*, it is difficult to account for the instrumental tenuity which from time to time leaves the ear so unsatisfied in *Dalibor*. It is perhaps this lack of orchestral amplitude and colour that makes this opera seem to an impartial critic rather immature and old fashioned. The Czechs, however, are right to love *Dalibor* for all it embodies of their own ideals and history.

There is now no occasion to dwell upon the polemic which followed the production of *Dalibor*. It was a futile passage of arms, because while sound and sympathetic criticism might have helped Smetana at this juncture, he was justifiably exasperated by the attacks of a man like Pivoda, a mediocre singing-master whose only claim to be remembered is the notoriety acquired by leading a yapping chorus against a great, if sometimes tactless, genius. Those who cried the loudest that Smetana had sold his birthright for the Wagnerian pottage, were those who, in the composer's own words, 'babble at random about Wagnerism without knowing what it means'. The result was not what these criticules expected—to frighten Smetana and rush him sheep-like back within the fold of comic opera. Impatient of public opinion, good or bad, as we have seen from his attitude to the admirers of *The Bartered Bride*, his answer to the detractors of *Dalibor* was a work which did actually approach much nearer to Wagnerian music drama—the Festival Opera, or *Festspiel*, *Libuše*.

Smetana had already treated the subject of Libuše, the virgin and sybilline queen of Bohemia, in two smaller works which were perhaps deliberate studies for the opera; the first of these, an Overture in C major, was written for the performance of Kollar's *Prophecy of Libuše*, and the second, *The Judgment of Libuše*, was intended to accompany a *tableau vivant* for a charitable entertainment. He had a very clear conception of the purpose to which his fourth opera should be put. In 1881 he says in a letter to J. Srb: 'I ask that *Libuše* should not be placed in the current repertory of the Opera, but kept as a festival work for special occasions.' Two years later he reiterates his wishes in his correspondence with the conductor Adolphe Čech: 'I have *never* given *Libuše* as a repertory opera; I desire it to be used only *for the festivals which affect the whole Czech nation.* . . . *Libuše* is not an opera of the old type, but a festival picture (*tableau*), a form of musical and dramatic sustenance.' His curious choice of the word 'sustenance' suggests that he attached to this work a kind of ritual significance. Elsewhere he says: 'It does not make the demands of a repertory opera, but it makes its own particular claims. . . . For the sake of a few florins I will not let a work of such importance in our literature be raked into the company of ditties that are whistled everywhere.' Once again, no greater literary talent than Wenzig seems to have been available for the libretto, which shares the weakness of *Dalibor* in the mingling of a rather impossible love-story with the loftier elements of myth and legendary history. The work is a kind of compressed trilogy: Act I, *The Judgment of Libuše*, was completed in September 1871; Act II, *Libuše's Wedding*, in February 1872; Act III, *The Prophecy*, in the following November. The national event for which Smetana destined his work did not take shape until June 1880, when the committee of the theatre offered a prize for the best opera suitable for the opening ceremony of the Národní Divadlo in the following year. *Libuše* won the competition and was first presented to the public in the new National Theatre, on 11 June 1881. Smetana was already too deaf to conduct the work himself, and this task was confided to Adolphe Čech.

Among the most ancient specimens of Bohemian literature is a fragment entitled *The Judgment of Libuše*, discovered as recently as 1817, at Kralove Dvůr in north-eastern Bohemia.[1] This poem relates the history of Libuše, the youngest daughter of Prince Krok, who has the gift of prophecy. The Virgin Princess reigns

[1] As with the Russian *Epic of the Army of Igor* and the Finnish *Kalevala* the authenticity of the Kralove Manuscripts has been hotly disputed.

in peace until she is one day called upon to settle a question of inheritance between two of her subjects. One of the brothers in the dispute, the rough, impetuous warrior Chrudoš, refuses to obey a woman's judgement. His insolence convinces Libuše that the country needs a male ruler and she resolves to marry. After consulting with her wise and elderly advisers Lutobor and Rado-van, she decides in favour of the virtuous and noble hearted peasant Přemysl, and founds the great dynasty of the Přemyslids.

Bearing in mind his intention of creating a festival work, Smetana laid out the introduction to *Libuše* on grandiose lines and called it a Prelude. It is in fact a condensed epic in itself, built upon two of the chief themes of the opera, the motive of Libuše and the virile motive of Přemysl. A brilliant fanfare on the chord of C major precedes these themes and creates an atmosphere at once archaic and reminiscent of the remote splendour of Libuše's Court in the Vyšehrad, perched high above the broad brown flow of Vltava. Later on, the motives of Libuše and Přemysl are united; the queen's melody being played by the violins while Přemysl's theme stands out chiefly in the brass. The whole opera is based on a framework of leading motives of which the two mentioned are of the first importance.

In the first Act, Libuše and her maidens are seen, attired in white, in the hall of the Vyšehrad. One of the queen's ladies, Radmila, relates the quarrel between the brothers Chrudoš and Štahlav. Another maiden, Krasava, daughter of the sage Lutobor, confesses that she has been the instigator of the mischief by pretending to prefer Štahlav to Chrudoš whom she really loves. A fanfare summons Libuše to the throne of judgement, and in the next scene she is seated under the sacred lime-tree, emblem of the Czechs, with the two rough and turbulent brothers, one on each side of her, and her counsellors grouped around her throne. The music expresses the defiance and obstinacy of the two warriors. The theme of Přemysl is foreshadowed when Lutobor and Rado-van confide in each other the need of a husband for Libuše. The realistic tendency which lies at the root of Smetana's art shows itself very clearly in the accompaniment to Libuše's recital. When she refers to the Sacred Tree, the Sword of Justice, the Cleansing Fire, the Undefiled Water, each object of the solemn rite evokes a characteristic passage from the orchestra. When she bids the brothers share their heritage in peace and goodwill, the insolent reply of Chrudoš (the motive of evil) dominates the musical situation. A chorus of indignation follows and then Libuše with great dignity announces her willingness to take a consort. While she is pondering her choice, Přemysl's theme creeps softly into the music. Finally the scene ends in a great chorus of exultant joy, based on the combined themes of the queen and the peasant.

The second Act opens in the gloomy forest, among the funereal barrows of the ancestors of Chrudoš and Štahlav. Lutobor arrives on the scene with his daughter Krasava. The violent theme of Chrudoš's jealousy and passion is contrasted with the serene and tender love motive of Přemysl. Lutobor now reproaches his daughter most bitterly for her duplicity. Krasava replies that she acted thoughtlessly out of pride and caprice, but that she truly loves Chrudoš. Her father bids her conciliate her lover and heal the quarrel between the brothers. Should she fail in this difficult task she will be for ever banished from his presence. The lovers meet in the gloom of the forest. At first Chrudoš is obdurate, but finally Krasava convinces him of her affection and the brothers are reconciled. The sustained musical interest, the dim, impressive setting of the forest burial-place, give a compensating value to this scene, which, from the point of view of dramatic structure, is actually an interruption to the main theme of the plot. The fourth scene brings us to the typical Slovak farm which is the home of Přemysl, at Stadice. The master is resting for awhile in the sunny entrance; a plough stands idle under a lime-tree; it is early summer. Přemysl is lost in meditation and the music with its frequent references to Libuše's theme reveals the subject of his thoughts. He has once looked upon his queen and ever since has loved her with a secret, respectful, hopeless passion; while his heart holds a perpetual memory of this pure, gracious, and inaccessible woman. His dreams are interrupted by some delightful pastoral music. The composer of *The Fields and Forests of Bohemia*, and the disciple of Beethoven, knew well how to cast the spell of nature over the reverie of Přemysl. The two ideas alternate for a time and the heroic theme of the lover hints that his hopes are growing bolder. Then a horn call brings the peasants on the scene and a simple dancing song is used as the thematic nucleus for the joyous episode which follows. When the peasants have departed, Přemysl is again left alone with his thoughts, which are now touched with a darker shadow of melancholy, as though he had some premonition that the peaceful and active life of the beloved homestead was drawing to a close. Soon the distant hum of voices and the distinctive fanfares announce the arrival of the deputation from the Vyšehrad. They confer; and when the peasant-hero's doubts and scruples are finally conquered, the Libuše motive rings out triumphantly. Přemysl takes leave of his home in simple and touching music which, if it sounds a little naïve to sophisticated ears, must be accepted as appropriate and veracious use of the folk element, since Přemysl, for all his natural dignity, remains a democratic hero. The crowd now acclaim him as the future husband and protector of their adored queen and the scene ends with a solidly constructed chorus at the close of which Libuše's theme stands out in an imposing climax.

The scene of Act III is the same apartment in the Vyšehrad where we first saw Libuše and her maidens. The curtain rises on the reconciliation of the brothers, when their respective themes are heard in harmonious combination. The trumpets presently proclaim the arrival of the bridegroom. The company hurry out to meet him, leaving Libuše alone. The prophetic spirit takes possession of her; she sees in vision the great destiny of her line, and invokes the memory of her father that he may intercede for the future welfare of the country. Her soliloquy is interrupted by the entrance of twelve maidens in white who attire the queen in her nuptial robes and sing a graceful epithalamium.

The opening fanfares of the Prelude herald the coming of Přemysl, no longer a hesitating lover in peasant dress, but every inch a king. He mounts the throne beside Libuše and his first act is one of clemency, when Chrudoš, conquering his pride, kneels at the queen's footstool and is formally pardoned by his new lord. The people burst into a great chorus of acclamation. Libuše the prophetess now rises and stands rapt and gazing into futurity. One by one the great personalities of Czech history are seen to pass by in the background: Břetislav and Jitka, Jaroslav of Sternberk, Otakar II, Charles IV, Žižka the Hussite, George of Poděbrad—a glorious procession, each accompanied by characteristic music, the whole culminating in a grand version of the old Hussite hymn 'All ye Warriors of God'. As the curtain falls the trumpets and trombones, which play as important a part in the opera as any of the human protagonists, since they embody the spirit of an old and indomitable race, blaze forth the ever-recurrent fanfare: the twofold affirmation of Bohemia's ancient glory and future freedom.

This *Finale*, which formerly roused the enthusiasm of the Czech public every time they heard it afresh, now excites an overwhelming display of triumphant rejoicing, since it has passed from the dusks of prophecy into the clear noonday of fulfilment.

By the time this national epic was staged at the new National Theatre the tragedy of Beethoven was repeated in Smetana. The pomp and splendour of sonority evoked in *Libuše*—which Ritter appropriately likens to a great stained glass window with all its heraldic devices of legendary and prophetic themes intertwined in a glowing decorative design—and the applause of a grateful populace, were inaudible to the composer.

I cannot agree with the writer quoted above that *Libuše*, written for the Czech National Opera House, must be kept a prisoner within its walls for all time. When a creative artist for some good and disinterested motive restricts his ambitions to geographical boundaries, he himself is apt to overlook the universal interest of his work, and others will follow suit. But if he has a flash of God-sent inspiration, there is bound to be that quality in his art which will appeal to more than one race, and will eventually overthrow the walls of indifference, or prejudice, which intervene between nation and nation. Moussorgsky cherished the not unnatural delusion that his *Boris Godounov* would prove a dead failure outside Russia; Borodin was convinced that 'we Russians, polar bears, eaters of tallow candles', could never reach the outer world in the character of producers. But time and facilities of communication have changed these exclusive conditions, and the war of 1914–18 broke up the great 'corner' in Teutonic music and gave the musical commodities of other countries a chance in the world market. It is indispensable, however, that the art-material exported should be of unquestionably sound quality. For that reason, while I should deprecate the introduction to this country of *Dalibor* as being an imperfect, if in many respects an interesting, opera, I believe that there is a sufficient reserve of dramatic and musical vitality in *Libuše* to make it acceptable even to those to whom Slavonic myth and history offer no special interests. While we are waiting for Czech opera to be tried experimentally in this country we might at least include the Overture from time to time in our concert programmes.

From the grand style Smetana next descended to the com-

parative triviality of drawing-room opera. His wish to endow the
National Theatre with a varied series of works accounts for *The
Two Widows*, a slight but carefully finished comedy opera in two
acts, produced at the Temporary Theatre on 27 March 1874.
Taking as his subject a little French play of the same title, by
Malleville, which had been acted in Prague in 1868, he had it
translated and completely adapted to Czech surroundings. Smetana describes it as 'an essay in an elevated drawing-room style
. . . the music of which is purely Czech and cannot be thought of
as belonging anywhere else than to Bohemia'. In spite of this
verdict, the work was afterwards produced by Pollini in Hamburg
(1881) in a German translation, the scene transferred once more
to French soil.[1] As in the case of *The Bartered Bride* Smetana
took great pains with the revision of this work, substituting recitative for the spoken text in the second edition, and adding a second
pair of rather superfluous lovers, Tonik, an under-gamekeeper,
and Lidunka, the innkeeper's daughter. The action takes place
at a country house belonging to Karolina Zaleska, a rich widow,
where her cousin Agnes, also a widow, is on a visit to her. Ladislav Podhajsky, a good-looking bachelor, has made love to Agnes
in her husband's lifetime without success. In order to approach
her once more he resorts to the stratagem of poaching on Karolina's estate, where he is caught by the head gamekeeper, Mum-
balm, and dragged into the presence of the ladies whom he is dying
to meet. Karolina enters into the fun of the situation and con-
demns the culprit to spend the rest of the day at the manor-house.
She even helps his suit with the doleful Agnes by starting a desperate flirtation with the young man which awakens her cousin's
jealousy so effectually that after a series of farcical misunder-
standings she succumbs to Ladislav's wooing. The leading parts
—the merry widow, Karolina, rapidly convalescent in an effective
white *toilette*, and the inconsolable relict who clings faithfully to
her weeds, even after she knows that her heart is hopelessly lost
for a second time—are nicely contrasted, and offer a charming
opportunity for two rival prima donnas to become reconciled—
on the stage. The music is better than the libretto, but it has not

---

[1] The alterations in the opera made by the publishers, Bote and Bock,
drew angry protests from Smetana: 'I am so annoyed', he writes to Prochazka in 1882, 'that I would gladly repay all fees received so far from
Pollini and return the contract. These gentlemen seem to think my opera
is a pure farce in the style of Offenbach.'

the spirit and witchery of *The Bartered Bride*. I heard *The Two Widows* in Prague in a performance under Kovařovic that was nearly perfect, and I found it a pleasant little opera that might easily be given in any country, and on any small stage, but it is not, to my mind, a sparkling gem of humour. The comic element supplied by the old gamekeeper, who blunders and jokes with wearisome persistency through both Acts, is more akin to buffoonery than wit, and overweighs the element of light comedy and the patrician touch which Smetana must have originally intended to give to this work, since in writing of it he says: 'aristocratic manners and customs should be learned from the stage'.

CHAPTER VII

WITH a new and vitally national existence spread out before them; with a Republic, at the head of which was President Masaryk, a sage, a practical politician of the widest outlook, a man who learnt toleration in the school of personal suffering—in a word an ideal leader; with a glorious reputation as fearless fighters in the cause of liberty; with so much achieved and it may be hoped still more in prospect, one would gladly turn down for ever one or two blackened pages in the social history of the Czechs. The martyrdom of Smetana is one of the darkest. At the same time, while we condemn it, we must in justice remember the atmosphere of suspicion, unfairness, and party spirit which hangs like a poison cloud over all countries whose development has been forcibly interrupted by conquest, and the tyrannical substitution of alien institutions for those which are theirs by right of inheritance and national volition. Envy, duplicity, timidity of public and private opinion, are the natural outcome of oppression. When a patriot arose in Bohemia there were always a certain number of opportunist spirits who found it easier to curse and swear with Peter: 'I know not the man'. While one party was carried away by Smetana's operas, another asserted that they were only insincere attempts to ape the composer of *The Nibelungen Ring* behind the mask of nationalism. The accusations of deliberate imitation of Wagner might have created only a passing irritation in Smetana's mind, but the charges levelled against him as chief conductor of the National Theatre were more corrosive. They ate their way into a heart and brain too sensitive to resist such foolish malignity.

In the autumn of 1874, the composer felt all the sypmtoms of total deafness gaining upon him. He wrote to Dr. Čížek, vice-president of the Committee of the National Theatre, detailing the condition of his hearing. He still hears a little with the left ear, he says; vertigo and a sound like the rushing of a torrent torment him constantly; a chorus is a confused mass of sounds in which he cannot distinguish the parts or individual voices. Consequently he begs the Vice-President to lay his case before the Committee and asks to be excused from conducting and rehearsing for the time being. 'If at the end of the quarter', he writes, 'my condition has grown worse, I shall of course be obliged to give up my work and submit to my unhappy fate. As I am forbidden also to give pianoforte lessons and shall be deprived of this source of earning which enables me to keep my family, I beg at the same time permission to draw on that part of my salary which the Committee has assured to the professors of the Opera School, and which is due to me for last year.' A few days afterwards, the news of his deafness having been spread abroad, a newspaper called *Politik* made a ruthless attack upon him, the abominable character of which can be shown in a few brief quotations.

'It is said that he receives a huge salary as a composer, first conductor, and artistic director of the opera, as well as for the post of Principal of the Operatic School. For all this he apparently does nothing but ask from time to time for a continuance of the contract and a rise of payment which his partisans and Dr. Čížek grant him without hesitation. . . . As a composer he works very little. . . . He is known to the public by his appearance at the Café Bendl, where he reads the papers all day, when he is not nursing his disordered nerves at home. . . . This is the first time that the Czech Theatre has been mistaken for a hospital, a public infirmary, or a pathological institute.'

Whether this cruel indictment hastened the final catastrophe or not, it followed very quickly upon it, for on the night of 20 October, complete deafness descended suddenly on Smetana, and although he visited the great aural specialists, Troltsch at Wurzburg, and Pollitzer at Vienna, and spent a sum he could ill afford on the pursuit of remedies, no improvement resulted.[1] Realizing the hopelessness of the case, Smetana left Prague and went to Jabkenice near Mladá Boleslav, in northern Bohemia, where his daughter was married to Josef Schwarz the intendant of the forests. Here he lived for the next ten years, in a seclusion and poverty which were not without compensation, at least for a time, in the mental and physical peace which the neighbourhood of vast woodlands can give.

In the healing quiet of Jabkenice Smetana wrote what many of his admirers consider his loveliest work, *The Kiss* ('Hubička'),

[1] In a letter to Mr. Thorne, a musician of Hobartstown, Australia, who had written kindly to the composer in his misfortune, Smetana says: 'all the doctors agree that it is paralysis of the acoustic nerve'.

a peasant opera of a very different type to *The Bartered Bride*. The libretto of the new opera, in two Acts, was written by E. Krásnohorská, its basis being a tale of rustic life by Karolina Světlá. The work is Smetana's first triumph over his tragic disability. Later on, deafness and cerebral complications made themselves increasingly felt in his music, but in *Hubička* there is still a perfect balance of radiance and shadow. The story of the young couple who nearly ruin their lives by a simple act of self-will is thoroughly Czech in character. Lukáš, a young peasant, has accepted out of filial respect the wife chosen by his parents, but he has always loved Vendulka. At the beginning of the opera, we learn that the young wife died when her first child was born, and Lukáš is free to marry his former love. The pair are passionately attached, but both are hot-tempered and unyielding. Vendulka's first act is to take charge of Lukáš's baby, put out to nurse, and to mother it. On the day of their betrothal Lukáš asks Vendulka to kiss him. She refuses, because she is dominated by an old, ingrained Czech superstition that a kiss given before marriage will cause the first wife to turn in her grave. Lukáš, who has never loved the dead woman and is impatient to possess the living one, grows angry and insists on his rights. Vendulka is obdurate. So the lover goes away exasperated, frequents bad company and brings shame on Vendulka. Having drunk too much at the village inn he arrives accompanied by some village girls of light reputation, and makes a scene outside the cottage where Vendulka is rocking the child to a lullaby which is broken by the strains of their ribald songs. Furious and disgusted she leaves the village and takes refuge with her aunt Martinka, the midnight carrier for a band of smugglers. Separation brings remorse to Lukáš and the spirit of forgiveness to Vendulka. In the wild and romantic setting of the mountains the pair meet again. At the sight of her lover the woman is ready to throw herself into his arms; but Lukáš has learnt self-control. He refuses the long-withheld embrace until he asks her forgiveness in the presence of the villagers. This accomplished, their lips meet in a kiss of reunion. The music of *The Kiss* is as national as anything Smetana ever wrote, but it has a stronger note of realism, and is overcast here and there by a shadow of poignant melancholy which sets the work in complete contrast to the light-hearted gaiety of *The Bartered Bride*. It is, however, equally a peasant opera, and, written in the rural surroundings of Jabkenice, the music seems impregnated with their freshness and perfume, and chequered with the flickering lights and shades of the forest. The subject offers opportunity for frequent emotional contrasts. The vivacity of the dialogue between the quarrelsome lovers, the tender cradle-song, the merry dances, full of the spirit of the people—these changes of mood carry us along from the first to the last bar of the opera; not, it is true, on the rise and fall of mighty waves of passion, but as on a level, breezy sea, now dancing in sunshine, now darkened by cloud shadows.

Smetana entitled *The Kiss* a 'comic opera', but its humour is of a totally different quality from that of *The Bartered Bride*, being much less naïve and rollicking. In *The Bartered Bride* the fun depends chiefly on the drollery, or even buffoonery, of one or two characters. When Vašek appears on the stage we are expected to laugh, and we are conscious of it, as we are with the appearance of the clown in the arena of the circus. The joke of Vašek, be it said, comes off very well. In *The Kiss* humour is blent with pathos. It is the situation which creates the comic element, not the charac-ters, none of whom is laughable. 'The tear and the smile' alternate throughout the opera, for the quarrel between the lovers, absurd and paltry as it seems at first, leads us eventually near to the edge of the gulf which divides comedy from tragedy. Lukáš and Vendulka are only absurd because they allow umbrage and superstition to take command of their thoughts and actions; but they are never risible, because their sufferings are real. The unity of the music is admirably preserved, the division into two Acts being practically a concession to theatrical exigencies.

Musically the work may be compared to a symphonic move-ment, beginning gaily with the betrothal of the lovers, with just a passing grave episode when Vendulka's father expresses some fear as to the future of such a headstrong couple; then the first hint of gathering storm when Vendulka refuses her kiss; and from this point the music flows on like a sunny river, gradually rising to full spate until the young people find their true selves again and the festal spirit of the opening scene returns in a happy con-clusion. Although the music is on the whole continuous, there are one or two songs that are detachable from its main stream. In the first Act Vendulka sings two little cradle songs which afford a rare instance of Smetana's treatment of the real folk-song. The songs, which are all too short, are separated, or rather perhaps linked, by a very brief psychological episode, when Vendulka pauses in rocking the cradle to think of her lover, and then starts again, a new melody ('white dove flew') in a new key. The other and even more popular solo is 'The Song of the Lark', sung by Barča, a servant maid, which is a thing of light-hearted unmixed joy that attunes us for the happy reconciliation of the lovers it precedes. Here it is the feeling, not the actual material, which emanates from the folk; although Barča is a true daughter of the people. All the characters in *The Kiss* are peasants and show themselves as such in their elemental joys and quarrels. Lukáš and Vendulka are not a village Romeo and Juliet; when Lukáš comforts his injured self-esteem at the inn and then rushes off to sing insulting songs under his sweetheart's window he acts according to his kind. When Vendulka shows her warm motherly instincts by adopting Lukáš's baby before they are married, and when her fear of offending the dead woman causes her to refuse a kiss to her lover, she is equally true to type. *The Kiss* rather than *The Bartered Bride* is, I think, the seed from which sprang several Czech operas which I shall deal with in a later chapter.

The Kiss ('Hubička') was first produced on 7 November 1876, at the Temporary Theatre, under the direction of A. Čech. It soon vied in popularity with *The Bartered Bride*, and not a season passed in Prague without its frequent repetition, for it may be counted on to draw a full house. It is probably one of the most transplantable of Smetana's operas and might be recommended to the attention of some of our opera companies.

The Secret ('Tajemstvi'), a comic opera in three Acts, the book by Eliška Krásnohorská, was begun and completed at Jabkenice between 1876–8. Another story of rural life is treated here, but it is less simple and touching than the subject of *The Kiss*. Twenty years before the tale commences Kalina was in love with Rosa Malina, but his suit did not prosper because her family did not think him rich enough. Kalina's feelings are hurt and he marries another girl. He becomes a widower and is left with one son, Vítek, who has lost his heart to Blaženka, the daughter of Rosa's brother, Kalina's old enemy who treated him so contemptuously in bygone years. Rosa has remained faithful to Kalina. She never knew exactly what had occurred between her family and her lover, only an old monk, now dead, told her that he had confided to Kalina a secret whereby he could be successful in winning her. This is the explanation of the title. There is still a great rivalry between the families of Kalina and Malina, and the villagers are all partisans of one or the other. In order to show that he is not so poor as his enemy supposes, Kalina has just rebuilt his house —on credit—and gives a house warming. The old pensioner Bonifác, who has carried off a broken plank from the former house, finds a bit of paper thrust into a crack of it and takes it to Kalina. It is the great secret of Brother Barnabáš! Kalina is to search a certain spot in the ruins of Bezděz for a treasure. Unfortunately he reads the letter aloud before he has realized that Bonifác is still there. He swears the pensioner to silence. But no sooner has Kalina gone, than Bonifác tells the mason, who tells the woman drawing water at the well, who tells the watchman, who announces it from the church tower through his megaphone. Thus are secrets kept in villages all the world over! At night Kalina carries out his instructions, not without some superstitious tremors. However, the desire for wealth drives him on and he penetrates into the subterranean passage indicated in Barnabáš's letter. The next day the villagers all assemble at Malina's for the festival of the hop harvest. Vítek, whose love-making with Blaženka under the ruined walls of Bezděz has been discovered thanks to the dissemination of the Secret, goes to take leave of his sweetheart; for since they cannot marry, owing to the family feud, he decides to emigrate. Suddenly a loud knocking is heard near the stove, and a little door, long since condemned, falls in with a crash and shows Kalina in the aperture. This underground passage to Rosa's home was the secret, and she was the treasure trove. Kalina, who had sworn never to cross his enemy's threshold, now finds himself obliged to do so. He steps into the room, and not only pleads successfully for the marriage of the two young lovers, but asks for the middle-aged Rosa for himself. There follows a scene of reconciliation and rejoicing.

Two leading themes form the basis of the work: the motive of the Secret and Kalina's theme. Smetana spent much care and ingenuity on the elaboration of the music, undeterred by the triviality of the libretto. It is evident that he now began to work with painful slowness. The last Act took nearly a year to complete, and there was no longer any question of 'tossing off' a comic opera, as in the case of *The Bartered Bride*. After the first performance Smetana added a monologue to the second Act, at the suggestion of the singer Joseph Lev, who took the part of Kalina. On the whole, the opera is less spontaneous than its predecessors. Ritter considers it the work of a man who is striving to convince himself 'that he is still capable of writing complicated music and weaving into a symphonic tissue an intricate criss-cross of motives'. The complications of the music are of course relative, for, in spite of its very slight touch of pedantry, *The Secret* would hardly be regarded as labyrinthine in these days of hyper-sophistication. While the music of the opera is less un-premeditated than is the case with *The Bartered Bride* and *The Kiss*, the psychology throws back to the earlier work. The humour of *The Secret* depends less on the irony of temperament and des-tiny than on comic types, clearly and realistically drawn. The music emphasizes the comic side of the characters, and, with the exception of the lovers, all the protagonists are labelled humorous. In the three subordinate characters, Bonifác, Skřivánek, and the stonemason, Smetana is said to have created three entirely new folk-types. But to appreciate such full-flavoured examples of national humour at their true value it is necessary to know the race very intimately. *The Secret* is richer in songs than *The Kiss*, and one of the cleverest pages of the opera is perhaps the charac-teristic drinking songs in which Skřivánek and Bonifác take part. The play on the names of Kalina and Malina is a comic device of the 'Box and Cox' kind. A night procession of pilgrims to the chapel of Bezděz gives the composer an opportunity of inter-polating an interesting chorus in the folk style.

It is impossible to go further into the details of these two comic operas, *The Kiss* and *The Secret*; I can only recommend my readers to make their acquaintance in the pianoforte scores. The first I hope we may see produced in England in the near future; the second is, I fear, by the somewhat naïve and local nature of its libretto fast bound to the land which produced it. The same judgement may be applied, I think, to *The Devil's Wall* ('Čertova Stěna'), another comic opera in three Acts, to yet another libretto by Eliška Krásnohorská. Smetana began the work in March 1881 and completed it in April 1882. On the score of the second Act these pathetic words are written: 'finished in spite of terrible and constant hindrances'. They explain the sense of fatigue and over-wrought nerves which hangs about the music like a thin mist and shuts out the sunny gladness and exhilaration to which the earlier works have accustomed us.

The Devil's Wall is a barrier of great rocks which stretches across Vltava at Vyší Brod and looks like the piers of a ruined bridge, which, indeed, local tradition says was thrown across the river in prehistoric times by the Devil himself. Apparently he still haunts the neighbourhood when the action of this opera takes place, in medieval times. Vok, lord of Rožnberk, remains a bachelor for the sake of a woman who refused him in earlier years. All his friends wish to see him married, for he is the owner of a great estate. His faithful squire, Jarek, vows that he will never wed his own sweetheart, Katuška, until his master sets the example by taking a wife. The one person who is content to keep Vok unmarried is the hermit Beneš, who for all his rumoured piety has his cherished ambition: to induce the nobleman to build a great monastery by the riverside, to endow it with all his wealth, and to make Beneš the first abbot. The devil (Rarach), wandering in search of mischief to be done, hears of Jarek's vow. Here, he thinks, is a fine opportunity of setting every one by the ears. He disguises himself as Friar Beneš, keeping his sleeves pulled down over his claws. There follows a long series of intrigues, rather confusing and not always amusing. The devil does his best to make Jarek break his oath and nearly succeeds. He becomes the double of the pious Beneš, so that nobody knows one from the other, and keeps the hermit in his power. Vok hears of the death of his first love, and that she has left him guardian of her daughter, Hedvika. She arrives on the scene in time to prevent Vok from listening to the advice of the real Beneš and retiring to a cloister. Hedvika has her mother's features and charm, and the middle-aged lord of Rožmberk falls in love with her. At first history repeats itself and she refuses his suit; but when Vok lets it be known that he means to become a monk the girl conquers all hesitation and declares her love for him. Beneš repents of his worldly ambitions, confesses his sins, and, being shriven, now has power to drive away his tormentor, Rarach, with the sign of the Cross. Jarek is free to marry Katuška.

Round this inconsequent story, which is reminiscent of the old romanticism with its barons and castles, demons and abbots, vows, devil's bridges, and whatnot, Smetana wove almost the last coherent music he wrote. He had the highest opinion of his work, but whether his judgement was really clouded by the rapid advance of cerebral disease or not, is a question that I leave to be answered by those who know the opera better than I do. Smetana wrote to his friend Srb in April 1882: 'I have no fear as to the effectiveness of the music. It is in a style peculiarly appropriate to the libretto. The more I revise and correct it the more convinced I am that it is good music which could have been written in no other way. The songs belonging to almost every role are, generally speaking, very expressive, and some are captivating; the orchestration is so varied and highly coloured that I admire my own patience in the work bestowed upon it.' He adds that only to a sincere friend and intelligent music lover would he dream of thus boasting of his work. In a letter to the conductor Ad. Čech he says: 'Although the music is not easy, especially as regards the intonation and the harmony, it swarms with agreeable melodies; there is hardly one ungrateful part.'

The reception of the opera on its production, in September 1878, must have disappointed the composer bitterly. His enemies were only too pleased to connect what they called the 'degeneracy' of *The Devil's Wall* with the master's failing health. Decency might have restrained them from inflicting this mortal blow upon Smetana. On the other hand the composer Fibich saw no signs of weakness in the opera and spoke of it as a strong, healthy work, at least as consistent as any other Czech opera of the time. I regret that during my visits to Prague I never had the opportunity of hearing *The Devil's Wall*, because—in the face of such divergent views—it is impossible to estimate the value of it to Czech music by reference to contemporary criticism. I do not think, however, that its restoration to the repertory of the Národní Divadlo is merely an act of respect to the composer's memory. Judgement has grown clearer and more moderate; moreover, it is one of the operas with the revival of which Kovařovic took most pains and produced the best results, so that under such conditions it would no doubt be a pleasure to hear it from time to time.

From the beginning of the 'eighties Smetana's physical and mental sufferings steadily increased. In his correspondence with Dr. Procházka and K. Srb he gives accounts of his condition which are as pitiable as they are medically confused. Deafness and continual noises in the head, high blood-pressure, and intense nervous irritability, were symptoms of which he frequently complains. In December 1882, he had two attacks during which he temporarily lost memory and speech. The doctor forebade any kind of musical work, or even thought. But the poor tormented brain refused to rest. In the summer of 1883, he accepted from Eliška Krásnohorská the book of another romantic opera, *Viola*, founded on Shakespeare's *Twelfth Night*, and proceeded slowly and laboriously to compose the first Act.[1] Absolute music he says is now an impossibility; once he lets himself go in pursuit of melodic material he loses all power of concentration; but a text acts as a guiding thread to his confused ideas. So he gropes his way with long pauses 'because I do not want to ruin my poor brain with overwork'. Gradually the score showed increasing signs of the composer's failure, until early in 1884 he ceased entirely to work at it. About this time a strange incoherent letter to Srb shows an alarming want of mental control. On 2 March a concert was organized in Prague in honour of his sixtieth birthday, but he was unable to be present. A few weeks later Srb took him to an asylum, in which, on 12 May 1884, he died. His grave in the famous cemetery on the Vyšehrad is a place of pilgrimage for all musical visitors to Prague.

Never did calumny stoop to invent a meaner and more foolish accusation than the charge of indolence brought against Smetana by his detractors. It is possible, on the contrary, that the quality of his work suffered through his indefatigable industry and his unresting determination—in which we may see a reflection of the traditional pedagogic bent of the Czechs—to supply his people with a series of musical exemplars to serve in every emergency. His zeal to found a national school led him occasionally to undertake tasks hardly worthy of his attention. I am not referring now to his numerous Polkas—the national dance of his people—which he ennobled by his treatment, as Chopin raised the Mazurka to the level of an art form. In his operas Smetana uses the polka as a means of psychological expression, as, for example, in *The Kiss*, when Lukáš vents his rancour outside Vendulka's cottage. But there exist a few compositions for which one grudges his expenditure of energy, while admitting that it was no doubt difficult for him in the face of his avowed policy to refuse those occasional pieces which the national party looked to him to supply; but since these lesser works are not likely to travel beyond Bohemia it is unnecessary to speak of them here. What is really astonishing, seeing the difficulties with which he had to contend, is that out of the 135 compositions enumerated in Dr. Karel Teige's Chronological Catalogue, such a large proportion are works of significance. From the beginning of his career he was attracted to symphonic music, and mention has already been made of his early

[1] Smetana's ninth opera stopped short at the first Act.

Symphonic Poems: *Richard III*, *Wallenstein's Camp*, and *Hakon Jarl*. In spite of certain temperamental affinities with Mozart, he never harked back to the influences which for so long had dominated Bohemian music. Even experimentally Smetana never essayed symphony in the formal sense of the word. The influence of Liszt, combined with the emotional realism of the Slavonic character, sent him always in search of a concrete programme; and with his realism was combined a touch of romanticism which lingered—and still lingers—in Czechoslovakia like the last ardent rays of sunset, reminiscent of a splendid noon that had passed, but left its trailing clouds of glory along the horizon. Realism, romanticism, and nationalism were the materials out of which Smetana fashioned his art. He used them deliberately and at the sacrifice of a more universal appreciation, or at least the patronage of the German neo-classical school; but, on the whole, because these qualities were inherent in him.

Side by side with his operas he left his people a cycle of Symphonic Poems under the title *My Fatherland* ('Ma Vlast') which have been of the highest importance in the cultural development of the Czechs. They contain some of Smetana's best and most inspired work, and though he elected to choose his subjects entirely from national history and landscape, this cycle has also served to carry his name farther afield than anything else of his, excepting always the popular Overture to *The Bartered Bride*. *Ma Vlast* is dedicated to the city of Prague.

The first of the cycle, entitled *Vyšehrad*, was originally produced at a concert of the Prague Philharmonic on 14 January 1875. As the explanatory notes to the Symphonic Poems were written by the late Dr. Zelený with the co-operation and approval of Smetana himself, it is important to reproduce them here. For the benefit of those who have never visited Prague I may add that Vyšehrad (literally—high castle) is the rock overhanging the river Vltava where tradition places the old Court of Libuše. The note which appears in the score of the work says:

'At the sight of the venerable rock Vyšehrad the poet's memory is carried back to the remote past by the sound of Lumír's harp. There rises the vision of Vyšehrad in its ancient splendour, with its gleaming golden crown, the venerable and proud dwelling-place of the Přemysl kings and princes, filled with the renown of warriors. Here, in the castle, knights assembled at the joyous call of trumpets and cymbals to engage in splendid tourneys; here the warriors gathered for victorious combats, their arms clashing and flashing in the sunlight. Vyšehrad was shaken by songs of praise and victory. Yearning after the long-perished glory of Vyšehrad, the poet now beholds its ruin. The unbridled passion of furious battles has thrown down its lofty towers, fallen are its sanctuaries, and demolished the proud abodes of princes. Instead of songs of triumph and victory Vyšehrad quakes at the echo of savage war-cries. The tempests are stilled. Vyšehrad is hushed and emptied of all its glory. From its ruins comes the melancholy echo of Lumír's song, so long silent and forgotten.'

Vyšehrad was composed after *Dalibor* and *Libuše*, and partakes of the character of both these works: the old-world, knightly atmosphere of the former; occasional reflections of the splendour of the latter; the whole work seen as it were through a mist of tears; the vision of a poet dreaming of glories 'dismantled and declined'. The introductory *Lento* is a *cadenza* for two harps, the second giving out chords which foreshadow the principal theme, while the first has sweeping passages ending in a loud descending scale which closes on the dominant seventh, when, after a pause, the harps lead into the *Largo maestoso*, 3-4. This introduction, reminding us of the harp of Lumír the Slavonic bard, is also a kind of formula which evokes the victim of the ancient castle. The subject of the *Largo*, strongly accentuated on the second beat of the bar, is given out by horns and bassoons. The harps continuing their chords give a rhapsodical atmosphere to the music. The theme passes to the wood-wind, which gives it a softer colouring. The first solo trumpet sounds a call, and is answered by the second trumpet. The fanfare swells in volume and the drum adds to the martial effect. This is lost in a new *cadenza* for harp. Between the sweeping passages, a quaver figure of importance makes its appearance in the wood-wind, the trumpet call being repeated against it.

Now the strings take part for the first time in a restatement of the principal theme *fortissimo*, a fifth higher, the brass makes a resounding call which brings the whole orchestra into action and a climax is built upon the leading theme, the cymbals and triangles adding to the general brilliance. Assuming the form suggested by the wood-wind figure, the theme is carried on by full orchestra, *grandioso poco largamente*.

After a further climax, the wood-wind deals with the first subject in its original form, the brass replying with the quaver figure. Both phrases die away softly as in the distance. The time changes to *allegro vivo ma non agitato*, 4-4, and the first principal theme is treated by the strings in unison in a strongly emphasized rhythmic version. Some contrapuntal devices are used in the course of this development. A chromatic passage for strings links this section with a restatement of the chief theme in the basic tonality of the work, the quaver figure being vigorously insisted upon by the basses. A kind of conflict seems to be depicted, for at a signal from the cymbals the brass seizes upon the quaver passage, while the strings ejaculate a short emphatic figure of protest, and, at the climax, a series of modulations takes us into C minor, in which key the second subject—long delayed—makes its entry (*più allegro e poco agitato*) in the wood-wind and horns. The strings keep up a semiquaver accompaniment to this cantabile melody; solo clarinets attempt softly to unite the first and second subjects; the trumpets renew their appeal, growing more and more urgent. Presently the first theme returns in a new version for strings. A supreme climax results, in which the principal subject rings out like a national song, impressively harmonized, over a tremolo in the strings. A swift *diminuendo* leads to a complete emotional change. The folk-song melody is heard *più lento*, no longer triumphant and exalted, but expressive and mournful from the clarinets in E flat minor. The rest of the wood-wind then takes it over, transferred to the major, with an echo-phrase for horns. The melody gradually broadens and subsides, making way for the principal subject (*lento ma non troppo*). A final crisis treated in much the same way as at the beginning of the poem dies down in both strings and wind, on a general pause. The oboes and bassoons join the strings in an expressive passage, the horns and clarinets call very softly; the basses glide down to the lower E and remain there to the end; the harps run up and down in zephyr-like arpeggios. There comes a last reminiscence of the chief subject, breathed in unison from the strings. Then the drums, taking courage, roll from *ff* to *pp*, and the poem dies out in a long soft chord, like the sigh given to a vanished dream.

After this eloquent evocation of the past, Smetana turned his attention to musical landscape, in which he was well fitted to succeed, both by his intimate knowledge of the varied beauty of his native land and his power of musical imagery. Compared with the landscape work of contemporary composers from Debussy onward, Smetana's attitude towards nature is simple and concrete. Less realistic and forcible in colour than Rimsky-Korsakov in such tone-poems as *Sadko* and *Antar*; far more definite in delineation than Debussy and Loeffler, or, to come to still more recent nature-lovers, Bax, Ireland, Malipiero, or Goossens; untouched by such moods of austerity and runic concentration as we find in Sibelius's pantheistic broodings; Smetana's pictorial music occupies a place of its own, nearer to the romanticism of Liszt and Berlioz than to the impressionism of the last quarter of a century, yet holding in its essence something of Slavonic sincerity and charm. The younger generation smiles patronizingly upon such a work as *Vltava*, labelling it topographical music, a page from a musical Baedeker, without mysticism or psychological suggestion. Mysticism it must be conceded is not characteristic of the Czech nature; but *Vltava* is not without atmosphere; a clear transparent light bathes this unpretentious landscape, beautiful as a dream in which the dreamer finds his way about, instead of wandering in a twilight maze.

The Vltava is the river which bisects Prague; which runs at the foot of Vyšehrad, and passes by the Hradčany hill and under the famous Karlův Most (Charles Bridge) whereon the statues of St. Ludmila, St. Prokop, St. Wenceslaus, and St. Adalbert are ranged among saints of less irreproachable Slavonic proclivities. In maps printed before 1919 the Vltava figures under the German name of Moldau.[1]

Smetana wrote the second of his tone poems in November and December 1874, and its first performance was at Žofin in the following April. Outside Czechoslovakia it is the best known of the cycle *My Fatherland*. The poetic basis of the work is as follows:

'Two small springs gush forth from the shadowy depth of the forest of Šumava. One is warm and swift; the other cold and lethargic. They are united; and henceforth their rapid wavelets chatter as they flow over the pebbles and dance in the sunlight. In its rapid course the torrent becomes a little rivulet,

[1] The old Latin name was Multava, written Mvltava, and the M being dropped we get the present form—Vltava.

the Vltava, which flows across the land of the Czechs, widening as it goes. It passes through dark forests, resounding to the horns of the huntsmen; it crosses the fresh meadow lands where the peasants are singing and dancing at some village wedding. By moonlight the water-nymphs (Russalki) sport in its glittering waters, in which are mirrored the frowning keeps and towers that once saw the glorious past in the days of famous knights and warriors. In the gorge of St. John it breaks into foaming cascades, forces its way between the rocks, and laps against the scattered boulders. Then stretching out in a wider bed, it rolls majestically past Prague, greeted by the old and solemn fortress Vyšehrad. Here in all its force and splendour the Vltava is lost to the poet's sight.'

The programme decides the form of the work, since the musical flow starting from the birth of the river is cumulative in effect and admits of various episodes which break the monotony of its course.

The solo flute gives out a playful thread-like figure, accompanied by very slight pizzicato chords for harp and violins. The phrase is indicated in the score as 'the first source of the Vltava'. The theme flows more freely and its undulations become more marked as other instruments swell its volume. Presently it passes as accompaniment to the strings, while oboes, bassoon, and first violins have a lovely melody against it. After a leisurely development, the horns are heard announcing the arrival of the hunt along Vltava's banks, the strings still simulating the onward movement of the river. The sounds of the chase draw nearer and mingle with the growing murmur of the water; then the horns become fainter and more distant, and a new picture passes before us introducing a lively dance tune. The rustic festival (G major, 2-4) reaches a climax of gaiety and then gradually subsides. With a change of key subdued harmonies in the wood-wind suggest the rising of the moon, after which the flutes give out the playful, ethereal motive of the Rusalka dance, over a sustained accompaniment for horns and muted strings, while the clarinets have a persistent lapping or undulating figure. Now and then the harps break in with a shimmering effect. The development of this idea is carried out with poetic feeling. Towards the end of the picture the brass steals in softly with a march-like rhythm. Sinuous passages in double notes for flutes and clarinets lead to the recapitu-

lation when the strings resume the wave-like figure, and we welcome back the serene and lovely melody of the river played as
before by first violins, oboes, and bassoon. The volume of tone
swells and the pace is accelerated and presently we come to the
St. John Rapids, where Vltava rushing between the rocks grows
agitated and impatient at the temporary constriction. With a
swift ascending passage for strings, over a drum roll, the waters
break free and spread out, depicted in a broad majestic section for
full orchestra. The motive of Vyšehrad is heard as the river
glides past the proud stronghold of the ancient kingdom, after
which it rolls along in power until in a gradual decrescendo the
sound and gleam of its waters are lost to view.

Šarka is the third of this cycle of Symphonic Poems. The work
was composed at Prague in 1874–5, and performed for the first
time at Žofin, 17 May 1877. The subject is taken from the legend
of the Czech Amazon who belongs to prehistoric times, a famous
man-hater who revenged herself upon the sex by simulating a
passion for the chieftain Ctirad, who discovered her bound to a
tree—actually the work of her own army of women. In a letter
addressed to his friend, the conductor Adolphe Čech, in February
1877, Smetana gives the following account of his Symphonic
Poem:

'The idea of my work is, in a word, the story of the young
heroine Šarka herself, which had been recalled to me by the
sight of the district that bears her name. I do not depict this
wild land, but being in the midst of it, I tell the tale of Šarka
over again. The beginning speaks of her rage against men, her
mortification, and wrath—the outcome of love betrayed—and
her vow to take vengeance. Ctirad and his soldiers now come
upon the scene (the March in A minor). He sees Šarka in
lamentable plight attached to the tree, and, astounded at her
beauty, falls in love with her. She deludes him and makes the
mercenaries tipsy (the 3-4 rhythm, D major). Their gaiety
ends in heavy sleep. The horn (in C) gives out Šarka's signal
to her women. Echo. The women fall upon the slumbering
camp. Their triumph. The massacre. Vengeance is accomplished. There is no moral. Each listener is free to follow his
own fancy and to add what he pleases to this broad outline.'

With the foregoing account before us, the work, which is
frankly programme-music, tells its own tale. We have only to

listen to it in order to recognize each phase of the story as set forth by the composer. At the same time it is a work which greatly depends on interpretation for its just effect. In the memorable performance by Karel Kovařovic and the orchestra of the Národní Divadlo, at the Czechoslovak Festival at Queen's Hall in May 1919, we were much struck with the fact that Šarka was not the hysterical virago we had supposed her to be, but a suffering and exasperated woman and, above all, a queenly character. Into the *allegro con fuoco ma non agitato*, with which the work opens, Kovařovic infused a dignity far removed from the Asiatic frenzies of Rimsky-Korsakov's *Joy of Vengeance*.

The leading theme of *Šarka* which is exposed in the opening bars of the poem, with its rugged rhythm and its drooping outline in the fifth bar, has a character of noble pathos. In its weighty development the wrath of Šarka against all mankind, the pain of love betrayed, and the vow of vengeance are definitely suggested. In the March (*più moderato assai*) of Ctirad and his warriors we hear an episode for clarinet—the lament of Šarka in her anguish. Shortly afterwards a *fortissimo* passage for 'cellos leads to the love-theme (*moderato ma con calore*) in the wood-wind and first violins, which works up to an ardent climax, and dies away in the violins to give place to the scene in Ctirad's camp. A resounding call from the brass opens this section, after which the wood-wind and strings come in with a wild theme beginning with leaping fourths and elaborated with much vigorous figuration. This barbaric episode is not unduly prolonged. The whole army is presently hushed in tipsy slumber, a descending passage for woodwind by which Smetana suggests the snoring of the soldiers. The grunting of the second bassoon on a sustained low C was a source of bewilderment to some of the old-fashioned pedants of Prague. The Director of the Conservatoire at that time desired to have it removed as an obvious error, and it was only spared when the critic V. J. Novotny explained its presence as a little joke which Smetana had confided to him! The slumbering camp is rudely awakened by Šarka's horn signal. A waiting passage for solo clarinet, derived from the Amazon's theme of vengeance, seems to indicate a momentary womanly weakness, a passing regret for the onslaught she has planned. It is too late for repentance, however, for immediately afterwards the whole orchestra is employed to depict the frenzy of the massacre. There is no slackening of the insatiable fury of the Amazons, but Smetana, more merciful,

H

or more concentrated, than many Slavonic composers, does not repeat himself much. A few pages suffice to bring this paroxysm to a culmination, when it concludes in an imposing unison.

In conception, completion, and performance *From the Fields and Groves of Bohemia* ('Z Českých luhův a hájů') seems to have preceded *Šarka*, although it is now numbered as the fourth of the cycle *Ma Vlast*. Written in rural surroundings at Jabkenice, it was completed in 1875, and produced as a novelty at a concert at Žofin in December 1876. But as early as the winter of 1874 Smetana had begun to consider the idea of a symphonic poem embodying the life of the Czechs at work and at play, something in what the Germans call *Volksweisen* or *Tanzweisen* (folk-style or dance-style).

The title of the work suggests the pastoral and joyous nature of the music, which is in complete contrast to the fierce emotions depicted in *Šarka* and may be more fitly compared to the broad and clear tone-painting of *Vltava*. There are several versions of the programme of this symphonic poem; but although they differ in detail they are fundamentally the same. The following is taken from Dr. K. Teige's annotated catalogue of Smetana's works:

'A sunny summer's day in the land of Bohemia. The flowing river, the joyous vibration and revivifying air fill the spirit with enthusiastic feelings. The atmosphere is impregnated with the simple and fresh expression of rustic happiness. Leaving the noisy crowd, we enter the forest steeped in shadow and silence. A light breeze sets the branches lightly in contact, until the whole woodland from end to end is rustling and mingling its music with the vibrations of the atmosphere and the trilling of the birds. Above this song of nature comes the plaintive sound of the horn from some distant forest.

'This majestic peace is broken by a louder rustling breeze. And now sounds of the peasants merry-making reach our ears. Soon we are in the midst of a joyous rustic festival. The true joy of life for the Czechs consists in dance and song. The expression of their happiness is heard across the fertile fields.'

Dr. V. Zelený, who has published some of the conversations he had with Smetana after he began to suffer from his terrible affliction of deafness, gives the following notes on the meaning of the work as the authentic utterances of the composer himself:

'The beginning (*molto moderato*, 2-4) is intended to convey the impression of arriving in the country. This is depicted by the vigorous opening built on the accentuated chords of G minor. Then in G major a simple country girl is pictured walking through the fields. At the change to 3-4 (*allegro poco viva*), the splendour of nature at noon on a summer's day, when the sun strikes directly overhead. In the forest there is deep shadow; only here and there a shaft of light pierces the tree-tops. A continuous figure (of ascending quavers) represents the twittering of the birds, which persists throughout all the counterpoint that follows, when the theme for the horns in F major appears above it. This was a great contrapuntal task, which I accomplished like child's play, for I have had so much practice in those kinds of things! The section in G minor depicts a harvest festival, or any kind of peasants' merry-making.'

Besides the leading theme mentioned by the composer, the work contains one or two melodies very typical of Smetana's style, as, for instance, the yearning motive (*dolente*) for clarinet in the first section of the poem; the horn theme which reflects a folk-song, in the 3-4 section, and the polka rhythm at the opening of the jovial *allegro*.

The fifth of the series, *Tabor*, was finished at Jabkenice in December 1878, by which time composition was becoming an effort to Smetana. From the grand old Hussite chorale 'All ye warriors of God' (mentioned on page 7), he drew inspiration and renewed energy for this task. The work was first performed under the conductorship of Adolph Čech at a concert in honour of Smetana's Jubilee in the hall on Žofin Island. Tabor, the picturesque little town that lies in a commanding spot on the plains in the direct line from Prague to Linz, is the scene of the famous general John Žižka's first stand against the Catholic army of King Sigismund. It is for ever associated with the desperate struggles of the Bohemians for religious and political freedom. The programme is brief:

'This song of the Hussite warriors, first sung in their city of Tabor, resounded throughout Christendom. There a strong-hold was founded which was to be a refuge for liberty, the fountain and safe retreat of their faith. The hymn fired the courage of the Taborites, who marched to do battle for their belief, and gave them confidence in the holiness of their cause. When it was heard amid the hottest of the fight, it struck terror to the heart of the enemy, and announced that the Taborites would perish rather than renounce the truth of God.'

The opening *lento*, 3-2, starts with long-drawn notes for lower strings and bassoons, and a grave summons from the horns in octaves over a drum-roll. The horn-call is repeated by the entire orchestra, and after a pause of one bar the strings and wood-wind respond in a figure which ascends from the lower to the higher instruments in succession. After some repetition of this the section comes to a grandiose conclusion. There is now a change to common time and a phrase for full orchestra, succeeded by four bars of the hymn-like theme, given out by the wood-wind *dolce* in the 3-2 measure. The full orchestra resumes in common time, and in the same solemn strain, until a new section is reached— *molto vivace*. The exposition of this animated movement is presently interrupted by three bars of the *lento* 3-2 measure for wood-wind, after which the quicker time is taken up again and the movement is developed at considerable length, the chorale-like theme being constantly in evidence. Towards the close of the section the time is accelerated. A climax of sonority is attained with a return to the *lento maestoso*; and now the theme is announced with full force by the wind, the strings being occupied with bustling semiquaver passages in unison. The excitement increases, trumpets and drums growing more insistent in their appeal, and the strings maintaining a persistent rhythmic figure of accompaniment. Gradually the volume of sound grows less, and some solo passages for the brass are heard. But a crescendo soon follows, and an emphatic passage for strings alone leads to the peroration of the work, which ends like a song of victory.

The following year Smetana completed the cycle with the sixth, and last, symphonic poem, *Blanik*. The old Taborite hymn still haunted his imagination, but, as he points out in a letter to Dr. Hostinsky in 1879, the chorale dominates the whole musical fabric of *Tabor*, whereas in *Blanik* there is only an occasional reminiscence of it, and the last verse, 'to triumph in the end with Him', is used as the theme of the exultant *Finale*.

In 1909 Sir Henry J. Wood introduced the entire cycle of *My Fatherland* in the course of the Promenade Concerts.

Smetana, as we have seen, from the outset of his career was

never attracted to the composition of music which had not some descriptive aim at the back of it. Therefore even into the realm of chamber music he brings a biographical significance, and gives to the two String Quartets (two violins, viola, and violoncello) the title *From my Life* ('Z mého života'). The first of the Quartets, in E minor, dates from 1876 and is therefore contemporary with some of Smetana's best music—notably *The Kiss*. The Prague Society of Chamber Music declined to produce the work because of its 'lack of form and insurmountable technical difficulties'. This seems to have stirred the composer to take up his pen in defence and explanation of his work. The Quartet always seems to me perfectly satisfying in the musical sense without a word of literary explanation. Nevertheless its programme, so fully set forth by Smetana himself in his correspondence with J. Srb, is worth giving here in a condensed form:

'As regards the style of my Quartet I gladly leave the judgement of it to others and do not feel annoyed if they do not like it. I had no intention of writing it according to a recipe, or according to the conventional formulas, with which, however, I am well acquainted, having worked at them when studying musical theory in my youth. With me the form of the work builds itself, according to the subject. Therefore this Quartet has created its own form. I wished to depict in music the course of my life.

'The first movement (*allegro vivo appassionato*) depicts the love of art in my youth, the romantic supremacy, the inexpressible yearning for something which I could not clearly define, and also a kind of warning of my future misfortune.

'The long drawn note in the *Finale* owes its origin to this: it is the fatal whistling in my ear in the highest registers that in 1874 announced my deafness. I permitted myself this little joke, such as it is, because it was so disastrous to me.

'The second movement (*allegro moderato a la polca*), a quasi-polka, brings to memory the joyful days of my youth when I composed dance music enough to bury the world, and was known as a passionate lover of dancing. . . . The third movement (*largo sostenuto*) reminds me of the bliss of my first love for a girl who afterwards became my faithful wife. The fourth (*vivace*) describes the discovery that I could treat the national element in music, and my joy in following this path until the catastrophe overwhelmed me; the beginning of deafness, with the prospect of so wretched a future; a little ray of hope in a passing improvement, but, remembering all the promise of my early career, a feeling of painful regret. This is more or less the meaning of the work, which is to some extent of an intimate nature and therefore written as a quartet that, in a small and friendly circle, may speak of what afflicts me so profoundly. That is all.'

The First Quartet soon found appreciation outside Bohemia. Liszt wrote that he had introduced it with great success at Weimar, while in 1882 E. Lemoine called the attention of Saint-Saens to its great merits, and it began to be known in France. It also met with approval at a performance in Hamburg in 1880. These events were a consolation to Smetana, buried away from the activities of the musical world at Jabkenice, for the neglect of his own countrymen. The Quartet came fully into its own with the foundation of the Bohemian (Czech) Quartet who made it known in every great musical centre in Europe and were naturally the first interpreters of this intimately emotional music.

The Second Quartet, in D minor, was written between 1882–3 and has not the charm of its predecessor. The first work is chequered with the sunny memories of youth and the shadowy presentiments of coming catastrophe. The second Quartet takes up Smetana's life-story *after* the catastrophe and is therefore sunless, and bears traces of the nervous fatigue and confusion of mind which beset him at this time. He was painfully sensible of this and wrote to Srb in June 1882: 'I have finished the first movement but as to its structure I am very doubtful, it is very peculiar in form and difficult to grasp; a sense of derangement pervades the whole movement and will give a good deal of trouble to the executants. It is the outcome of my unhappy life. I feel tired and drowsy, and I fear I am gradually losing the vitality of my musical ideas; it seems to me that all that I work at now in music is veiled in a kind of mist of worry and pain.'

Later on he began to take a more hopeful view of the Quartet and says 'It is good and full of melodious moments, emotions, and novelty'. In his own private list of his works he observes of the second String Quartet: 'Composed in a nervous condition, which arose from my deafness'. It was played for the first time on 3 January 1884, in the hall at a chamber concert of the Arts Club

(*Umělecka Beseda*), but it has never taken its place beside the first of these two autobiographical works. Nor has it figured as often in the performances of chamber concerts organized by the Bohemian Quartet as the early Pianoforte Trio in G minor, which has a certain romantic charm and melancholy, and was written in 1855 in memory of his eldest daughter Frederica, who died at five years of age, but who had already shown signs of an unusual musical gift.

Among his latest works is the Introduction and Polonaise for Orchestra which was intended as the Prelude to an important Symphonic Suite, *The Carnival in Prague*, 'a series of purely musical scenes which, like *My Fatherland*, may be presented individually or as one great symphonic poem'. The project was never realized. *Our Song*, a chorus for male voices, and the two Mottoes for the choral society 'Hlahol', both, by reason probably of their comparative brevity, show less sign of mental weariness than the longer compositions.

CHAPTER VIII

OF the three most striking figures which dominate the middle renaissance of musical activity in Bohemia—Smetana, Dvořák, and Fibich—the last named was by far the least consciously influenced by national impulses and patriotic inspiration.

Sdeněk Fibich was born twenty-six years later than Smetana, in 1850, at Sebonice, near Časlau, in the midst of a thickly wooded country where his father was head forester. The forest atmosphere was in the blood of generations of Fibichs, and the boy absorbed something of the calm, the sylvan freshness, and the twilight charm of his early surroundings. The nature touch in his music, without being crudely realistic, is always sure, with the certainty of direct and unforgettable experience.

His musical gifts, early demonstrated, were also early cultivated. A song, *Le Printemps*, published as Op. 1, dates almost from childhood, and at fourteen he is said to have conducted a movement from a symphony of his own composition at a concert in Chrudim. He was sent to preparatory schools in Vienna and Prague, where his musical education was not neglected, and, as it was obvious that his heart was set upon an artistic career, he went direct from school to the Leipzig Conservatoire, where his uncle Raymond Dreyschock was professor of violin. He spent two years at the Conservatoire, studying the piano with Moscheles, harmony with Carl Ludwig Richter, and counterpoint with Jadassohn. From Leipzig he went to Paris for a year (1868–9) and finally to Mannheim, where he worked under V. Lachner, and returned home in 1870, unusually well equipped for his start as a professional musician. For three years he taught music at Vilna, in Poland, before he was appointed second conductor at the National Theatre in Prague, and later on he acted as choirmaster of the Russian Church in the Bohemian capital. Soon after his thirtieth year he relinquished all his appointments in order to devote himself wholly to composition. These are all the available details of his uneventful external life. Judging from the regularity with which his works were produced in Prague within a few months of their completion, he does not seem to have had any of the struggles or setbacks which sometimes beset the young composer's career.

When we glance at the list of Fibich's teachers we are prepared to find him enter upon his creative career influenced by the already debile school of German romanticism. Fortunately it was to Schumann rather than to the languishing band of his imitators and followers that the youth was directly attracted in his student days. We are conscious of this affinity in the early chamber music, the pianoforte pieces, and the overtures; just as a little later on the first Symphonic Poems show the working of Liszt's spell upon a young and progressive talent.

His first essay in chamber music, a Pianoforte Trio in F minor, dates from 1872. Two years later he produced a pair of works which showed an immense advance upon the earlier effort. The String Quartet in A minor is remarkable as containing a novel experiment in the use of the national Polka rhythm by way of a Scherzo. The E minor Pianoforte Quartet, Op. 11, found its way beyond the Bohemian frontiers. Hanslick, whose appreciation of his countrymen's music was usually in reverse ratio to the measure of nationalism which it contained, wrote of this work some twenty years after its composition: 'a strong and sympathetic personality speaks in this Quartet . . . echoes of folk-music are almost entirely lacking to this composition, which we welcome as a valuable addition to modern chamber music'. The work has but three movements: an opening *allegro moderato*, followed by an *adagio* which is an air with variations, and winding up with a spirited *allegro energico*. It is cyclical in form, certain recurrent themes in modified versions being common to all three movements. Though somewhat discursive, the Quartet has much charm and colour. It was introduced to this country at a Saturday Popular Concert by the Bohemian violinist, Mme Norman-Neruda, Charles Hallé, Strauss, and Piatti. It was frequently in the repertory of the Bohemian String Quartet and the Ševčik Quartet. A later String Quartet, which bears however an earlier Opus number, is in G major (published as Op. 8). Its distinct touch of national colour, most noticeable in the Scherzo with its Trio in polka style, may be accounted for by the fact that Fibich composed the work in the country, while recovering from a serious illness in 1878. It is a pleasant, melodious, and cheerful example of his early manner. Nearly sixteen years elapsed before Fibich again interested himself in chamber music, and the Quintet in D, Op. 42 (1894), is an experiment in instrumental combination. The addition of the horn and clarinet to the piano, violin, and 'cello gives a romantic colour to this semi-orchestral work; but the form is on the whole pure and true to type. There is some very grateful writing for the wind instruments, and it is surprising that the work is so completely neglected by the organizers of chamber-music concerts.

Besides these compositions, Fibich left a set of Variations in B flat major for String Quartet (1883), a Sonatina for Pianoforte and Violin, Op. 27 (1868), a Romance for the same Instruments, Op. 10 (1879), and a few other small and unpublished things.

Fibich wrote no great works for piano. If we except the Sonata, Op. 28, the rest of his work is in the miniature style which Schumann introduced with his *Carnival*, *Kinderscenen*, &c.

By far the most interesting of Fibich's contributions to pianoforte literature are to be found in the Collections which he published from time to time under the title of *Moods, Impressions, and Memories* ('Nálady, Dojmy a Upomínky'), containing about 350 separate pieces. None of these is as perfect as the best of Schumann's short pieces, or the emotional epitomes of Chopin's Preludes, but they are on a far higher level than the lilliputian swarms which were published in Germany from the pen of a Reinecke, a Scharwenka, or a Theodore Kirchner about the 'eighties of last century. Fibich jots down in music what others may do in a written diary. and the result is a kind of musical day-book in which we may read with considerable entertainment. Here are marches, dances, such as polkas, furiants, valses; reminiscences of some modal tune; experiments in rhythm and harmony; folk-melodies real or evolved from a long familiarity; obvious parodies; quotations from other composers, as a painter might preserve the memory of another artist's masterpiece in his own sketch-book. A heterogeneous collection, delightful and amusing as a bric-à-brac shop, in which we may at any moment light upon a small gem. The thirty-three pieces, Op. 44—the middle volume of the *Moods, Impressions, and Memories*—are called *Novelle* (a Novel) and contain a Foreword, Introduction, Four Chapters, and an Epilogue. Some of the short pieces are the seeds from which larger works have germinated. The Collection will give pleasure to those—more numerous than they care to confess—who, repelled and puzzled by the strange crossings and inflexes of modern musical horticulture, and baffled by the idiom of a Malipiero, a Berners, or a Stravinsky, still like to wander at ease in a garden of normal and comparatively old-fashioned blossoms.

Fibich's songs clearly indicate the various stages in his creative progression. The early lyrics are imbued with the folk spirit. Later albums (Ops. 36 and 45) show that he had studied the songs of Schumann and Brahms to some purpose. A choral setting of a romantic ballad, *The Bride of the Wind*, by Kinkel, gave him an opportunity to write picturesque music describing the three elemental forces which come to woo the Daughter of Giants: the Water Sprite, King Salamander, ruler of Fire, the Spirit of Earth —each of which is dismissed in turn, until the Spirit of the Wind comes, breaking his way through the forest, and carries her away by his impetuous wooing. Other choral works there are, belonging to his first period, but they are not of the first importance. In this sphere Fibich is not the equal of most of the Bohemian composers. He only found himself when it came to the union of music with the drama.

Like most of the modernists of his day Fibich was disposed to believe that Beethoven had laid the defunct form of the Symphony in a grave whence it could never rise again. This accounts for the fact that, prolific as he was, he only three times attempted a formal symphony.

The First Symphony in F, Op. 17, is dated 1883, but much of it was undoubtedly written earlier. It is nature music—essentially of the forest; pleasing in its thematic material rather than original. The Scherzo is like an elfin dance in some twilight glade; the slow movement has a romantic ballad-like melody for oboe, accompanied by harp.

The Second Symphony, in E, Op. 38, finished in 1892, when Fibich was forty-two, is a growth springing from far deeper roots. It owes its balance and unity of style to its methods of construction on the basis of a motto-theme, given out in the first movement by the horns and constantly reappearing in some fresh and ingenious guise. The form of this movement is exceptional in the absence of a recapitulation, although it is lengthened out by a *Coda* developed with unusual fullness. The mood of the slow movement is subdued and reflective; but its pensive melancholy is shattered by a loud trumpet-call which ushers in a spirited Scherzo with a Trio in the minor that overcasts its first flush of gaiety. The combination of the motto-theme with an augmented version of the actual first subject of the *Finale* is effectively carried out. The instrumentation of the work is by no means colourless, but Fibich had not yet learnt the mastery of the orchestra which he acquired from his great melodramatic experiment—the Trilogy

Hippodamia. In 1898 Fibich completed a Third Symphony, in E minor, Op. 53, dedicated to Hans Richter.

The group of Overtures which mostly belong to the ripe period of Fibich's earlier style—before the production of *Hippodamia*—is worth study. The Comedy Overture suggested by Vrchlicky's *A Night in Karlstein*, Op. 26 (1886), is a lively and attractive work, developed with remarkable command of technical craft, used to clarify rather than to complicate the material from which it is woven; material with more than a tinge of national colour and touched with humour. The period of Vrchlicky's play is that of the great Emperor Charles IV, who built Karlstein Castle as a kind of retreat, dedicating it more or less to religious uses. In consequence he forebade the presence of any woman within its walls. The Empress Elisabeth, devotedly and jealously enamoured of her husband, managed to force an entrance to the semi-monastic stronghold, with results more diverting than tragic.

A still better work is the Overture written for the Komensky (Comenius) Festival (1892) on the third centenary of the birth of the great educational reformer and apostle of Bohemian freedom. The Overture is built upon a chorale taken from Komensky's Cancional published at Amsterdam in 1659. C. L. Richter speaks of the work as 'an interesting treatment of the profound spirituality of the Bohemian Brothers'. In any case the *Komensky Overture* has musical value apart from its merits as an occasional piece. The Dorian theme reappears three times in the course of the work, each different aspect depicting a phase in Komensky's character. The theme of the *Allegro* in D minor reflects the fighting spirit of the reformer, his wanderings, risks, and courage as a propagandist; when it comes back transformed in the quiet and tender section in B major, it depicts the mild and philanthropic character of the sage and his teaching; the closing section is frankly national in colour and works up to a great *Coda* prophetic of the ultimate triumph of Komensky's marvellously far-sighted and progressive ideals. This is a work that seems to have been unaccountably overlooked in our orchestral concerts.

There are several other Overtures: *The Jew of Prague* (1871), *A Comedy Overture* (Op. 35), and the *Overture to a Tragedy* in D minor, but they need not detain us. I must pass on to another phase of Fibich's work.

Under the influence of Liszt he began early to cultivate the Symphonic Poem. His first effort in this line, *Othello*, Op. 23, was written at the age of twenty-three. It had no great success at first, but many years later, in 1896, Trenkler revived it in Dresden, and it eventually found its way back into the repertory of the Czech orchestras.

Another Symphonic Poem based upon one of the much-discussed folk-legends of the *Kralove Dvur* manuscripts deals with the story of 'Zaboj, Slavoj, and Ludek'. Though published as Op. 37, it is said to date as early as 1873, in which case it might claim to be the first symphonic poem inspired by a purely national subject, for Smetana's cycle *My Fatherland* only started (with *Vyšehrad*) in 1875. The conflict between the two representative heroes is depicted with considerable power, two opposing themes being employed; one somewhat violent and archaic in its rhythmic character, the other a noble flowing melody suggesting a more cultivated nature.

Toman and the Woodnymph, Op. 49 (1875), is the outcome of a popular ballad of the same title by Čelakovský. *Toman a lesní panna* deals with one of the many Slavonic legends of the supernatural forces that lurk in the forest, the stream, or the quiet woodland pool, ready to exercise a baneful influence upon mortals who venture too near to their haunts. The musical picture is tuneful and fresh, and much use is made of an old national wedding-song.

Spring, Op. 13, did not appear until 1881. It is a sketch of rustic life containing a lively polka-intermezzo and a dance of elves in the forest.

At Twilight ('V podvečer'), Op. 39, is another idyll of the spring, written in rondo form. The chief theme is announced in G major by horns and violins over a long pedal. A brisk Scherzo follows, and with the return of the first subject there is a *cadenza* for solo flute, a realistic bird song. The second section introduces an amorous melody linked to a counter subject. On the final appearance of the *Rondo* subject there is some skilful combination of it with its own subsidiary motive. C. L. Richter points out that towards the close, the poem refers to the leading theme of the Second Symphony, which 'seems to have some persistent inward meaning for the composer since it crops up in so many of his works'. I recall a very poetic interpretation of this unpretentious tone poem given by Karel Kovařovic and the orchestra of the Národní Divadlo at the Czechoslovak Festival at Queen's Hall in 1919.

All these symphonic poems belong to Fibich's fluctuating tendency towards nationalism which ebbed and flowed periodically throughout his career. Works which have no direct patriotic inspiration are *The Tempest* ('Bouře'), Op. 46 (1880), based on Shakespeare's play, the material of which served him some years later for an opera on the same subject, and *Vigilae*, Op. 22 (1883) two rather original and characteristic records of 'nights spent in poetic reverie'. They are purely subjective music of varied emotional expression, sometimes dreamy, sometimes glowing with passion; distinctive and interesting works to those who are still tolerant of the romanticism which carefully skirts the domain of the supernatural and artificial without touching it.

Smetana's example and the opening of a Provisional Theatre, followed at a short interval by the establishment of the Národní Divadlo, turned the attention of most young Czech composers towards dramatic music. Fibich was no exception to the rule. In the opinion of C. L. Richter he was a born dramatic composer who gravitated inevitably towards the medium through which he could most convincingly express himself. My personal feelings about his art are that he was naturally a lyric musician, stirred to dramatic ambitions by the Wagnerian atmosphere in which he lived, and endowed with such gifts of perception and intelligence as enabled him to find his way through successive experiments to 'the purple heights' of dramatic achievement. But in whatever way we choose to express ourselves on his musicianship, it is this side of his work that has assured him a high place in musical literature. Comparing him with Dvořák, Richter says: 'whereas to Dvořák's artistic temperament the text hinders his free flight through the sphere of music to which he is attracted by the inspiration of absolute music, Fibich's art, on the contrary, finds its greatest power when linked to words. The two elements are only welded together where this natural gift exists.'

There is not a great deal in his first opera *Bukovín* (1870), first produced in 1874, which foreshadows the works to come. Various influences show that he was far from having decided on a definite method of dramatic construction. The powerful magnetism of Wagner had not as yet touched his art. Mozart, Beethoven, and Weber, whose *Freischütz* has a particular significance for this son of the forest, all contributed some ingredients to *Bukovín*. How could it be otherwise in a work commenced at sixteen and completed in his twentieth year? Nor was he very fortunate in the libretto by Karel Sabina; though it is comprehensible that a text by the librettist of *The Bartered Bride* proved an attractive bait.

His second opera, *Blaník*, is inspired by a book of Eliška Krásnohorská upon the old Czech legend which Smetana has also used for one of his Symphonic Poems. Composed between 1875-7, its breadth of line and the definite use of leit-motifs point to the fact that Fibich had now studied Wagner's operas to some practical purpose, although Smetana sometimes haunts its pages and Weber is not quite forgotten. Emanuel Chvala speaks of it as a legacy from the composer's 'Sturm und Drang' period, displaying an unpruned luxuriance of imagination and emotion, picturesque qualities and a refreshing youthfulness. 'The glowing eloquence of the love music and the poetic atmosphere touch us deeply. Such a love lyric as Fibich gives us towards the close of Act I is rarely met with in opera; it is not only genuinely inspired but valuable as music.'

In *The Bride of Messina* (1883, first production 1884) Fibich has plunged head and heels into the stream of Wagnerism. He has here the advantage of a text by one of the first writers on aesthetic questions, Dr. O. Hostinsky, and has produced a serious and, as regards all the technical side of his art, a very successful music-drama. But excellent as it is in structure and decorative effects it lacks the passionate individual accents of *Blaník*. It keeps so close to the Wagnerian model as to be perilously near imitation. For the first time we become aware of his naturally lyric tendencies being deliberately yoked to the service of declamation. Perhaps Fibich himself realized that he had chosen the cul-de-sac of Wagnerism at the risk of losing his own individuality, for a considerable interval elapsed between *The Bride of Messina* and his next composition for the stage.

During this period he worked out to a logical conclusion the theories inspired by his Wagnerian studies and they appeared to him to lead convincingly in the direction of melodrama. Melodrama from the time of Benda was something of an inherent tradition among the Czechs. The form, aesthetically condemned in many directions, has been accepted in Bohemia. Modern composers have attempted it in many instances with signal success, as we shall see in the later chapters of this book. Nešvera, Foerster, Kovařovic, and others have produced melodramas on a modest scale, often for one reciter only, with pianoforte or orchestral accompaniments, which, if they were furnished with careful and telling translations of the texts, might prove an acceptable change from the over-familiar hackneyed repertory arias.

On these simple lines Fibich made his first experiments. *Christmas Eve* ('Štědrý den'), Op. 9, Freiligrath's *Der Blumen Rache* ('Pomsta květin'), *Eternity* ('Věčnost'), Vrchlický's *Queen Emma* ('Královna Emma') are written with piano accompaniment. Erben's poem *The Water Sprite* ('Vodník'), Op. 15, and *Hakon* demand an orchestra. All these works preceded the ambitious melodramatic effort *Hippodamia*. *Christmas Eve* is a picture of folk life, well carried out with a direct expression of joy and pathos in the music. A gay dance theme accompanies the Christmas revels; then two maidens consult some Yuletide oracle as to their future; for one we hear a wedding march, for the other a dirge.

Vodník is altogether more dramatic and complex. It is the old story of a mortal—this time a girl, for whereas in Russian legend the supernatural agent is generally a Russalka, in Czech folk-literature the watersprite is often a maleficent male creature—lured to a watery grave by the song of the Vodník. But the tale is complicated by the mother's love, for she, having warned her child in vain, resolves to follow her to the cold haunts of the watersprite. The poem is the outline of the picture; the orchestration the colour which fills in and enhances the design.

Although Fibich had progressed far on the path of dramatic music, he seems at this point to have reached an impasse with regard to opera. Wagner had been his model for *The Bride of Messina*, and it was not possible that a work should more closely resemble its prototype without becoming imitative; the alternative courses before him were sterile repetition, or a rapid move in a new direction, since he never dreamt at that stage of retracing his steps towards a lyric style. In spite of all his diversity and almost fatal fluency of invention Fibich never worked in an aimless, fortuitous fashion. 'He now held in his hands the threads of opera, and the threads of melodrama', says C. L. Richter. The former had not given him quite the results he desired; in sung music-drama he was trammelled too much by the Wagnerian theories; spoken music-drama would surely leave his individuality free expression. The fault of the old form of melodrama was the continuous alternation of declamation and music. The two elements tripped each other up, as it were. There was no inevitable fusion of words and music, but one struggled with the other for predominance, as in an ill-matched marriage. More recent experiments, such as we find in Beethoven's *Egmont* or Mendelssohn's *Midsummer Night's Dream*, were limited to the occasional relief effects of music as an accompaniment to words. Fibich solves—or goes a long way to solve—these difficulties in his Trilogy by a skilfully contrived continuous musical commentary, 'in which the leit-motif, like a live wire, runs alongside the spoken text, flashing a succession of messages which elucidate the shifting ideas and emotions of the protagonists'. In this way the moods and reflections of the music cling closely to the words, lending them greater depth. 'The melodrama as Fibich created it', continues Richter, 'proceeds in a direct line from music-drama as its only logical result.' He contends that the basic idea in both forms is identical: to give the greatest possible prominence to dramatic expression and a complete equality between the two co-operating elements—the poetic and musical. In this he claims for Fibich almost complete success. The difference between melodrama and music-drama is free declamation as opposed to recitation on determinate notes. Richter favours the former, since 'in sung music-drama, even at the best, eighty per cent. of the text is lost, whereas in melodrama at the worst only twenty per cent. becomes inefficient'.

For his culminating effort in melodrama Fibich chose the classic story of Hippodamia in Vrchlický's version. The form of the work, a Trilogy consisting of three separate dramas intended for performance on three consecutive evenings, seems like an attempt to out-Wagner Wagner, and its impracticability, with the labour involved in its performance, has no doubt militated against the success of this melodrama. Its first production at the Národní Divadlo was, however, piecemeal, each section being presented as it was completed: *Pelops' Wooing*, in 1890; *The Atonement of Tantalus*, in 1891, and *The Death of Hippodamia*, in 1892. The first section was performed by the artists of the Národní Divadlo at Vienna in June 1892, and in the following year it was well received in Antwerp. Most of the leading Viennese critics agreed that the work did much to sweep away the long-standing prejudice of the aesthetes against melodrama.

Vrchlický in building his trilogy upon the old legend of Pelops has succeeded in combining the pure classic outline with modern colour and emotionalism. Fibich's music accompanies the text throughout, vitalizing the movement of the drama and clothing

I

the words, as it were, in a flexible garment that is never permitted to muffle them in a noisy obscurity.

The first section, *Pelops' Wooing*, tells how Oenomaus, King of Pisa, resolves to give his daughter Hippodamia in marriage only to the suitor who can conquer him in a chariot race, the unsuccessful candidates being put to death. Pelops sees Hippodamia walking by moonlight on the walls of the city where hangs the decapitated head of her father's last victim, and (forgetting his wife) determines to win her. She favours his suit and makes a bargain with Myrtilos, the king's charioteer, who is also in love with her, and willing to do her bidding—at a price. He contrives that the wheel of the chariot shall come off when going at full speed. The king, falling under the horses, is trampled to death and dies, cursing Pelops, who of course is innocent of this crime. The lovers journey to the home of Pelops, but when Hippodamia confesses that she arranged the tragedy herself, he grows jealous, and demands from Myrtilos on what terms he agreed to assist. He offers half his kingdom for the truth; but Myrtilos demands a share in the bride, and Pelops, infuriated, hurls him into the sea.

Readers who wish to study *Hippodamia* in greater detail can do so in C. L. Richter's monograph on the composer.

The first section of *Pelops' Wooing* opens with a Prelude in which an energetic theme depicts the hero setting out on his journey. The tissue of leading motives is closely woven and almost too intricate. Besides Pelops' principal theme, the barbaric King Oenomaus and his daughter have representative phrases of their own; Myrtilos has two—one which indicates his shifty nature, the other in a brisk and curious rhythm suggesting his occupation as charioteer. Then there are the themes of the King's Curse, of Pelops' Innocence, and of the Crime. All these occur in Part I of the Trilogy and engender other subsidiary motives. The antique Chorus takes part in the drama and to it is entrusted the task of describing the headlong chariot race with its disastrous end to Oenomaus. From the musical point of view the music which accompanies Hippodamia's visit to the city walls, and the Intermezzo from Act III with its lovely violin solo, are the most attractive pages in the score. There is also a fine Festival March sometimes heard as a separate item in the concert hall.

Part II of *Hippodamia*, entitled *The Atonement of Tantalus*, shows the palace at Argos where Tantalus is anxiously awaiting the return of Pelops. He is weighed down by the curse which he incurred, some say, by having stolen nectar and ambrosia from the table of the gods and given them to his friends. For this breach of the laws of hospitality he is relentlessly pursued by the Furies. Pelops now returns bearing the message of the Delphic oracle for Tantalus: the sin will only be atoned for by a sin. Pelops brings home his new bride, Hippodamia, who immediately begins to persecute her predecessor, Axiocha. The first wife takes refuge by the Altar of Hospitality which Tantalus in his remorse has raised as a refuge for the helpless. But Hippodamia is no respecter of sanctities and she pursues her victim even there. The consequences of Hippodamia's crime against her father are beginning to tell. Pelops, ever restless, jealous, and suspicious, calls up the shades of the dead in the hope of learning how to solve the painful perplexities of his life. He learns that Myrtilos is still alive. He also sees the spirit of Axiocha, who implores him to save their child from Hippodamia's hatred. Tantalus takes charge of the boy and saves him from death, and this act of humanity wins him the forgiveness of the gods on his death-bed.

The Atonement of Tantalus shows a surer hand than *The Wooing of Pelops*. There is nothing tentative in the working-out of this drama which offers so many fine occasions for musical illustration. The framework of representative themes is transferred from Part I of the Trilogy with more intensive developments. New leading themes make their appearance as the figure of Tantalus comes more and more into the foreground, and in contrast to the music which centres round Hippodamia we hear the gentle feminine motives which stand for the devoted and despised Axiocha.

The work opens with an orchestral prelude depicting sunrise upon Argos. Pelops and Hippodamia arrive and the humiliation of Axiocha begins. The music which accompanies the incantation scene is penetrated with a strange, chilly, crepuscular atmosphere; the outcome of Fibich's skilful orchestration. The exorcism of the Furies brings a fine choral incident in the solemn chanting of the priests. The whole drama proceeds step by step to its final climax—the death and transfiguration of the suffering Tantalus. We naturally think of Amfortas at this juncture, but there is no conscious imitation of Wagner here, and this scene is generally acknowledged to be Fibich's masterpiece. The sun-shot music of the Prelude returns effectively at this climax; but the serene and luminous theme of Tantalus's translation to the spirit world is ingeniously derived from the gloomy motive of the Furies.

The Death of Hippodamia (Part III) shows constructional weaknesses which are absent from the well-planned plots of the earlier sections of the Trilogy. Time had to be allowed in order that the seeds of the crime committed by Hippodamia should ripen to fruition. But the unexpected resurrection of Myrtilos and his reappearance as the instrument of supreme vengeance after a quarter of a century's delay are not convincing. Pelops and Hippodamia now reign in splendour at Olympia, but the shadow of the past darkens the inner lives of themselves and their children. The later developments of the original themes of the guilty pair are psychologically admirable. There is also a new motive for Hippodamia significant of her state and material triumph. The new thematic material includes representative phrases for her two sons: that of Atreus, her favourite, suggests a proud and intractable nature; while Thyestes' theme shows his cunning and guile. Chrysippos, Pelops' son by Axiocha, is depicted by a new version of his mother's leading motive. An altogether new character is that of the beautiful young hostage Airopa, beloved by all three brothers in turn; first by Chrysippos whom she discards; then by Atreus who marries her; and finally by the wily Thyestes who elopes with her. The reappearance of Myrtilos is announced by the old, alert, and rhythmically capricious theme of Part I, now transformed to suit the character of the blind and ailing old man. Myrtilos quickly sows the seeds of mischief in the house of Pelops. He tells Chrysippus the story of Hippodamia's treachery to her father and how Pelops profited by it to become king. At the marriage feast of Atreus and Airopa, Chrysippus, embittered by the bride's deception and inflamed with wine, tells the tale and asperses Hippodamia's fame. Atreus slays his half-brother and, called before the king's judgement-seat, is condemned to exile. Thyestes, who knows himself equally guilty, escapes with his brother's wife. The banishment of her favourite son turns Hippodamia against Pelops. She resolves to murder him. But both are linked together by their common fear and hatred of Myrtilos. The old charioteer takes refuge from them in a deserted hut by the sea shore. The opening of this scene is accompanied by some effective sea-music which merges into the expression of anguish and foreboding when Pelops arrives at the hut and finds his wife, who has just said farewell to Atreus. Hippodamia is prepared to kill Pelops with her own hand, but pauses when she hears him calling to the blind Myrtilos to warn him of his presence. 'Be thou accurst', cries the old man. 'That have I been long since', replies Pelops. Again he implores Myrtilos to tell him the truth about his relations with Hippodamia. The old man, knowing that silence is the cruellest revenge, refuses to speak, and Pelops, exasperated, stabs him to death.

The opera closes with the death of Hippodamia, who, with a final curse upon the whole house of Pelops, puts an end to her baneful life.

In addition to the music which accompanies the monologues of the actors, *The Death of Hippodamia* contains several salient musical features: a March which precedes the inauguration of the Olympic games, the touching funeral music for the death of Chrysippus, and some animated scenes for the populace.

It has not been my good fortune to witness a performance of the work. It has been revived at the Národní Divadlo from time to time, but it does not seem to have become a necessity to the musical life of the Czechs as certain operas of Smetana, Dvořák, Kovařovic, and Janáček have done. Fibich, whose art was fastidious and whose aims were universal, neither found his inspiration in the life of his own people nor penetrated their hearts with his music. In planning *Hippodamia* he obviously aspired to carry dramatic music a step farther than Wagner. He won the praises of the German critics, who were pleased with this ambitious compliment to their musical deity, but the Germans never made up to Fibich for the sacrifices entailed in this experiment by frequent productions of the Trilogy. It has been left more or less on the shelf; a revered relic displayed occasionally to the composer's compatriots, but not a chalice from which to drink delight and encouragement day by day. To offer a definite judgement on a work primarily intended for stage production when one has conned it only in the study is perhaps presumptuous. Personally, the more I look into *Hippodamia* the more doubtful I feel as to its complete success as an organic art form, but the more I am convinced of the interest and value of much of the music. It would not be difficult to test the present day value of some of the music of *Hippodamia* in our concert rooms. The preludes to several of the Acts of the Trilogy, such as the Sunrise in Part II, the Sea-Music in Part III, or any of the eight Marches which occur in the course of the work would be easily detachable from the whole.

That Fibich himself was left in doubt about the complete success of his excursion into melodrama may be assumed from the fact that he never returned to this form. Into the three operas which rapidly succeeded the Trilogy he brought all that he had assimilated from Wagner, all that he had acquired of dexterity in the use of leading motives, all the mastery of orchestral colour and deftness in following the emotional changes of the spoken word, which were the rewards of his apprenticeship to melodrama. But now the use of *cantilena* comes into its own and flows freely through the later works, which proclaim clearly that the musical element has again triumphed over the purely declamatory.

I have already spoken of Fibich's Symphonic Poem based upon Shakespeare's *The Tempest*. He now resolved to write an opera on the subject, and was again indebted to Vrchlický for a libretto. The gifted poet did his work in a reverential and tactful manner. Not so the German translator, who made a botched version of the wonderful play. In *The Tempest* ('Bouře'), which was composed in 1894 and performed the following year, Fibich uses only a few leit-motifs as the skeleton of the work: motives which are recalled only from time to time as landmarks in the melodic progress of the opera. Here and there a lyrical episode, complete in itself, stands out from the main movement of the music. The subject suits the imaginative lyricism of the composer. The characters are clearly outlined in their respective musical portraiture. Ariel's entrances, visible or invisible, are depicted in delicate phrases of rapid graceful figuration which tell unmistakably of 'my dainty, my delicate Ariel'. But the composer has tactfully refrained from attaching a musical label to his wings. Prospero is a dignified figure kept well in the foreground of the picture by means of a threefold theme: (*a*) denotes his Magic Powers, (*b*) his Princely Dignity, (*c*) his Lofty Virtue and Gentleness.

Through Caliban's music runs a vein of tragic pathos which contrasts at times with a harsh grotesque element and touches of broad humour in the scenes with Trinculo and Stephano. The supernatural plays a large part in *The Tempest* and there is some charming elfin music. Ariel's song, 'Full fathom five', with its

simple orchestration and uncertain tonality, accompanied by a
pianissimo chorus and the hollow resonance of the *glockenspiel*, is
one of the gems of the work. A pompous March announces
Prospero's arrival for the judgement in his magic robes. Prospero's farewell to the island is a touching and dignified monologue. The opera concludes with the chorus of the liberated
spirits.

Hedy (Haidée), written in 1895 and first produced in 1896,
is written round an episode from Byron's *Don Juan*. After the
fantastic philosophy of *The Tempest*, comes the wholly erotic
mood of *Hedy*. C. L. Richter, who thinks that the subject expresses the inner feelings of the composer at that period of his
life, describes this work as 'the Czech *Tristan and Isolde*'; and,
like its predecessor, an epic which recounts the ecstacy and fatality
of a great inevitable and unhappy passion—an epic, however,
without the atmosphere of northern mysticism; a Southern love-
tale. Here the lyrical element has its own way in what is practically
a long love-duet. It is hardly necessary to re-tell in detail the
well-known tale of Don Juan's wreck, of his discovery on the
shore by Haidée, of his reawakening to love and life in her arms,
and the subsequent anger of her father, the pirate Lambro, who
sends him into slavery.

The introduction depicts the wild free life of the pirates and
the curtain goes up to a brisk chorus of the seafarers. The sombre
clear-cut motive of Lambro is then heard followed by Haidée's
lament for her solitude. When Juan returns to consciousness
a discreet reference to Mozart's masterpiece is heard. The
theme of his awakening to life becomes later the theme of
the first kindling of love, and is heard again as a violin solo in
the Prelude to Act II. Another and more obvious reference to
Mozart occurs in the scene in which Juan enlightens Haidée as
to his identity: 'I am a nobleman of Spanish blood—Don Juan
Tenorio.'

These reminiscences, which have been naïvely mistaken for
plagiaries, are of course conscious acts of homage offered by a
Czech to the master who loved Prague and endowed it with his
best. To lengthen out the material and add some general interest
to the continuous love-music, Fibich has introduced a ballet-
pantomime which comes quite logically into the scene in which
Haidée, having had news of her father's loss at sea, takes Juan to
her home and installs him as master of the house. The folk

assemble to do honour to them and the ballet falls appropriately
into place. The most piquant number is the fiery Sword Dance:

> The Pyrrhic dance so martial
> To which the Levantines are very partial.

There is a fine dramatic ensemble when Lambro suddenly reappears on the scene.

The last Act (IV) of the opera brings us back again to the
rocky strand with the ship that is to carry Juan away lying off the
shore. The Introduction opens with the theme of Lambro's
ruthlessness. Then a plaintive horn solo seems to presage in its
sad sweet melody the end of a great passion. Presently a fisherman
is heard singing a melancholy song in the folk-style *a capella*.
Juan is torn from Haidée's arms and carried on board, and the
ship fades slowly from sight in the distance. The remainder of
the scene is taken up with the death of the broken-hearted and
distraught Haidée. At first her lament mingles with the fisherman's song, but her growing despair and her wandering thoughts
are afterwards expressed in very poignant music. When the last
flame of love flashed light into her darkened mind, the motive of
Juan's return to life and sunshine accompanies her peaceful
departure from a troubled world. The fisherman then resumes
his melancholy song—the elegy of a great love tragedy:

> Alas for Juan and Haidée! they were so loving and so lovely.

Fibich's finest operatic work is *Šarka*, which was completed in
1896 and produced in the following year. His return to a national
subject does not imply a use of the folk-song element in the style
in which Smetana employs it. The charm of the popular melody
as we find it in *The Bartered Bride* and *The Kiss* is its spontaneous
flow from the heart of the composer where it seems to be preserved as in some sealed and inexhaustible spring. Such a natural
and homely effusion would have been impossible to Fibich at this
mature stage of his existence after years of work in the broader
fields of comprehensive, international art. The story of Šarka
attracted him more by all that it offers of strong emotional contrast and picturesque setting than by the fact of its being a national
saga. The legend has been told in these pages in connexion with
Smetana's Symphonic Poem on the subject; but it differs somewhat in the operatic treatment.

Libuše, the foundress of Prague, surrounded herself with a council of virgins who were the guardians of the tables of the law and the sacred fire and water used for sacrificial purposes. After Libuše's death Prince Přemysl thought it expedient to keep the government in male hands and banished the women—a survival of his wife's first years of spinster rule—from the precincts of the Vyšehrad. This gave rise to a fierce conflict between the sexes, and Šarka became one of the leaders of the Bohemian women warriors.

The Overture to the opera is solidly planned and adheres broadly to rondo form. It exposes two of the three basic themes on which the work is built up: the pathetic motive of Libuše's death (*adagio non troppo*), and the strongly marked rhythmic motive of the male warriors (*marciale non troppo mosso*). Another significant theme is the war-cry of the Amazons; while the third of the primary themes from which *Šarka* is evolved is a vehement motive which first appears on the entry of the women warriors and is subjected to many interesting psychological variations.

The first act brings out the contrast between the two leading women—Vlasta, grave and sweet, and the fierce, untamable Šarka —but both are equally determined to uphold feminine power. After their public mourning for Libuše in the sacred grove, and the invocation of the gods to help their cause, a group of masculine warriors is seen approaching, headed by Přemysl, to offer sacrifices on behalf of his army. Šarka, in a fury, forbids them, and scatters their offerings far and wide. The soldiers seek to kill her for this sacrilege, but Vlasta intercedes, and the magnanimous Přemysl pardons Šarka, but insists that in future the country shall be governed by men. Šarka will not compromise; she challenges the hero Ctirad to meet her in single combat and let the gods decide the issue. When he scornfully refuses, she attacks him with drawn sword. Vlasta again intervenes, and declares that the quarrel must be settled by fair and open war.

In the second act, Vlasta and her warriors are assembled in a glade, and she sings an epic ballad celebrating the exploits of fighting women and lamenting their dead. Radka, a ruthless and savage Amazon type, now enters, bearing in triumph the head of a male victim. She is followed by a group leading a woman in chains, and telling how they stormed the wedding feast of Ctirad's friend and carried off the bride. But Ctirad is behind them in hot pursuit. Šarka cries out that 'the hour of vengeance is come', and begs Vlasta to put his fate in her hands and leave her alone in the forest with only one or two faithful women at her side. Šarka then has a long solo, which ends in her asking the women whether she is really as beautiful as men say. The lovely melody now heard in the orchestra suggests their reply. Šarka then makes her resolve: Ctirad shall be lost through her beauty. She lets her dark hair fall over her shoulders, loosens her girdle, and bids her maidens tie her to an oak-tree and leave her alone. Ctirad enters singing an old Bohemian folk-song, but when he sees her bound to the tree, the climax of the opera begins. Moved by pity, he approaches, and she implores him to slay her, as she would rather die than fall into the hands of one to whom she is an object of contempt and scorn. Ctirad breaks into a passionate recantation of his scorn, and warms by degrees into a glowing confession of love. With a triumphant cry Šarka tells him to release her, and overcome, half by fatigue, half by unwilling love, she sinks into his arms. Soon, however, the Amazon flames up once more in Šarka, when in a moment of reaction she snatches a dagger from the folds of her dress and tries to kill Ctirad. But the power of love unnerves her hand. Šarka suddenly realizes Ctirad's danger and bids him escape before the wild women return. The hero refuses to run away from female warriors. They rush in, led by the implacable Radka, who succeeds in wounding Ctirad. But Šarka saves his life by claiming him as her special prize.

In the Prelude to Act III we are reminded by a harsh dissonance of Šarka's broken vow. This is followed by references to the battle hymn of the men warriors, and finally by broad lamenting *cantilena* which seem to foreshadow the tragic catastrophe to come. Šarka now enters leading Přemysl and his army to the narrow rocky pass where they can intercept the women as they march through. She bewails her role of traitress, undertaken as the sole method by which she can save her lover's life. The men hide in the woods. Now the women warriors arrive leading Ctirad a prisoner, and after a dignified and pathetic monologue from Vlasta, he is condemned to death. The hero's farewell to life and love is a touching episode. The women, in a strange and sinister chorus in the Dorian mode, evoke Morana, the Slavonic goddess of death. Vlasta has just raised her sword with the words, 'Morana accept thine offering', when Šarka throws herself as a shield in front of Ctirad. Vlasta, filled with horror and indigna-tion, expels Šarka from the ranks of the women heroes with a solemn curse. Šarka signals to Přemysl's soldiers, who emerge

from their ambush to the rescue of Ctirad. In the fierce fight
which follows, the women are forced into the narrow pass and
massacred. In the closing scene of the opera Vlasta's curse begins
to take effect. We see Šarka rapt in a terrible vision in which the
spirits of her dead comrades alternately pursue her and call on her
to join them. Her remorse and horror are depicted in powerful
music. Ctirad tries in vain to comfort her with his protestations
of love. Šarka cannot escape Vlasta's imprecation, or the stabs of
a guilty conscience. Breaking away from her lover's arms, she
mounts a high rock and hurls herself into the abyss below.

In *Šarka* we find the perfect palinode of Fibich's long adher-
ence to Wagnerian theories. Musically he has now arrived at his
fullest independence. This is most clearly shown in his treatment
of the vocal parts, through which the individuality of his characters is now revealed directly, without undue reliance on the
orchestra for salient relief and illumination. Melody runs like a
line of light above the depth and sonority of the modern orchestra.
Šarka is undoubtedly a fine achievement. If we admire the perseverance with which the composer pursued his dramatic aims
along the path which eventually culminated in *Hippodamia*, still
more must we marvel at the courage of his return to opera and its
just fication by such a work as *Šarka*.

Fibich's last opera *Pad Arkuna* ('The Fall of Arkuna'), although
well received in Prague and accorded a place in the permanent
repertory of the Národní Divadlo, is, musically, something of an
anticlimax. It is based on an episode from Danish history which
tells how Dargun, a young priest of the god Svanovit, ill requites
the hospitality of his host by seducing his daughter Helga. Svanovit is a kind of superman, and his lofty ambitions, his vows of
celibacy and contempt for the woman who fell an easy victim to
his charms, cause him to refuse the idea of repairing his ill-doing
by marriage. He kills Helga's father, who seeks to avenge his
daughter's wrongs. But Helga has another champion in the
Danish warrior Absalon, to whom she was originally betrothed.
Years later, when Dargun has become high priest of the temple
of Svanovit and virtual ruler of the Island of Rujan, Absalon,
converted to Christianity, leads an expedition against him. He
takes with him Margit the daughter of the unhappy Helga.
Dargun seeing her by accident imagines that he has had a vision
of the woman he injured. When he has learnt who she really is,
Margit, reconciled to her father, endeavours to persuade him to

embrace Christianity and escape before Absalon's forces begin to attack the capital of the island, Arkuna. But the proud, unyielding old pagan clings stubbornly to his faith in Svanovit. In the end he sees the city sacked and the temple of the god in flames, ere in wrathful despair he overthrows the idol he has served and dies in the ruins. The young Prince Jaromer, who has been kept in subordination by Dargun's ambitious intrigues, saves Margit's life. The new faith having triumphed over paganism, Jaromer is proclaimed King of Rujan and marries her. Thus Helga is avenged.

The last year of Fibich's life was an active one, and saw the completion of a Symphonic Poem on a folk-tale, *Oldřich and Božena*, and a popular Suite for Orchestra, *In the Country*, consisting of five movements: Moonlight, Ländler, On the Mountain-tops, Happy Hours, and Open-Air Dance.

Fibich died at the age of fifty when he had just attained the height of his powers. He left several distinguished pupils—Karel Weiss, Kovařovic, and others—but the measure of his influence on Czech music as a whole cannot be compared with that of Smetana or Dvořák.

CHAPTER IX

In a hollow among the smooth, rolling plains of north-east Bohemia, which stretch between Prague and the Saxon frontier, lies the village of Nelahozeves, the birthplace of Antonín Dvořák. The sheltered, old-world hamlet, situated by the river Vltava, is dominated by an old castle which belongs to the Lobkovic family.[1]

Dvořák's father, František (1814–94), a native of the district, settled here in early manhood in the double capacity of butcher and innkeeper. In the old farmstead in the main street, where František carried on his dual business, the future composer was born on 8 September 1841. The Dvořáks were not, like the Bendas, numbered among the professional rural musicians of Bohemia, but through several generations the family could always boast one or more lovers of music; some of them played the fiddle, and František was something of a performer on the zither. Such itinerant musicians as passed through Nelahozeves naturally paused at the inn, and, from a very early age, Antonín showed the keenest delight when they played their plaintive folk-songs or gay polkas. There was no question about his inborn love of a tune.

Like all Bohemian dominies the village schoolmaster, Josef Spitz, was able to teach the children the rudiments of music, and from him Dvořák received his first instruction as a fiddler. The boy's progress pleased his father, but did not, however, modify his plans for Antonín's future. It was decreed that the lad should follow the more or less traditional occupations of the Dvořáks as butchers and innkeepers. But in order that he might have a better education than his forefathers, Antonín at twelve years old was sent to live with an uncle at Zlonice, a few miles to the north-west of his native hamlet. In his new home he was fortunate enough to become the pupil of A. Liehmann, an enthusiastic musician who was quick to discern the unusual gifts latent in Dvořák. At this time he appears to have taken up the viola, the piano, and the organ. About two years later Antonín's father removed him to Česka-Kamenice in order that he might learn

[1] A portion of this vast house was later opened to the public, as a museum containing many treasures accumulated in the long history of the Lobkovic family.

German. Here he studied with the local organist Hancke. He left Kamenice stronger in music than in German, but his education, from the point of view of the elder Dvořák, was now quite sufficient for his future walk in life. He returned, not to Nelahozeves, but to Zlonice, where his father had opened a new shop in this busy mining district and needed the help of his sturdy son of fifteen.

There is ample evidence that all Antonín's teachers considered him very gifted on the musical side and regretted the wasting of his talents in a butcher's shop. Seeing, however, that for a Czech the conditions of artistic life in 1855 meant too often exile and starvation, a wise parent could hardly be blamed for discouraging in his son any notion of becoming a professional musician. Externally the boy resigned himself to his fate. Inwardly the love of music burned like a secret fire in the background of his prosaic life. Every leisure moment he spent with his former teacher, Liehmann, and often acted for him as deputy organist, while he was always in demand for any local musical festivities, and still made an occasional appearance at 'the castle'. After a year, the importunities of Liehmann and Antonín's uncle prevailed, and, in the autumn of 1857, his father consented to his entering the Organ School at Prague. Karel Pitsch, then at the head of this institution, was a man of seventy; fossilized in the old régime, speaking not a word of Czech. In Dvořák's second year Pitsch was replaced by Josef Krejči who, though a Czech by birth, was not sympathetic to his compatriots. The youth was more fortunate in his other masters: Blažek, who taught him theory; Josef Foerster, an excellent musician and sound patriot, whose name is associated with the reform of Bohemian Church music; and Zvonař, conductor of the singing class. In Prague, as in the provinces, every musician who came in contact with Dvořák was impressed by his abilities. In 1859 he left the Organ School with the second prize of the year. The Director summed him up as a pupil in these words: 'His talents are excellent, but mainly practical. He takes pains to acquire executive skill and knowledge. In theory he is weak.' This judgement need not be regarded as seriously disparaging Dvořák. 'Practical' musicianship was, after all, the aim and object of the Organ School; and it must be remembered that the stricture on his theoretical deficiency was passed by one who never left the narrowest path of classical convention. We have it from Dvořák's fellow-students—even if we did not see

it for ourselves in his early works—that he soon showed himself
a rebel against the strict rules of harmony as taught by the pedantic director of the Organ School.

At eighteen, with a certificate from the Organ School in his
pocket, Dvořák fared forth to battle for his livelihood in Prague.
The pity was that his pocket contained practically nothing else,
for the funds from home had gradually dwindled and were soon
altogether to cease. Business was not very flourishing in Zlonice,
and Antonín had other brothers to be put out in the world. But
perseverance and a strong will sustained him through the next
few years and he started his career at a moment when a ray of light
was falling on the dark pathway of native talent in Bohemia.
Smetana was the torch bearer. Already the permanent orchestra
of the Provisional Theatre was coming into existence and Dvořák
was lucky to find a place at one of the desks, which constituted
the best possible training for him.

Another stroke of luck which befell him at this time was the
friendship of Karel Bendl (1838–97), a musician who was beginning to make his way in the Bohemian capital, having passed out
of the Organ School soon after Dvořák entered it. Mendelssohn
and Schumann left their mark upon Bendl's part songs and lyrics,
nevertheless the former were very popular among the choral
societies of his own land, especially his choral ballad, *Švanda
Dudák*. As an operatic composer he passed through many phases.
He began with a grand opera, *Lejla* (1868), in which the oriental
colouring was something more attractive and fresher in those
days than it has now become, since every tyro has learnt the trick
of it from the Russians. In *Starý Ženich* ('The Old Bridegroom'),
1883, he emulated Smetana's humorous folk-operas; while in
Mati Mila ('Mother dear'), 1895, he produced a realistic one-act
opera, and in *Dítě Tabora* ('Son of Tabor'), 1892, an historical
opera on the subject of the Hussite Wars.

At the time when Dvořák first became intimate with him,
Bendl had recently been appointed conductor of the Choral
Society 'Hlahol'. Lifted above grinding poverty, and possessed
of a good musical library, perhaps the greatest of all the benefits
Bendl conferred upon his young friend was the loan of scores he
could not possibly have afforded to buy. Working night and day
for a living wage; living uncomfortably in his aunt's house;
afterwards sharing a room with several other students; knowing
no peace; possessing no piano—Dvořák at this time managed to

continue his musical education in the only way open to him. His chief text-books were the borrowed scores of Beethoven's Quartets, and it was in chamber music that it seemed most natural to take his first steps as a creative musician. The trifles which he wrote almost in his boyhood—such as the *Forget-me-not* Polka—need not be considered here; nor the Polka and Galop composed for Komzák's restaurant band in 1860. Dr. Otakar Šourek in his great book on Dvořák[1] gives 1861 as the year which saw the production of his first serious work, a String Quintet, by no means devoid of promise. So far, with the exception of Smetana's early Pianoforte Trio in G minor, this field was uncultivated by the Bohemian composers. In this neglected soil Dvořák began to work as steadily as Smetana was working for dramatic music. As the former laid the foundation of national opera, so Dvořák produced a series of chamber works, one of the most beautiful contributions to Czech art, in which, as Šourek says, 'the Czech spirit pierces like a meteor through the depths of a starless night'. The Quintet was followed in 1862 by a String Quartet in A, Op. 2, somewhat influenced by the exuberant eloquence of Schubert. Emil Chvala, writing in 1888, says that it confirms the prophetic opinions of those who believed that Dvořák was a great master in the making. 'It is impossible to speak of it as an immature essay, the ebullition of a youthful talent in strong ferment. . . . It is not so grateful to play as Dvořák's later Quartets, but an ardent spirit burns in the work.' Soon after these first attempts in chamber music, came the Songs published as Op. 2 and Op. 3. The Cycle entitled *The Cypress Trees*, words by Pfleger-Moravsky, were closely connected with Dvořák's first, and last, love story. He first met Anna Čermáková in 1864, but the engagement was a long one, and not until he was appointed organist to the church of St. Adalbert, in 1873, was he able to make a home where he could take his wife.

A Symphony in B flat, Op. 4, dedicated to Karel Bendl, and an opera in three acts, *Alfred the Great*, engaged his attention at this period. Operatic development, which in Germany seemed to have come to a culmination and to pause on the heights to which Wagner had carried it, was fresh and vigorously active in Bohemia; being one of the channels through which circulated the renewed life-blood of the Czech people. It was natural that

[1] *Život a dílo Antonína Dvořáka* (The Life and Works of Ant. Dvořák), 3 vols. Published by the Umělecká Beseda, Prague, 1916–29.

vořák, sitting night after night at his desk in the orchestra of the
rovisional Opera House, should have felt that the nearest way to
.e hearts of his compatriots was through dramatic music. It was
qually natural that, overshadowed by the presence of Smetana
id still unsure of himself in this new sphere of activity, he
iould have kept his first attempt a secret even from his intimate
iends. He had begun by basing his self-education simply and
icritically on the classics. Now, at thirty, he found himself in a
elter of conflicting opinions. The fact of hearing Smetana
used for his Wagnerism, led him to study for himself the music-
amas that were revolutionizing musical opinion. He saw and
:ard Liszt when he visited Prague, and he was playing in the
chestra when Smetana conducted the first performance of
iszt's *St. Elisabeth* in the Bohemian capital. How naïve were his
:ws on opera at this time is shown by his first essay in dramatic
usic. In some old German magazine Dvořák found Theodore
orner's *Alfred*, and on this romantic foundation proceeded to
instruct an opera which should embody his enthusiasm for the
odern theories. It was long believed that he had burnt the
anuscript, and that there the matter ended. This was not the
se, however, and those who are interested in the immaturities
great composers—an interest only a degree less unprofitable
an the exhumation of posthumous works—may find a fairly
ng analysis of *Alfred*, and quotations of most of its leading
emes, in Dr. Otakar Šourek's book to which reference has
ready been made.

In 1871 Dvořák came boldly into the field with a second opera
rál a Uhlíř ('King and Collier') which, while pseudo-Wagnerian
style, was national in character. Smetana, after the first
tempt at rehearsal, courteously returned the score to the com-
ser. Dvořák was not born a Czech to no purpose. Like most of
s compatriots he never accepted defeat. This time he really
irnt the ill-fated manuscript, and then proceeded to rewrite the
ork from end to end. Some of the faults of the original opera
ill persisted: the literary material which would have served well
iough for a short rustic comic opera is stretched to the require-
ents of grand opera and laid out in monumental scenes; the
iportunities of contrasting Court life with village life are
iglected, and the characters are feebly sketched. The new ver-
on of *King and Collier* was produced at the Provisional Theatre
1874, conducted by Adolphe Čech, who had then succeeded

K

Smetana as musical director. It was played four times, and re
vived in 1881 and again in 1887, but it never took a lasting hol
on the public taste.

The failure of *King and Collier* was compensated by the succes
of a new work which breathed an inspired patriotic sentiment an
at once set the composer in the full tide of the public favou
Hálek's hymn, *The Heirs of the White Mountain* ('Dědicové Bí
Hory'), which combines both lyrical and epic elements, ha
appeared in 1869, and made a profound impression on a natio
just reawakening to the hope of spiritual and political freedon
The text expresses in simple but poetical language the sufferin
of a race 'born to eternal tears' and the reaction from despair
a resolute faith in its ultimate victory, and rises towards the clo
to a climax of patriotic rejoicing. Dvořák's music is fine
adapted both to the shadow which overcasts the opening of th
work and to the blaze of light in which it culminates. Broad an
flowing melody, rhythmic balance, pregnant harmonies, chara
terize the first section, the solemnity of which is relieved by since
warmth of emotion. The music then begins to mount by a gradu
transition to heights of aspiration, until the twin summits of ho
and certainty stand out, touched with the glory of a new dawn
the final outburst of the concluding bars. In this work Dvoř
sheds the last traces of his apprenticeship and becomes sudden
mature. The Hymn was produced on 9 March 1873, at one
the concerts of the Choral Society 'Hlahol' under Karel Bend
and the composer's reputation was made forthwith. Dvoř
revised the score when the work was given at a Slavonic Conce
at Žofin in 1880.[1]

After this success Dvořák returned to opera. *The Pig-head*
Peasants ('Tvrdé Palice') was finished in 1874, and *Vanda*, O
25, composed to a Polish text adapted by Beneš-Šumavský,
1876. The manuscript of this 'grand opera in five acts' was pu
chased by the firm of Cranz of Hamburg who did not publish
and for many years only the sombre Overture was occasional
heard in the concert hall. *Vanda* was produced at Prague, und
the conductorship of Adolphe Čech, in 1876, but met with
marked success. It was repeated in 1877, and again in 188
after which it dropped out of the repertory. When Kovařov
was appointed chief conductor to the Národní Divadlo he ha

[1] The work in this revised form was published in 1885 by Messr
Novello & Co.

an idea of reviving this opera, but it came to nothing. It has, however, seen the light once more at the commemoration of the twenty-fifth anniversary of the composer's death (1929).

The subject of *Vanda* is closely allied to that of Smetana's *Libuše*. Vanda is in fact the same Slavonic heroine in a Polish guise, the Czech version of the legend being the more human and pathetic of the two. The similarity provoked comparisons which were not to the advantage of Dvořák's work.

In the same way the likeness between Dvořák's comic opera composed at this time, *The Pig-headed Peasants*, and Smetana's *The Kiss* has been often commented upon to the detriment of the former. The fate of *The Pig-headed Peasants* proved happier than that of *Vanda*. Unreasoning obstinacy plays its part in Dvořák's *Pig-headed Peasants* as in Smetana's *The Kiss*, but the first is based upon a libretto which tends to farce, whereas *Hubička* is comedy, verging at moments upon a tragic catastrophe. There is very little character-drawing in Stolba's text of *The Pig-headed Peasants*, which simply relates how a farmer and a widow, the one with a bachelor son, the other with a daughter of marriageable age, plot to make a match between the young people. Tonik and Lenka are really rather disposed to like each other, but, irritated by parental intrigues, they refuse to 'keep company'. Rericha the village matchmaker finally intervenes. He succeeds in awakening a flame of jealousy in both their hearts, and, after a lovers' quarrel, the pig-headed pair find out that they are indispensable to each other's happiness. The sketch of rustic life is rough and lacking in psychological depth. The music rattles along in a succession of bright and vivacious melodies; it is more jocose than witty, and offers no such moments of poetic contrast and relief as the charming Slumber Songs in *Hubička*. Composed in 1874, *The Pig-headed Peasants* was not produced until 1881, but it has maintained its popularity and was often heard at the Národní Divadlo.

Indisputably at this time the influence of Smetana was stamping the work of Dvořák in more than one direction. *The Bartered Bride* was still enforcing its triumphant, light-hearted appeal upon a naturally gay, but artificially repressed, people when, in 1877, Dvořák received from Vesely a humorous text which had a good deal in common with the story of Smetana's masterpiece in comic opera. *Šelma Sedlak* ('The Peasant Rogue'), Op. 37, is less natural than *The Kiss*, because it deals with the love of a nobleman for a peasant girl and lets in a strain of sentimentalism rather of the novelette order. That the dramatic expression is musically vague proceeds perhaps from the tentative and somewhat broken use of leading motives. But the music shows a great advance upon the preceding operas, for here the vocal element is not merely supplementary to the orchestral, but, on the contrary, the whole melodic structure derives more or less directly from the vocal line and makes for a greater unity of effect. Without concurring in Šourek's eulogistic view, that the workmanship of *Šelma Sedlak* is so delicate and the purity of expression so translucent that the score of the opera almost belongs to the category of 'the most refined chamber music', we may admit that it has charm, and an appealing simplicity which is saved from over-naïveté by the sparkling and clever orchestration—comparing it, of course, with the instrumentation of those days.

In all other branches of his art, the 'seventies was a period of rapid advancement for Dvořák. In 1875 the composer applied to the Austrian Ministry of Culture and received a small grant which enabled him to take the risk of resigning his post at St. Adalbert's and giving all his time to composition. The first outcome of his liberty was the beautiful *Stabat Mater*, one of Dvořák's most sincere and valuable contributions to musical literature. The first sketch of this work occupied the composer from 19 February to 7 May 1876. It was undoubtedly the outcome of a genuine spiritual impulse, originating in some unproclaimed, inner sorrow which craved for religious consolation. But after the completion of the sketch, he did not perhaps feel equal to moulding this impulse into a definite form; for the task was laid aside while he took up the instrumentation of his Symphonic Variations.

In September 1877, the serene and happy course of Dvořák's domestic life suffered a terrible shock. His first child—a son of three and a half—died by a tragic accident. In his overwhelming sorrow the composer now returned to the *Stabat Mater*, in which he found a vent for his grief and a source of consolation. All who knew Dvořák intimately agree that his life was rooted in a firm belief in God and in the efficacy of prayer. This attitude gives a peculiar quality of sincere tenderness and human sympathy to his art, bringing it into relationship with that of other great believers, Bach, Mozart, and César Franck. At this date he was still enjoying the happy freedom which is the compensation for comparative obscurity. No external motives governed his choice of subjects in those days; nothing did violence to his natural tendencies; there were no commissions to hasten his work unduly; therefore the *Stabat Mater* was a perfectly spontaneous creation, carefully and lovingly worked out, in the spirit in which the Angelicus Pictor decorated the walls of San Marco in Florence. The composer's unquestioning faith knew no reservations and was untouched by intellectualism. He belonged, as Bartoš says, to the simple company of pre-Beethoven classicists 'who were pious and composed much, with the rosary in their hands'. Frequently at the end of his compositions is to be found the old Slavonic formula: 'Finished with God's help'; and to him God was actually present in the inception and conclusion of all his works. Kittl, who spoke the funeral oration over Dvořák's grave, said: 'He had a heart of gold and was honest in the highest sense of the word. Maybe his words were rough, his speech vehement and uncouth; his heart was good and crystal-clear. His great success did not trouble the depths of his spirit, nor efface the fundamental purity of his character, nor spoil his simplicity and piety.' This simple, large-hearted candour is, however, occasionally wanting in his music. The force of circumstances now and then urged his natural temperament and his musical invention along parallel roads where they could never hope to meet. But again in many instances they converge and fuse in a beautiful and inseparable union and nowhere is this utter interdependence between the man and his art more complete than in his *Stabat Mater*.

Šourek thinks that the work falls into two clear and distinct emotional and musical sections. The first is realistic and dramatic, although without a touch of the operatic manner which sometimes jars against the medieval feeling of the text in the settings of Rossini and Verdi. The first number, with its bare F sharps rising octave by octave to the highest register, seems to lift our eyes to the Christ raised upon the Cross, while the rising and falling of the chromatic passages which swell in steady crescendo depict the heart of the suffering mother, now sinking in anguish, now uplifted in love, until the pent-up emotion bursts forth unrestrained when the whole orchestra crashes down on the chord of the diminished seventh. There is dramatic feeling too in the low breathless accents of the chorus with their reiterated 'Stabat Mater dolorosa'. The poignant sorrow lightens a little when the tenor transfers the tonality from the sombre colour of B minor to D major and the wood-wind bring in a lovely, comforting theme.

Profound grief, objectively conveyed, pervades also the exquisite lamentation 'Quis est homo', for solo quartet, in which the theme is continually caught up from the voices and imitated by various orchestral groups—sometimes in contrary motion. There is a very telling though quiet passage in the middle section of this number where the trumpet—immediately echoed by the oboe— is heard in conjunction with the trombones ('Pro peccatis'). The close of the number is unforgettable, when the quartet declaim *pianissimo* and in unison 'Vidit suum', over the sustained chord of the wind, and the drum gives out a throbbing figure, faint as the last pulses of dissolution. In the final orchestral *tutti* the opening theme steals back with its suggestion of transience and mortality. The same spirit of realism permeates the third number ('Eia Mater', C minor) which with its halting, rhythmic subject has something of the character of a funeral march. After this number, the composer seems less concerned with musical iconography than with the expression of intimate personal sorrow. There is no sudden break in the emotional expression, for the 'Fac ut ardeat' (No. 4) begins with a bass solo, emphatic and gloomy, and a dolorous rising and falling of the accompaniment. But with the entrance of the female chorus, and the mild and comforting tones of the organ, we are conscious of a lamp held up in the darkness; a flame which flickers, but never totally fails us again. The chorus 'Tui nati vulnerati' (No. 5), with its pastoral character, is a transitional movement preparing us for the depth and intimate tenderness of the 'Fac me vere' (No. 6), in which the tenor solo alternates with male chorus, the latter supported by a delicate moving figure of accompaniment in the strings. In the duet 'Fac ut portem' (No. 8) we are uplifted on broad and noble structural lines from the gloom of Golgotha, and before us lies the freedom and fervour of the 'Inflammatus', which combines clear-cut majestic rhythm with an impassioned and exalted melody. The moving octave figure for strings seems, at the close of the number, to symbolize the uplifting of the human soul to the heights whence the angelic hosts sing of the glories of Paradise. Just as we begin to feel that the music has left the opening mood of the work far behind and below in its soaring flight towards the transfiguration of sorrow, Dvořák recalls the sense of despairing anguish once more in the Quartet and Chorus 'Quando Corpus' (No. 10). But with the words 'Paradise gloria' the light returns, and through the key of G major we are led to the great

'Amen' in D major, and in this Handelian style of rejoicing, says Šourek, the work comes to an end.

In the *Stabat Mater* Dvořák seems suddenly to have matured. Nothing he achieved before it, and few of the works which immediately followed it, show such clear and definite lines, such finish in structural details. It has been judged as a purely cosmopolitan work, showing Italian influence. This is not the attitude towards it of the Czechs themselves, with their long traditions of church music. To them it is the first modern and native religious work; the foundation stone of modern Czech oratorio, just as Smetana's dramatic works form the basis of Czech opera.

The first performance of the *Stabat Mater* took place in Prague at Christmas 1880, by the Society of Musical Artists, to which it is dedicated. Its success was immediate. On 10 March 1883, the Musical Society, conducted by Joseph Barnby, introduced the work to London, where it broke like a flash of light and warmth into the grey monotony of the contemporary oratorio industry of Great Britain. The composer was invited to direct a kind of monster performance at the Albert Hall, with an orchestra of 150 and a chorus of 900, in the following season. The *Stabat Mater* was also included in the scheme of the Worcester Festival of 1884. We may question the scale of the Albert Hall performance, but it gave the first impetus to Dvořák's popularity in England and the work was published by Messrs. Novello in an edition which made it accessible to all our choral societies.

The external circumstances of Dvořák's life so far retarded his development that the works produced before he was thirty, while showing promise, point also to unsettled convictions and delayed maturity. His period of artistic ferment began late, and he was still hovering between various influences at an age when most composers have settled into some distinctive style and method of their own. The Quartet in A minor, Op. 10, written in December 1873, seems to have been his last, and most successful, attempt to apply the cyclic sonata form to chamber music. But his neo-romantic tendency was already on the wane and the experimental form of Op. 10 is quite as likely to have been suggested by the study of Beethoven's C sharp minor Quartet (Op. 131) as by Liszt's influence. The reaction to classicism coincided with a period of great creative activity in chamber music, so that his progress between 1870–80 can best be followed in this branch of his art. It was just at the crisis of Dvořák's career that he was fortunate enough to find a staunch friend in the influential critic Dr. Ludevít Procházka, who was one of the first to call attention to the new composer in the press. Procházka's clear judgement and sound advice were of great assistance to Dvořák, floundering at the moment from tendency to tendency. The Pianoforte Trio, Op. 13, was the first outcome of this friendship, and shortly afterwards there followed the String Quartet in A minor, Op. 16, dedicated to Procházka, and said to be the first example of Czech chamber music to find its way into print. It was published by Emil Stary in 1875.

Between this Quartet and the Quintet in G, known as the Quintet for double-bass, Dvořák wrote his opera *The Pigheaded Peasants*. The Quintet shows a touch of the operatic spirit in the principal theme of the opening *allegro con fuoco*. It had originally two slow movements, one of which the composer used later on as a separate work—the Notturno, Op. 40. The Quintet in G was originally numbered Op. 16, but when it was published in 1888, Simrock, wishing to bring it into line with other and more recent works issued at the same time, gave it—not without protest from Dvořák—the advanced number, Op. 77. Although in its clearer form and free expression this Quintet is an advance on all the chamber music which preceded it, the suggestion of its maturity falsely conveyed by the high opus number must have been a source of wonder to those who know Dvořák only by his later chamber music.

The Pianoforte Trio in B flat major (1875), Op. 21, marks a still greater step in advance. The form is not yet unimpeachable, but the general style is on a higher level than that of the Quintet. The *adagio molto e mesto* shows a Beethoven-like breadth. The *allegro scherzando* moves in a lively Polka rhythm and has an admirably contrasted Trio. The composition is the first which actually foreshadows the beautiful and imaginative series of chamber works which were to follow in the course of the next few years. Late in the 'seventies a strong infusion of nationalism found its way into Dvořák's music. The tendency is first noticeably present in his *Bagatelles* ('Maličkosti'), Op. 47, written for pianoforte, four hands, in 1878, and published in its final form, for piano, two violins, and 'cello, in 1880, by Simrock. But between the period of more or less conscious imitation of the classical masters and the composition of the *Bagatelles*, comes a work which Bartoš regards as transitional and 'embodying a conflict between

Slavonic and cosmopolitan elements'. This is the Pianoforte Quartet in D major, Op. 23, which Dvořák wrote in 1875. Nothing could be more satisfactory than the happily contrasted themes of the opening *Allegro moderato*. The *Andantino* consists of variations on a simple and touching theme. At a first glance the Quartet appears to have only three movements; but obviously the Scherzo is included in the *Finale* which has two distinct sections—an *Allegretto scherzando*, in triple time based on a half-melancholy dance tune, and an *Allegro agitato*, 4-4. This Quartet waited five years for its first performance, which took place at a concert given by the Arts Club (Umělecká Beseda), Prague.

Its immediate successor, the Pianoforte Trio in G minor, Op. 26, is attractive by its freshness and clarity, and remarkable for a greater economy of thematic material than is usual in Dvořák's early works. The slow movement is built on a broad melody given to the 'cello, and has a middle section enriched by some interesting figuration. The movement works up to a great central climax and then slowly subsides to a *pianissimo*. Dvořák has written few movements to equal in spontaneous gaiety the *Scherzo* of this Trio, in a triple dance measure. The *Finale* leaves something to be desired. Almost all the last movements belonging to this period show some traces of the obstinate conflict which he had to wage before he succeeded in giving to his *Finales* the concentration, brilliance, and firm-handling which were needed to make them into convincing and clinching perorations of his fluent eloquence. The G minor Trio dates from 1876. A pair of String Quartets, one in E major, originally Op. 27, but published as Op. 80, the other in D minor, Op. 34, belong to the same year as the G minor Trio. The earlier work is so mellow in musical thought, and so finished in workmanship, that it may well be regarded as the first of the series of really great Quartets—Ops. 87, 96, 105, 106, which continue to live in the affections of all lovers of chamber music; and here the advancing of the opus number from 27 to 80 awakens no suspicions in our minds. But it is well to realize that the apparently long pause in the opus numbers before we come to another chamber work is due to the methods of Dvořák's publishers, who thought it more profitable to pass off old lamps as new, and does not actually indicate a break in the continuity of his enthusiasm for this form of composition. In spite of its major tonality the Quartet known as Op. 80 is clouded with sadness. The opening *Allegro* is tranquil. The chief theme, given after some canonical treatment to solo violin, soon shifts to the minor. The second subject, pregnant with yearning regret, is only lightened by the *pizzicato* figures for viola and 'cello. The *Andante con moto* (A minor) recalls Dvořák's incursions into the folk-melody of the Jugoslavs a year or two earlier.[1] There is no attempt here to build up a broad Beethoven-like slow movement. The touching themes are brief and lyrical. In the *Allegro scherzando* the signature of E major is a kind of ambush behind which lurks the key of C sharp minor, which emerges boldly into the open when the Trio is reached. Even the vehemence of the *Allegro con brio* of the last movement seems prompted by the energy of grief rather than of joy. The leading theme is given out in G sharp minor and does not appear in E major until the thirty-second bar; the final climax is in C sharp minor, and only in the penultimate bar does the composer make a belated snatch at the original key.

The two Quartets, like many a pair of astronomical twin stars, are quite different in colour; while the general tone of the E major is sombre, the D minor, Op. 34, often gives out a clear brilliance. In the *Scherzo*, Dvořák pays a tribute to Smetana by introducing a polka rhythm, damping down the exuberant spirits of the opening section by changing from 2-4 to 3-8 in the Trio. The *Adagio* is a touching movement; the emotion is fervent and sustained; the heavy, moving figures for the 'cello *pizzicato* add to its impressiveness. In the *Finale* Dvořák lets himself go on a full tide of gaiety. The completion of this Quartet coincided with Brahms's kindly expression of his appreciation of the Moravian Duets, and Dvořák responded by dedicating this work to the master whom he greatly admired. This was the starting point of the friendship between the two musicians—a pleasant page in the musical relations between Slav and Teuton.

The national sentiment, tentative in the D major Quartet, Op. 23, becomes intensified in the Sextet in A, Op. 48, for two violins, two violas, and two 'cellos, composed in 1878. The success of the Sextet for Strings, which was the first example of Dvořák's chamber music to be performed outside his own country, contributed greatly to Dvořák's fame. Jean Becker, leader of the well-known Florentine Quartet, approached him immediately afterwards with a request for a new work, with the proviso that it should again be in the 'Slavonic' style. The Quartet in E flat,

---

[1] The Four Serbian Songs date from 1872.

Op. 51, was the result, and turned out to be one of the most attractive and individual of his chamber works. Unlike the melancholy Quartet in D minor, the work reflects the composer's lofty sensibility and wealth of ever-changing inner emotions.

The thought of Brahms's two Sextets for Strings (1862 and 1866) may have been in Dvořák's mind when he decided on this form of chamber music; but there is no imitation in the contents of his work. The birthday party of Dvořák's Sextet must have been unusually interesting, for it was played for the first time, in July 1879, at Joachim's house in Berlin, the host himself leading and the executants consisting of the other members of his Quartet, Hegermeister, Witt, and Robert Hausmann with the addition of two of his pupils—Kottek and Diepert. Afterwards Joachim introduced the Sextet to London. The immediate enthusiasm awakened by this composition, which is now unjustly neglected, was partly due to its novelty of construction. Here in the middle movements Dvořák uses for the first time in concerted music the forms which the public afterwards came to expect from him as a matter of course: the Dumka and the Furiant. Strictly speaking the Dumka is not of Bohemian origin. It is the name given by the Malo-Russians to a lyric or epic song of elegiac character. The Furiant is a genuine Czech dance form of rapid and whirling *tempo*, with sharp accentuations and unexpected changes of measure. As early as 1789 Turk speaks of it in his *Klavierschule* under the name of *Furie*. Dvořák never confined himself strictly to the use of such purely home-grown folk forms as the Polka and the Furiant. In his nature dwelt a broader feeling than mere national consciousness; he was *race-conscious*, and the popular songs and dances of all branches of the Slavonic family appealed to him. His patriotism was neither noisy nor aggressive, and seemed to the fiercer propagandist spirits of the national movement to be insufficiently militant. But from the moment when the publication of the Moravian duets opened up the prospect of a wider fame, he spoke more and more clearly in the language of his native land and expressed the spirit of the whole Slavonic race. Dvořák happily could afford to be a less restricted and strenuous propagandist than his immediate predecessors. His position was analogous to that of Tchaikovsky, for he came into the field of musical activity in Bohemia after Smetana had cleared a path— at any rate at home—for the advancement of native music; just as Glinka did for the Russian composers who followed in his wake.

Dvořák rarely loses the sense of his Slavonic descent. As Josef Krejčí truly says of his art: 'his lyricism knows the dreamy melancholy of the wide steppes; his oratorios and cantatas seem at times inspired by the roar of mighty rivers; in his dance-themes pulses the hot blood of youth—of young semi-cultured, semi-barbaric races'; and he might have added that the best of his operas are based on Slavonic history or folk-lore. Even those works which have misleading titles—such as the *New World* Symphony—bear witness that heart and memory are perpetually haunted by the spirit of Bohemia.

Dvořák, however, never claims any superiority for his art on the ground of its national character. Obviously for him the ground-work of his music was his first conscious consideration. Were the foundations firmly, clearly, nobly planned? This sense of design he acquired by labour, humility, and perseverance. We have seen how in the case of works disapproved by those whose judgement he respected he made no outcry against the injustice of those in authority, delivered no tirades against the unsympathetic attitude of the world to young and inexperienced artists; but set to work to correct his errors of technique. Much of his workmanship improved greatly by the sharp, if wholesome, criticism of Smetana. But his earlier compositions suffered from constant and often unfair comparison with those of Brahms. The standards by which both men tested their compositions were the same, but the colouring of their materials was necessarily quite different. Tradition refined, if it did not repress, any riotous element in Brahms's sense of colour and rhythm almost in his cradle; Dvořák inherited both elements from a race to which the juxta-position of bright tints is a joy, not an offence, and whose dance-rhythms are fiery and undisciplined.

Since, to the outer world, Dvořák will always be numbered among the composers who have embodied the folk-spirit in their art, it may not be out of place to consider here the works in which he shows himself most openly in touch with the music of the Slavonic nationalities. These remain the most popular of his compositions.

It is among Czech critics that we find Dvořák's claim to be regarded as a representative national composer most seriously challenged. The ultra-nationalists who reacted to Smetana seem to think they can best pay him honour by belittling Dvořák. The process of enthroning and dethroning idols is not peculiar to

Czechoslovakia; we may see its workings at home, accomplished with indecent alacrity. A study of Czech musical criticism reveals two distinct points of view: one which asserts that Dvořák was too classical, too cosmopolitan, too much preoccupied with the conquest of form to give out a clear and genuine echo of the folk character; but for this very reason these writers incline to put him on a pedestal; the other school maintains that he sprang too directly from the folk to forget his early impressions, and never grasped the need for refining and idealizing sufficiently the crude material of their songs and dances. Bartoš, an intelligent, but harsh, and often biased, critic of Dvořák, compares him with other national poets in an interesting page of his critical study of the composer: 'Smetana,' he says, 'who reveals himself in every bar as a dramatic composer, saw in the dance a vehicle of dramatic pathos; Chopin, a Pole in soul and body, could never forget the vanished glories of his country and enshrined the memory of them in idealized dance-forms. Both of them were distinguished and polished artists who kept in mind that dances, though composed in the folk-spirit, must bear the stamp of individual creation. Undoubtedly there has been among the people an occasional musician who has filled us with wonder; but it has never been possible to claim that one of the folk created anything we could classify as a *style*; it is precisely the criteria of style that is lacking to the masses. The task of both Smetana and Chopin was to fill out and complete the rough suggestion of the folk-music by stylistic additions. Dvořák's outlook upon the folk-song was quite different. He remembered the time when he lived among the people, and the village schoolmasters who had been his teachers. He, the man of instinct and intuition, was from the first filled with admiration at the peculiar rhythmic character of the folk-dances. The whole basis of Dvořák's temperament was rhythmic . . . it was only possible for him to regard the national dances from the rhythmic standpoint. He did not understand that the folk-material needed remodelling. His idealization merely emphasized and reinforced the rhythmic movements of the folk. Therefore, when the original material met him half-way—that is to say when the rhythmic music lent itself directly to idealized interpretation—Dvořák wrote dances which are electrifying on the rhythmic side; but when the original matter lacks this suggestive quality he writes in a grey and commonplace manner.'

Few will concede that greyness is a frequent fault in Dvořák's music, but we are sometimes conscious that his musical thought has not been fastidiously winnowed, and that there may be some truth in the idea that he stood in too close an intimacy with the folk-material to see the need of separating the chaff from the corn, at least in his earlier years.

One of the first evidences of his national tendency may be found in the Slavonic Rhapsodies. The idea of this series was almost certainly suggested to him by Liszt's Hungarian Rhapsodies, and occupied his mind as early as 1874. He laid it aside in a moment of dissatisfaction with his first attempt, the Orchestral Rhapsody in A minor, and only returned to the project after his skill in handling such material had greatly developed. The *Three Slavonic Rhapsodies*, Op. 45, are delightfully fresh and glowing with exuberant vitality. Each has a distinct individuality. No. 1, in D major, was finished in March 1878. Šourek thinks that it depicts the remote past of Bohemia, the peaceful agricultural days when Libuše and her peasant consort ruled the land. The pastoral character of the leading theme flowing on serenely in the wood-wind and presently enmeshed in a series of delicate figures in the muted violins does not contradict this idea. The second theme, worked to a fine climax, with resonant passages for brass, reflects the spirit, heroic but not militant, of that remote period. The middle section (*tempo di marcia*, B flat) brings another joyous climax. But the work ends in the quiet mood of the opening.

The Second Rhapsody, in G minor, seems to recall a later phase in Bohemian history. It plunges us into a time of conflict and agitation in which the calmer moments are only episodes, constantly interrupted by martial music, moving on to victory. The first subject is abrupt and fiery; the second, more expressive, is rather reminiscent, perhaps intentionally, of the Czech national hymn, 'There, where our home is'. A third theme is more tranquil and sustained. These materials are elaborated in a series of short picturesque sections. But there is no sense of patchiness, the continuity of thought being well maintained.

The third and most brilliant of the Rhapsodies is more kaleidoscopic than either of its predecessors. Its dignified fundamental theme first rings out from the harps, reminding us inevitably of the introduction to Smetana's Symphonic Poem *Vyšehrad*. An ingenious transformation of this *Andante maesto* forms the lively subject of the *Allegro assai*. There follows an animated and brilliantly orchestrated section, its leisurely development broken by the tones of a solo violin which seems to reveal a passing pang of sorrow and nostalgia amid the liveliness and glitter of some chevalresque pageant. This is soon dispelled by a showy fanfare, and the stately introductory theme returns and is heard softly in the wood-wind. The *Allegro assai* follows. After much brilliancy and variety of treatment the Rhapsody, save for the final chords, ends quietly, like the receding of a vision. Šourek finds in it echoes from the patrician life of medieval Bohemia: the tourney and the chase, festal gatherings, gallantry, and dancing. The Rhapsodies, if this view of them be permissible, have the same imaginative basis as Smetana's symphonic cycle *My Fatherland*, but without any explicit programme. Hans Richter did much to make them widely known, and outside Bohemia they still vie with the Slavonic Dances in universal popularity.

Soon after the publication of the Moravian Duets by Simrock, in 1878, Dvořák began the First Set of Slavonic Dances, Op. 46. Like Brahms's Hungarian Dances they were originally written for pianoforte, four hands. In this set of eight pieces, Dvořák has treated several different traditional dance-forms, but with the exception of No. 2, in E minor, which betrays its Jugoslav origin in its rhapsodical moods of alternate reverie and naïve joy, the series is typically Czechoslovak. There are two examples of the vehement and brilliant *Furiant*-form, No. 1 in C and No. 8 in G minor; we recognize that form of wild Slovak jig or spring-dance called the *Skočná*, in which the dancers leap and shout in the exuberance of their animal spirits, in No. 5 (A major) and No. 7 (C minor); the gaiety of No. 6, a Polka in A flat, is more refined; while Nos. 3 (in D) and 4 (in F major) are instances of the *Sousedska*, or Styrienne. The dance-tunes are entirely of Dvořák's invention, though he has been careful to keep to the simple melodic construction of their prototypes. After completing one or two numbers, he discovered the need for orchestral colour. In this new form, Nos. 1, 2, and 6 were given to the public in May 1878 under the baton of Ad. Čech; the remainder were orchestrated by the following August.

The Second Series of Slavonic Dances followed some years later. Actually the next nationalistic work was the Czech Suite in D major, for small orchestra, Op. 39, consisting of five numbers: Pastorale, Polka, Styrienne, Romance, and Furiant. It is an effective work which does not make too great demands on orchestral means. The Romance is described by Hostinsky as 'a lovely song without words', and the *Furiant*, although it has not escaped expert criticism as regards its rhythmic characteristics, makes a brilliant *Finale*. August Manns was—I believe—the first to produce the Czech Suite in this country, at the Crystal Palace, and subsequently Richter introduced it at the Royal Philharmonic Society.

Two compositions dating from this period—the Serenades, Op. 22 and Op. 44—are links between the chamber music and the symphonic works. In point of fact the first Serenade, in E major, comes between the Quintet with double-bass, Op. 77 and the Pianoforte Trio in B flat, Op. 21, and was numbered before its publication, Op. 18. Šourek says Dvořák wrote it at a time when his music was being temporarily disregarded by the musical world of Prague, 'which did not, however, cause him undue mortification of spirit, as he continued to compose in quiet self-confidence'. The Serenade for Strings is free from any sense of strain or haste, and bears witness to the advantages of an occasional period of public neglect in a composer's life. Dvořák handles the pleasant old form, which Mozart, Beethoven, and Brahms had used before him, with great success. Unlike Brahms, who made the Serenade a stepping-stone to his first symphony, Dvořák chose the form spontaneously, having already composed three symphonies. The Serenade for Strings has five movements, the first (*Moderato*) and the last (*Allegro vivace*) are in somewhat lightly woven sonata form; the intermediate sections include a graceful *Tempo di Valse*, a spirited and whimsical *Scherzo*, and a *Larghetto* of contrasting sweetness and serenity. The second Serenade, in D minor, Op. 44, was composed three years later, 1878, and here Dvořák revives the original form of Cassation, or Evening Music, intended for outdoor performance by a small band of wind instruments. The scoring is for two oboes, two clarinets, two bassoons, double bassoon, and three horns, with the addition of 'cello, and double bass. Humour, rather than passionate declaration, seems to be the characteristic of the Serenade in D minor. Mischief lurks in the theme of the first movement (*Moderato quasi marcia*) with its veiled mockery of pompous importance, and becomes obstreperous in the final *Allegro molto*, in which movement there is a reference to the principal subject of the opening *Moderato* of the Serenade for Strings. Dvořák dedicated the work to Louis Elhert, whose appreciative notice of the Slavonic Dances helped to spread their reputation in Germany.

After having reviewed the chamber music, and the works—chiefly in dance form—in which Dvořák worked off the first spate of his national enthusiasm, we may gather the remaining compositions of this earlier period into one comprehensive group. Some of these may be dismissed in a few lines. The Overture to his first operatic essay, *Alfred*, was not published until 1912, when Simrock issued it with other posthumous works under the ill-advised title of *A Tragic Overture*. It is built up on themes from the opera itself and the two leading subjects represent respectively the Britons and the Danes, the music being mainly martial in character. Another early Overture, *Romeo and Juliet* (1873), was destroyed by the composer. Of the Three Nocturnes for Orchestra, Op. 18, the second, entitled *A Night in May*, was produced at a concert of the Prague Philharmonic Society in 1873, shortly after the production of Halek's Hymn, and became a popular concert piece.

As early as 1863–4 Dvořák made an attempt to write a Symphony, in C minor, which he contemplated calling *The Bells of Zlonice* ('Zlonické zvony'). He was supposed to have subsequently burnt the manuscript, but in 1923 it was discovered in the manuscript collection of Dr. Rudolf Dvořák and submitted to Dr. Šourek, who says of it: 'it is the work of an artist who has an innate feeling for all that is concise, ample, and lofty in his art'. He considers that it foreshadows the mature Dvořák, and equals the second Symphony in B flat, in the distinctive quality of its instrumentation.

This second attempt at a Symphony, the one in B flat numbered in the manuscript as Op. 4, would have shared the fate of the earlier work but for the intervention of the conductor, Anger. It was consigned to oblivion for many years until Dvořák revised it in 1887, when it was produced at a concert at the Rudolfinum, Prague, by Ad. Čech.

Seven years elapsed before the composer, encouraged by the success of the Hymn, took up the idea of a new Symphony in E flat. The manuscript which was first numbered Op. 20, and later Op. 10, is inscribed: *Beilage zum Gesuche des Anton Dvořak aus Prag um Verleiten eines Künstlers-stipendium.*[1] The work is in three movements: the first (*Allegro moderato*) and the Finale

[1] 'Enclosed with the appeal of Anton Dvořák for an Artist's grant.' There is neither an inscription nor an opus number on the score issued by Simrock in 1911.

L

(*Allegro vivace*) are in sonata form, somewhat laxly interpreted, while the *Adagio molto* (*Tempo di marcia*) is in three distinct sections and has the character of a funeral march.

A stronger and better balanced work is the Symphony in D minor, originally Op. 13 (1874), but later published without opus number, in which Dvořák shows that the conflicting influences of the 'sixties are at last giving way to personal convictions. Dvořák was thirty-three when he wrote this work, the earliest of his well-planned and formally balanced symphonies, which, unlike its predecessor, has a full complement of four movements. There is purpose in the plan of the opening *Allegro* which is in definite sonata form, built upon two admirably contrasting themes of equal musical value. The first subject, pithy and energetic, stands out boldly in a powerful exposition which closes in a vigorous climax. The second subject is an expressive melody in the national style with a delicate *pizzicato* accompaniment. The *Andante e molto cantabile* has a beautiful theme for wind instruments which lends itself well to variations, and the movement is an early study in that form of which his Symphonic Variations is the finest example. In the *Scherzo* (*Allegro feroce*) the contrasts are very striking. The fiery rhythm of the *Scherzo* is succeeded by a comparatively quiet *Trio*, touched with pleasant humour and original orchestral colour. The *Finale* (*Allegro con brio*) starts well with a brisk opening subject, against which is set a flowing *cantabile* melody, but after the exposition of these principal themes, when the first subject is recalled, it wears rather thin by prolonged development and passes through so many keys that we almost seem to lose sight of the basic D minor. No third theme is introduced, and after the recapitulation, the work ends with a *Coda* (*Più mosso*) in D major.

The Symphony in F major, originally numbered Op. 24, is usually accepted as the third of Dvořák's five greater and more familiar symphonies; but its conception actually dates from 1875, and the advanced opus number 76, by which it is known, is purely arbitrary, as in the case of most of that group of early works published by Simrock in 1888. It was first performed in Prague by the Academy of Literature and Art in 1879, but without much success. Seven years later Dvořák revised the work and dedicated it to Hans von Bülow.

In many respects the Symphony in F is superior in design and workmanship to the one in D major, Op. 60, which is in point of time the later of the two (1881). The mood of both works is, on the whole, optimistic. Šourek finds in the first movement of the Symphony in F 'the voice of the rustling woods, the song of birds, the fragrance of the fields; the strong breath of nature rejoicing and a sense of mortal well-being'. Here the themes instead of contrasting seem to complement each other. Both are given out in the tonic, and while the first is typically pastoral, the second is more spirited, but still retains an idyllic character. Kretschmar said of this Schumanesque subject that it was like 'thanksgiving for happiness'. The elegiac melody of the *Adagio con moto* suggests a gentle sadness that does not lacerate. This movement represents perhaps the germ of the *Dumky* as developed later on by Dvořák, reaching a climax in the *Dumky* Trio, Op. 90, where the alternating moods of this form pass over us like sweeping lines of light and shadow on an April day, and touch the limits of vivid musical contrast and emotional mutation. The fresh and cheerful atmosphere of the third movement has characteristic moments of tenderness which could only have emanated from a Dvořák. The Trio, with its delightful, provocative dialogue between wood-wind and strings, is distinctively personal. The opening theme of the *Finale*, strong and martial in character, is opposed to a broad and gracious melody—the second subject—beginning in the clarinet. The final coda in which, under cover of a ringing fanfare from the trumpets, the trombones recall the principal theme of the first movement, is an early instance in Dvořák of this method of imparting unity to a work. Henceforward we shall find him having recourse to it more frequently. In view of the confusion caused by the renumbering of Dvořák's works at the time of publication, it is interesting to remember that this fine Symphony, a direct link in the chain of structural development through Haydn, Mozart, and Beethoven, originated at least two years before Brahms's First Symphony.

By the close of the 'seventies, Dvořák had acquired a mastery of classical form second only among living musicians to that of Brahms, and a proficiency in orchestration second to none of his contemporaries. From the Slavonic Rhapsodies onwards, his scoring ceased to be in any way tentative; while the sense of orchestral colour was more innate in him than the sense of design, he never at any time looked upon the orchestra as a loom to weave a brilliant vesture wherewith to clothe poverty of ideas. Whether he combines his whole orchestra to build effects of rich sonority, or sets a few individual instruments discoursing in an intimate and witty dialogue, Dvořák's use of the orchestral groups is always most felicitous. His wood-wind colour is entirely satisfying; he does not hesitate to ask of the horn the most difficult and delicate services; he knows how to subdue the lusty salience of the trumpet until it becomes a discreet glittering thread in his rich orchestral tissue. He is very sure, sound, and generous in his orchestration, and although this element of music has now almost degenerated into virtuosity, and our appetite for orchestral effects is overstimulated to the point of satiety, Dvořák's scoring in the later symphonies, in the Slavonic Rhapsodies and Dances, in the *Husitska*, *Carneval*, or *Othello* Overtures, and, above all in the Symphonic Variations, wears remarkably well.

It was probably his consciousness of a ripe mastery of tone-colour which led Dvořák to compose the Symphonic Variations for Orchestra on an Original Theme, Op. 40. Besides using the form occasionally in his chamber and symphonic music, he had already written an independent set of Variations on a theme of his own for pianoforte solo, Op. 36. Comparison between the Symphonic Variations and Brahms's Variations on the *Chorale St. Anthony* appear inevitable. Although Brahms's work dates from 1874, three years earlier than that of the Czech composer, it had not yet reached Prague in 1877, and there is no ground for supposing that Dvořák was consciously apeing the German composer when he produced a set of Variations so individual in conception and treatment as the Op. 40. We find one striking difference between the two works: while Brahms limits himself to the fundamental key of his Variations, alternating between major and minor keys only, Dvořák permits himself a much wider scheme of tonalities. The atmosphere of the Symphonic Variations is more romantic, the orchestral colour richer, than in the Variations of Brahms. Without any ostentatious promulgation of his opinions, Dvořák wrote here in a deep vein of national feeling.

The theme which he took from a chorus for male voices, *Ja sum Guslar* ('I am a violin player') composed a few months before, is not perhaps of great intrinsic value; but this melody in the folk style had a suggestive power, and enabled Dvořák to evolve from it a whole series of mood pictures, most of them, as Šourek asserts, stamped with the image and superscription of a Czech. The theme is given out *Lento e molto tranquillo*, by strings in octaves, and in the second strain flutes, clarinets, and bassoons double the strings.

As the Variations proceed, the material grows freer and the individual motives take on a physiognomy of their own. Yet all the while the generative theme is kept in sight, preserved in the structure and most often in the harmony. The emotional range of the Variations is wide: humour, 'pawky' and whimsical, is to be found in Nos. 5, 6 (with its delightful dialogue between strings and wind), and 7; No. 11 is full of a dreamy sadness; No. 14 (*Lento*) expresses in its quiet chords and the solos for horn and bassoon the deep religious sentiment that was part of Dvořák's self; No. 19 is a Valse; there is a touch of the grotesque in Nos. 20 (B flat minor) and 21; No. 22 is a love-song for solo violin; No. 24 seems like a sombre ballad cast in the form of a funeral march; No. 25 is in the folk style. All these variations are emotionally simple and eloquent. In No. 27 a return is made to the original key of C, and the way is prepared for the closing fugue. While this is being firmly and boldly built up, new counterpoints appear, and at one point the composer interrupts the continuous development of his material to let in an unmistakably Czech polka. The theme returns, in unison and octaves, over a tonic pedal for brass and drum; and later on, it is given in augmentation by trumpets and trombones over a dominant pedal, with splendid effect.

The Symphonic Variations were produced in Prague in 1877 by Procházka. For ten years they were completely forgotten until, in 1887, they were revived at a Slavonic Concert with immense success. It then occurred to Dvořák to send the work to Hans Richter. The conductor was on the point of leaving Vienna for England, but he hastened to reply: 'I had already been thinking of asking if you had anything to give me. Now your Symphonic Variations have come, and they will splendidly enrich my programmes.' The work was given in London under Richter's direction in May 1887.

The curtain was now about to be rung down upon the first act of Dvořák's life, in which we have seen him, a simple Bohemian peasant, fighting his way through poverty, ignorance, and obscurity to the front rank of native composers. The process of his evolution from a national to a universal composer, with its advantages and drawbacks, its triumphs and almost fatal errors, belong to another chapter of this book. But before closing this account of his earlier years—so commonplace apart from his musical activity—it will be interesting to glance for a moment at the most important event of this period: his intercourse with Johannes Brahms.

The two musicians have been aptly likened to a pair of plants sprung from the same seed, the one raised in a conservatory, the other a growth of nature. The contrast between the temperaments and training of Brahms and Dvořák could not indeed have been sharper than it was. Brahms was born into musical surroundings and received from his early years not merely systematic musical instruction, but an excellent general education. Dvořák, as we have seen, developed to a great extent intuitively. With all its wealth of invention and nobility of tradition Brahms's music reflects the aspect of his nature which Hanslick once described as exalted to austerity. As years went on he grew increasingly exclusive and pessimistic. Clouds of doubt and disillusion drifted over his works and dimmed the joy of life and his faith in himself; his last musical message to the world—the *Four Serious Songs*— begins with a melancholy question: 'Who knoweth the spirit of man that goeth upward, and the spirit of the beast that goeth downward to the earth?' A question which is not too convincingly answered by the assertion that death is acceptable as an alternative to the miseries of life; nor even by the exhortation to live seriously and soberly with which the cycle concludes. Compare the spirit of these songs with Dvořák's Biblical Songs. Dvořák's whole outlook on life was fresher and more spontaneous. His eyes were never holden from the joy and splendour and human happiness of this existence and his unsophisticated piety lasted to the end. All this is embodied in his music. But in one ideal these two opposite spirits found communion: both believed in the sempiternity of 'absolute music'; both participated in the heritage of Beethoven and Schubert. Lesser influence shot with varied colours their respective works; Brahms felt the influence of Schumann while Dvořák passed in turn under the yoke of Wagner and Liszt, and reflects Smetana in many secondary ways. But when Brahms spoke in generous praise of the Moravian Duets and other works by Dvořák, he recognized not merely a gifted and promising contemporary at the parting of the ways, but a mind in harmony with his own upon the fundamental principles of music. They both drew freely and gladly at the source of Beethoven's inspiration; Brahms preserved the precious fluid in a chiselled cup of wonderful form and craftsmanship; while Dvořák brought to the spring a bowl of Bohemian glass, richly coloured, sparkling, and transparent. From his early years Brahms knew his own mind, decided which paths he intended to tread, and kept to them logically and consistently to the end of his career. Dvořák spent much time in experimental excursions to the right and left, and even when he had fairly set his feet in the path of classical tradition and pure music, he was often tempted aside by dramatic ambitions and a fleeting hankering after a programme.

Dvořák undoubtedly owed much to the study of Brahms's music in the balance of his symphonic movements, in the selection of ductile thematic material, in the interplay of his motives, and in other details of his craft. But for the essentials of his art he borrowed nothing from his German contemporary. That Dvořák's profuse invention and less reflective and less fastidious attitude towards life and art led him to leave some tares among the rich harvest of his works is indisputable. But his music reached the outer world at a time when the Brahms cult was at its height, and, reviewing the criticism passed upon it during the last two decades of the nineteenth century, it is noticeable to what a great extent the comparative method is used to the disparagement of Dvořák. Of late years the bulk of his work has suffered unmerited neglect, and the time has perhaps come to test the value of his music once again; but the selection must be judiciously made.

Brahms and Dvořák were the two great conservative influences of their time; the re-animation, not the destruction, of traditional form was the identical aim of both of them; and though Dvořák did not entirely share what Mr. Colles calls Brahms's 'immutable devotion to abstract musical form', the dignity of his art was equally dear to him, and his influence has curbed and ennobled the work of a younger generation of Czech composers. What wonder that these two champions of abstract music clasped hands in a friendship which lasted until the death of Brahms, who predeceased Dvořák by seven years.

CHAPTER X

THE help and influence of Hans Richter must always be gratefully recorded in the story of Dvořák's early years. He was among the first to recognize the strong and original personality revealed in the *Stabat Mater*, the Moravian Duets, the Slavonic Dances, and the Symphony in D, Op. 60, which Dvořák dedicated to him in recognition of his practical aid. Writing to him later about another work (the Symphonic Variations for Orchestra), Richter says: 'I gladly avail myself of this opportunity of coming into touch with a composer by the grace of God.' The first meeting of the two was in 1879; and it was largely through Richter's activities that so many of Dvořák's works were made known to the public outside Bohemia, and even in England before his first visit to this country.

The Symphony in D was produced in Prague on 25 March 1881, and though originally intended for the Vienna Philharmonic Concerts, was finally first introduced to England at a concert of the Royal Philharmonic Society on 15 May 1882, under the direction of Richter, who wrote enthusiastically of the performance to Dvořák. This was the composer's first success with symphonic music in any foreign country. Dvořák was busy at this time with several new works, including the opera *Dimitrij*, the *Scherzo Capriccioso* for Orchestra, Op. 66, and the *Husitska* Overture, Op. 67, but as none of these was ready for Richter's London concerts in the season 1882–3, only the Slavonic Rhapsody in G minor was given on 11 June. This, says Richter in a letter to Dvořák, 'was received with acclamation by the London public. . . . The orchestra (which is a good one), although rather puzzled at first, soon found pleasure in your beautiful work; when once the musicians had come to feel at home with the melodies and the rich rhythmical life of the Rhapsody, they played it with the right fire and spirit.'

The Opera *Dimitrij* remained on hand for several years. Begun in the spring of 1881, Dvořák made frequent revisions of the work, which was at the time severely criticized, and it was given in its final revision at the Národní Divadlo as late as 1894. The idea of reviving the work in its original musical form was realized by Kovařovic in 1906. The complete and thorough study of both scores left him resolved to reproduce the first with only a few changes in the musical content of the entire work, as first conceived by the composer. In this form it had a great success, and has always maintained its place in the repertory of the National Theatre in Prague.

Dimitrij is planned as a 'grand opera', rather conservative and Meyerbeer-like in style, on the subject of Dimitrij, the pretender who figures in Moussorgsky's *Boris Godounov*. The libretto was arranged by Marie Červinkova-Riegrova, and its gay and limpid flow of verse lent itself admirably to Dvořák's strongly individual setting. The music is coloured with both the Russian and the Polish elements that enter into the story. The plot turns upon the struggle between the Russians and the Poles after the death of Boris Godounov. Dimitrij the Pretender, seeks to usurp the place of the Tzar's rightful heir, whose cause is loyally upheld by his sister Xenia and the Prince Shouisky; but the situation is complicated by Dimitrij's love for Xenia, issuing in a bitter conflict with the claims of his wife Marina and his Polish supporters. To the main thread of the narrative various minor intrigues and clashes of national feeling are skilfully woven in, and the effect is vivid and dramatic to a high degree. Most of all are we struck by the rich melodic treatment of the successive themes, built up by masterly orchestration into brilliant and powerful climaxes. In no other opera has Dvořák given us a greater number of haunting melodies, which remain in the memory associated with the chief actors in the tale. Musically the personalities of Dimitrij, Xenia, and Marina are distinctively brought out, and the contrast between the aristocratic Marina and the more gentle and unassuming Xenia is well maintained. There is also much excellent character drawing among the minor parts, such as the Patriarch Job with his beautiful old-world song, and certain more or less tipsy Poles who make a difficult handful for their leaders. Some of the choral numbers are perhaps over-long, but there is no lack of movement and animation as the story is unfolded. Dvořák was much criticized at the time for his free use of declamation, but he never fails to make it appropriate and expressive. *Dimitrij* soon won, and has never lost, its high place in Czech opera, and is now generally recognized as one of Dvořák's finest operatic works.

While working upon *Dimitrij* in 1881, Dvořák laid the opera aside in order to write in haste the String Quartet in C major,

Op. 61, which he had seen announced in the papers for one of Hellmesberger's concerts on 15 December. Though the work was eventually given for the first time in Prague, the fact that it was composed for Vienna may have accounted for its fine, strong, Beethoven-like construction. Here Dvořák's technical powers touched high-water mark; for firm structure, expressive plasticity, and rich working out of themes, only Brahms had equalled it. As the definite racial and national flavour increased in his work, his creative spirit seemed, as it were, intoxicated with the growth of conscious power, and able to rise through the material into the spiritual world. There his soul, warmed and ennobled, communing only with itself, reached the pure meditative beauty and sublimity which permeate the whole C major Quartet. In the union of poetic inspiration with technical mastery this Quartet surpasses the one in E flat, Op. 51, yet at the same time appeals to us as equally delightful and intimate.

Following the Quartet, but in complete contrast to it, Dvořák wrote the incidental music to a national drama by Samberk, *Josef Hajetan Tyl*. This play, with the incidental music, was produced at the Provisional Theatre on the eve of Tyl's birthday, 3 February 1882; and the Overture, later published by Simrock, was very popular on account of its strong national colour.

The cycle of Five Choruses for a Mixed Voice Choir (Op. 63), composed to texts selected from Vitezlav Hálek's poem *Amid Nature*, must have been a congenial task to Dvořák, who loved the country life of Bohemia so deeply. There is an impressionistic atmosphere in some of these choruses which is rare in his music, and is specially noticeable in the one beginning 'At Eve the Forest Bells ring out'.

By this time Dvořák's works were constantly appearing in the programmes of concerts both in Prague and in other towns in Bohemia; in fact his fame in his own country was well established. The composer's German friends, who wanted to see him represented on the German stage, naturally deplored his national and racial leanings. Hanslick in particular would have been pleased to see him cast aside all his national tendencies and become a purely cosmopolitan composer—which would certainly have been the easiest road to success abroad. Therefore when Dvořák, rejoicing in the success of *Dimitrij* at home, looked forward to seeing it produced in Vienna, Hanslick, who had shown appreciation of the work in his criticisms, now thought it 'politically' unsuitable. But it was suggested that if Dvořák would write an opera to a German text it might meet with success. To this end Baron Hoffmann, Intendant of the Vienna Opera House, sent him one or two German texts to select from. This was indeed to set him at the cross-roads; for Dvořák knew well enough that to refuse this offer might prejudice all his future introductions abroad. Nevertheless he refused it, and again defended his deliberate choice of Czech subjects with which he had been reproached before. The conflict between the patriot musician, eager to express and interpret the soul of his own country, and the composer who longed at the same time to rise above the local and temporal into great universal art, was bound to be painful and long. Amid this conflict his mother's death afflicted him deeply. There could be no doubt as to the final resolving of his inward strife. Its importance is witnessed, however, by one or two works in which the feelings of this period are reflected—feelings of indignation, Promethean defiance and passionate doubt, poignant suffering and quiet resignation, and finally the feeling of victorious decision. The path which led from the Pianoforte Trio in F minor, Op. 65, through the *Scherzo Capriccioso*, Op. 66, and the Overture *Husitska*, Op. 67, to the Symphony in D minor, Op. 70, speaks to us eloquently of the individual phases of inward struggle at this time.

The Pianoforte Trio in F minor, one of the finest examples of Dvořák's instrumental works, abounds in direct and passionate feeling, and surpasses the intimate outline of chamber music in its powerful symphonic design. The content of the work is suggested entirely by the mood which then prevailed in the composer; a suppressed, passionate defiance, indignant doubt, and continual stubborn questioning. Throughout the first movement runs an atmosphere of agitation, conflict, and pathos, rising to great emotional climaxes. The *Scherzo* shows Dvořák's unity of style in all his works; it is not the usual hearty, joyous *Scherzo* of his earlier works, but its whole mood grows out of the content of the first movement. The opening theme of the *Adagio* is gloomy as though it echoed the trouble in the composer's breast; the second theme, still sad though in a gentler fashion, is treated canonically between violin and 'cello. The defiant mood breaks out again in the middle section, but the calm and quiet of the opening returns before the end. The *Finale* (*allegro con brio*) starts again in an atmosphere of conflict and excitement, which, however, subsides with the entry of the second theme—a beautiful *cantilena* bringing peace and resignation with it. And from resignation to reconciliation is but a step which we feel is taken at the closing bars of the work.

After the composition of this Trio Dvořák seems to have somewhat thrown off the winter of his discontent, and in the almost contemporary work, the *Scherzo Capriccioso* for Orchestra, Op. 66, returns to a mood of unfettered joy and *bonhomie*. The work seems to have been rather unjustly banished from the concert room, since it gives to the various instrumental groups an opportunity of showing their skill and demands great virtuosity.

The *Husitska* Overture, Op. 67, may be regarded as the palinode of Dvořák's patriotic doubts and hesitations. It is the outcome of a wave of triumphant enthusiasm which swept through musical circles in Bohemia when the Národní Divadlo raised its walls once more after the disastrous fire which destroyed it. The work was given for the first time at the reopening of the National Theatre on 18 November 1883, and introduced to this country under the composer's direction at a Philharmonic Society Concert in March of the following year. Though F. A. Subert, Director of the National Theatre, had suggested to Dvořák the idea of writing an orchestral Prelude for a dramatic trilogy, the work contains no descriptive programme of the Hussite Wars. It presents a beautiful symbol of an heroic and solemn epoch in Bohemian history, and may be summed up as a struggle for the great national ideal of freedom. The work is built upon motives from the old Hussite hymn, 'All ye warriors of God', and from the Chorale, St. Wenceslaus, which Dvořák has treated with epic breadth and sureness of touch, and with all his accustomed richness of orchestral colour. Dvořák was, as we know, a devout Catholic. He was possibly, like Bach, one of those rare pietists who can discern the essential God in both Catholic and Protestant churches. He was intensely patriotic and the Hussite Wars were wars for freedom.

In the early 'eighties, Brahms, Ehlert, and Hanslick, however much the last two may have deplored Dvořák's stubborn nationalism, had between them done a good deal to establish the Bohemian's reputation in Germany; and now at Easter 1883 a new victory was at hand, the conquest of the British public. To the liberty-loving Czechs England and her large traditional policy has always been held in respect, and her sympathy sincerely desired.

Writing of his first successes in England, Dvořák says: 'Already I may predict that now I can look forward to new, and let us hope very happy, times here in England, which I trust will be fruitful for Bohemian music in general. . . . The English are a kind, sincere, music-loving people, and it is a remarkable fact that if they once take to anybody they remain true to them. God grant that it may be the case with me.'

But between an enthusiastic welcome and a clear critical judgement based on deeper knowledge of the artist lay a great gulf. We lost no time in stretching Dvořák on the bed of Procrustes. Festival commissions, with their aimlessly benevolent, infelicitous conditions, were pressed upon this gifted and unsophisticated child of the Bohemian plains. Had we really understood Dvořák as essentially different from a Spohr or a Mendelssohn or a Gounod, as being on the one hand a racial composer and on the other a simple and devout Catholic, how differently we might have invited him to serve our interests!

Fortunately, however, the sum paid to Dvořák by Simrock, and the profits of this first successful journey to England, had so increased the composer's possessions that his dream of securing a modest country dwelling in some Bohemian district where he could work in peace was now realized. His choice fell upon Vysoka, where he had already spent several summer holidays, and here he eventually settled for part of each year and composed many of his best works.

Following the performance of the *Stabat Mater* he conducted other concerts at the Royal Philharmonic Society and at the Crystal Palace, when his Symphony in D, the *Husitska* Overture, the *Scherzo Capriccioso*, and the Slavonic Rhapsodies were all enthusiastically received. This induced him to pay us a second visit in the autumn, when he conducted the *Stabat Mater* and the D major Symphony at the Worcester Musical Festival, celebrating the eight-hundredth anniversary of the foundation of this Cathedral.

After this second visit Dvořák found time in the quiet surroundings of Vysoka to complete a new choral work, *The Spectre's Bride*. Those who can look back to the earliest performance of this secular cantata at the Birmingham Festival in 1885 will remember that the first and deepest impression derived from the work was that of its absolute freshness. We listened to it then as we might listen with mingled fascination and curiosity to a strange, euphonious speech of which we did not fully comprehend the roots or the idioms. It pleased as much as it surprised those who had been brought up upon Mendelssohn and kindred musical utterances. England welcomed Dvořák's music, as we have seen, more cordially perhaps than any other country save his own; but, glancing over the criticisms of the period when it first became popular here, it is noticeable that few writers realized that its beauty and charm were rooted in its nationality; that Dvořák's leading qualities, his originality, his sense of orchestral colour, the fascination and fertility of his melody, the pungency and richness of his harmony, were all part of the heritage of his Slavonic descent.

Smetana was the leading spirit of the renaissance of Bohemian music which was the outcome of the political movement of the early 'sixties. He deliberately sacrificed his chances of European fame by preferring to remain in Prague and endow his own people with a series of genuine national operas. In every patriotic musical movement somebody must needs be content to accept the lesser rôle which the world is apt to call with misplaced contempt that of 'the local composer'. Only in this way can the foundation be made secure for those who come after. Dvořák, having received from his predecessor the essential spirit of national music, could afford to dilute it somewhat to suit the tastes of the world at large. In later years, surrounded by cosmopolitan influences and successes, the source of his originality was almost lost in his moderate use of national characteristics. But *The Spectre's Bride* belongs to the most interesting period of Dvořák's development before he had begun to write the kind of music dictated to him by circumstance rather than imagination. Its worst fault, a certain prolixity, the result of the chorus being made so constantly to echo the textual, and even the musical, phrases of the soloist, must be attributed to a great extent to the original poem, which follows the Slavonic style in the matter of repetition. The same may be said of the threefold incident between the maiden and her lover, each version of which is more surcharged with horror than the last. But it is the dramatic power and success of the work as a whole, not its weaknesses, that astonish us when we remember how ill suited Dvořák was in this particular form. There is no doubt that it must have been an exceedingly difficult task for Dvořák to adapt himself to cantata form, since in his free and self-directed development he had already advanced beyond the older forms which festival commissions now forced upon him.

Since he could not find a national subject suitable for oratorio, his choice fell upon fruitful material in Karel Erben's version of a legend common to the romantic folk-literature of all Europe. The choice was highly characteristic of Dvořák. Erben was no text-monger, but a true poet, imbued with the folk-spirit and able to give this almost universal legend a peculiarly Czech colouring to which the composer instinctively responded. Here he found scope for a work of festival proportions. The poem is convincing and full of vitality; it shows the intense realization of death and the unquenchable belief in the supernatural characteristic of the Slavonic races, together with a religious element which appealed to Dvořák no less strongly.

The manuscript of the work was sent to England as soon as it was completed in 1884, and it first appeared in the English edition published by Novello. Later in the autumn it was issued with Czech and German words; but it was not till August 1885 that the Cantata received its first performance in England at the Birmingham Festival, when Dvořák was again invited to England to conduct the work.

Meanwhile two works on a large scale were commissioned for England: the Symphony in D minor, Op. 70, for the Philharmonic Society, of which he had been made an honorary member, and the Oratorio *St. Ludmilla* for the Leeds Festival.

The Symphony in D minor was begun in December 1884 and finished in March 1885. Not counting his first symphonic essay *The Bells of Zlonice*, this was the sixth of the composer's symphonies, though published later as his second, 'composed for the Philharmonic Society of London', and received its first performance at the St. James's Hall, 22 April 1885, conducted by the composer. There was no waning of the enthusiasm with which the work was received both by public and critics alike. Many set the Symphony above those of Brahms, 'one of the greatest works of its kind produced during that generation'. There is no doubt that a fervent desire to write a new symphony had been growing in Dvořák's mind for some time since he first became acquainted with Brahms's Third Symphony. That his admiration and love of this work counted for something in his own creative impulse is clear.

'Style in a musical work is marked by the agreement of all its constituent parts with one supreme impression.' In spite of the criticism of Dvořák's opponents in his own country to the contrary, this Symphony is a striking example of how in Dvořák's work every part is organically joined to the rest. With him, the whole work grows out of the fundamental mood; and either he produces—as in the D major Symphony—a work of radiance and joyous life; or one of tenderness and clarity such as the Quartet in E flat, Op. 51; or another in a melancholy mood such as the E major Quartet; or a work full of defiant movement, uncertainty, and passionate emotion like the Trio in F minor. In the latter, whether in the slow movement, the Scherzo, or the Finale, all is penetrated by one basic elemental mood; everywhere he makes answer with corresponding lights and shades, colours to colours, and all combined in the vision of one great idea—unity of style. We find the same in the Symphony in D minor—a work so delicately and passionately laid out, rich in musical ideas, ingenious in workmanship, and powerful in form and conception.

An interlude of lighter compositions and revisions followed the D minor Symphony, including the Ballade for Violin and Pianoforte, published by Urbanek in Prague as Op. 15, No. 1. At this time, too, occupied with his garden which was then in all its midsummer beauty and enjoying the music and perfume of the surrounding woods, he received a request to set to music Dr. Karl Pippich's *Hymn of the Czech Peasantry*. This was a congenial task, and he set this fine text for a four-part mixed choir with accompaniment for two pianos. Simple, yet beautiful in harmony and melody, it has become one of the most popular repertory pieces of the numerous choral societies throughout the country.

About this time Dvořák found himself in conflict with Simrock as regards the publishing of his works without Czech titles. The quarrel was precipitated by his determination to compose a new oratorio on a subject from Czech history. Settled again in Vysoka after a short visit to England, he took up once more the text which the poet Vrchlický had written for him on the subject of St. Ludmilla. He was particularly anxious to write an oratorio that would appeal to his own people. He wanted it to be penetrated by the Czech spirit, to celebrate some important historical event, not only in the religious but in the national sense. Thus it might become for his countrymen a national epic such as Smetana's *Libuše*. He had already considered basing it upon the life of St. Vaclav or Jan Hus.

The story of St. Ludmilla deals with what the historian Palacky calls 'the most important event in old Czech history'—namely the conversion to Christianity of the Czech Prince Borivoj and his wife Ludmilla, and the ensuing victory of Christianity over paganism throughout the land. Musically *St. Ludmilla* is a work in one cast, cut from a single block, in firm, strong, and noble lines which are precisely defined by a lofty style, suited to the lyric and dramatic needs of the story. That the work was composed for England, whose great church and choral choirs sometimes inspired Handel and were themselves a pledge of choral power, had not a little to do with Dvořák's choice of a model. He found that the poem lent itself to a succession of broad, flowing numbers for solo and chorus, using inherited and traditional forms, but filled at the same time with a new content of individual and national character. Even in this work he did not try to build a new form which might intentionally break up the connexion between his work and the oratorios that preceded it, but aimed at union with the spirit of the most prominent works already existing in this sphere. As in his symphonies and chamber music he started from Schubert and Beethoven, so in oratorio he turned to the great Handelian period as a model.

Dvořák was again in England in October 1886, when he conducted the first performance of *St. Ludmilla* at Leeds Festival, the Symphony in D minor at Birmingham, and *The Spectre's Bride* at the Crystal Palace. This cantata was also given at Nottingham a few days later, but Dvořák was obliged to return home for an important concert in Prague, and the work was conducted by Richter. Writing to friends in Bohemia after the Leeds concert, Dvořák says: 'Well, to-day it went off gloriously! This enthusiasm—this English enthusiasm—was such as I have not experienced for a long while. At the close of the performance I had to bow my thanks again and again. . . . And then to speak a few words in English, heartily congratulating the chorus and orchestra. . . . I heard that at Ludmilla's aria "O grant me in the dust to fall", which the famous Albani sang divinely, the public was moved to tears.'

After the success of *St. Ludmilla* at Leeds, Dvořák seemed to be resting and gathering strength for his next period of creative activity. Among the first results of the quiescence was that gem of chamber music, the Pianoforte Quintet in A major, Op. 81. This work, characteristically Slavonic in its alternating moods of rhythmic gaiety and dreamy sadness, soon won popularity with its lively and buoyant melodies and its vivacious first movement,

M

eloquent of sunshine and joy. The second movement, in rondo form, changes to a mood of happy reverie, as if anticipating some new delight. Instead of an *Adagio* there is a characteristic Dumka, followed by a spirited Czech Furiant, leading in the *Finale* to a whirling and enraptured dance, in which the composer gives full rein to the jubilant impulse of the hour. The Quintet was followed by a Pianoforte Quartet in E flat major, Op. 87, written in an equally happy mood but with a stronger sense of energy and power, as if seeking emotional balance and true poise between the sentimental and the austere.

In his next opera, *The Jacobin*, Dvořák again attacks a new subject in the historical field. Marie Červinkova-Riegrova once more provided the libretto. The story dates from the old feudal days, and relates to a lord of the manor, Count William of Harasov, and his dependents. The Count drives away his son Bohus whom he suspects of revolutionary tendencies, and a cunning nephew Adolf supplants him in the old man's affections. Bohus goes to Paris, but after many years returns with a wife, Julie. The old Count refuses to receive him, and the travellers take refuge with the village schoolmaster and organist, Benda by name. Julie and Benda together visit the Count and plead the cause of Bohus—'The Jacobin', as Adolf has nicknamed him. Finding that entreaties are useless, Julie goes to the harp and sings an old lullaby which her husband has taught her—it is the song with which his mother used to sing him to sleep. Here Dvořák uses the Lullaby which he wrote as a separate song a year or two before. This quickly touches the heart of the old Count; he becomes reconciled to his son and Julie, and at the same time realizes the shabby part played by Adolf, who has always abused and traduced Bohus in his absence. Side by side with this narrative there is the love-story of Benda's pretty daughter Terinka and her two suitors, the elderly Burgrave Philip and the Count's young huntsman George. Their rivalry yields some very effective musical scenes, but Terinka remains faithful to the younger lover. These two sympathetic characters are admirably depicted in the melodies allotted to them, and the discomfiture of the elderly suitor is treated with robust humour and gaiety. On the other hand the scenes between Bohus and Julie flow in broad and tender lines, full of deep feeling which culminates in the beautiful lullaby, 'My darling, my world'. The environment is peculiarly happy and congenial to Dvořák. He, too, had been a Czech music teacher, and rehearsed the village choir. All his own early memories have been poured into the character of Benda, and one of the most delightful scenes is the practising of the serenade to be sung at the castle in the last act. It has been well said that this section of the opera 'is an apotheosis of the Czech Cantors of the past, and a graceful tribute on the part of a great musician to the teachers of his youth'.

The Jacobin was finished in 1888, and in the following year Dvořák wrote the Symphony No. 4 in G major, Op. 88, a work of idyllic and joyful moods. It opens (*Allegro con brio*) with a dignified introductory theme which inaugurates each structural section and reappears each time in the same form though varying in its orchestral treatment, especially at the climax of the development, where it stands out in majestic splendour. The main subject of the movement follows this introductory idea. At first it sounds mild and playful, but presently gathers force, and breaks out into unrestrained joy. A sudden change of key, from G minor to B minor, brings in a charming middle section, in which a simple melody tinged with sadness is heard from the clarinets. This theme is cut off at the climax by a third theme in B major, which leads to an effective return to the principal subject, and then to a quiet reappearance of the introductory theme.

Dr. Šourek, commenting on the romantic character of the next movement (*Adagio*) says that its first subject, grave and lofty in mood, seems to suggest a series of silhouettes of an ancient castle seen in various aspects, now melancholy, now impressive and proud. The second subject, given by flute and oboe over a soft *staccato* accompaniment for strings, he regards as a love melody sung by some noble knight serenading his lady within the castle. The return of the leading subject is majestic, and a brilliant trumpet fanfare conjured up a vision of chivalric splendour. The love theme is repeated, this time by the violins accompanied by wood-wind. In the *Allegro grazioso* Dvořák seems to be expressing something of his love of country life. The first section is a quiet rustic dance, which flows happily from the violins over an undulating accompaniment for wood-wind; the next is in a serene and tender mood, enlivened by a melody which recalls a song from Dvořák's folk-opera, *The Pig-headed Peasants*; and the third recapitulates the first section with a short *Coda*, in which the theme of the G major section returns as a dance. The *Finale* is very national in sentiment. A strongly rhythmic and unmistakably Czech theme predominates, and the movement combines free sonata form with variation form. Many technical devices are here introduced, and the scoring has the true Dvořák colour and fullness of tone.

Soon after he had finished the Fourth Symphony, Dvořák was invited by the Committee of the Birmingham Festival to write a work for 1891, and they suggested as a possible subject Cardinal Newman's poem, 'The Dream of Gerontius'. Dvořák did not feel drawn to this material, but wrote instead a solemn *Requiem Mass* for solo voices, chorus, and orchestra, Op. 89. He began work upon this in January 1890, and came over to England to conduct the first performance at Birmingham in October 1891. So nearly a contemporary in composition, it could not escape comparison with the *Requiem* of Brahms, but it remains an original and characteristic product of Dvořák's middle period. We have seen how his normally gay and humorous temperament was often overshadowed by moods of deep seriousness and melancholy; and with advancing years he turned increasingly to consideration of 'the last four things'. In the *Requiem* he does not follow closely the traditional form of the Roman Mass for the Dead. He keeps the terrors of the Last Judgement in a subordinate place; and the musical motive which has been called the 'remembrance of death' is coloured by resignation rather than fear.

Once more a sharp contrast is produced by the work that followed—the '*Dumky*' *Trio*, Op. 90, written in 1891. Here Dvořák, to whom the contrasting moods of sadness and gaiety in the form of the dumka appealed, has woven a complete work of dumka movements. It has been said that the Slav spirit tends to idyllicism rather than tragic conflict; and Dvořák's music expresses gladness in all its aspects, from the gentle smile of pleasure to boisterous revelry and mirth. F. V. Krejci has truly said of his work: 'His musical lyricism expresses the melancholy reverie of the vast steppes, just as in his oratorios and cantatas we hear the roar of the sea, the rush of mighty waters; while the hot blood of barbaric or semi-civilized races pulses in his dance rhythms'. The Trio might be described as a Dance Suite in six movements, and though not strictly adhering to the traditional Trio-form, there are thematic links between the various dumky. The work bears ample witness to Dvořák's colourful writing for both violin and violoncello.

Early in 1891 Dvořák was appointed as teacher of composition in the Society for the Encouragement of Music in Bohemia, then the leading Conservatoire in Prague. He took up his duties with great enthusiasm and with the most encouraging results. In the same year he received an honorary degree from the University of Cambridge, and soon afterwards a similar one from the University of Prague. But his work as a teacher was soon interrupted, for a two years' visit to America, where he had accepted the post of Director of the New York Conservatoire of Music, followed in the autumn.

This sojourn in the 'New World' was to give him the title and the inspiration for what has become one of the most popular of all his works. His Symphony No. 5 in E minor, Op. 95, was first performed by the Philharmonic Society of New York on 15 December 1893. Much has been said about his alleged use of certain folk-melodies derived from negro music. But from whatever source he drew his themes in this work, the Slavonic idiom is dominant and unmistakable. It is difficult to understand why this Symphony, with its glowing emotion and lavish colour, its fine sincerity and deep underlying poetry, did not immediately take a hold upon the public taste, but within another ten or fifteen years it was to become one of his greatest and most popular successes.

Once arrived in America, Dvořák was very soon beset, as in England, with invitations to produce new works on given subjects or for special occasions, pressed upon him with the kindliest motives, but sometimes with more zeal than discretion. Happily Dvořák did not allow himself to lower his own high standards by a hurried or too prolific output. He had already accepted two important American commissions—a *Te Deum* composed for the Columbus celebrations in New York (Op. 103) and conducted on his arrival there; and a Festival Cantata entitled *The American Flag*, Op. 102, to words by Rodman Drake. When the rehearsals and performances of these were over, and he had settled down to the composition of his 'New World' Symphony, he found a summer residence at Spillville, Iowa, where in this Czech colony, surrounded by his own compatriots, he escaped the rush and whirl of New York life.

In these works we get the impression that Dvořák has come into contact with a kind of life entirely new to him, and has responded to it by seeking a musical idiom farther removed than he has ever yet gone from traditional form and character. Without forfeiting anything of his individual style, he here absorbs and reflects the vivid, hustling, and exotic aspects of the 'new world'. His chamber music dating from this period also shows the influence of his surroundings, as does his symphonic work, but it is equally a mistaken theory to imagine that he made any attempt to found a new American national music in these compositions. That he evolved fresh themes in the spirit of the Indian and negro folk-tunes, blending them with his own familiar national idiom, is not surprising. Of the two chamber works which were composed during the summer months of 1893 at Spillville, the String Quartet in F, Op. 96, carries us still farther from the classical style, for here Dvořák has made use of the aeolian, or mixo-lydian seventh, and other developments far removed from his former polyphonic form. The effect of the Quartet is one of impressionistic virtuosity reaching to almost barbaric force. In the Quintet in E flat, Op. 97, with two violas, a new element is introduced. The slow movement has a definitely religious character, similar to that of the *Biblical Songs*, which were conceived and sketched out at about the same period. Apart from this movement the Quintet betrays nothing beyond earthly revelries drawn out in brilliant instrumentation and haunting rhythms.

These works were followed by a small group of lighter compositions—a Sonatina for Pianoforte and Violin, dedicated to his children; a Pianoforte Suite in A, thought by some critics to reflect American local colour; and the ever-popular and delightful *Humoresque for Pianoforte*, Op. 191.

The last important work to be finished in America was the Violoncello Concerto in B minor, Op. 104. This was completed in New York in February 1895, and dedicated to Wihan, but he never performed it. It was first played in London in March 1896, by Leo Stern, who also introduced it to Prague in the following April, at a concert of the Czech Philharmonic Society conducted by Kovařovic. The work, which certainly contains much rhythmic and melodic writing for the solo instrument together with the composer's rich and brilliant orchestration, has won and retained its place amongst 'cellists.

But in spite of the appreciation shown to him in America and the creative musical activity which originated there, Dvořák was ever mindful of his strong national ties, and in 1895 gladly returned to his homeland.

Unlike his great predecessor Smetana, Dvořák concerned himself very little with programme music until the close of his career. After his return from America he seems to have experienced a change of outlook, and, using the national ballads of the Czech poet, K. J. Erben, as a literary basis, he wrote three Orchestral Ballades: *The Water Sprite* ('Vodnik'), *The Midday Witch* ('Polednice'), and *The Golden Spinning-Wheel*; also a pair of Symphonic Poems: *The Wild Dove* ('Holoubek') and *A Hero's Song* ('Pisen bohatyrska'). All date from the years 1896 and 1897. Critics of the school of Hanslick, who regarded Dvořák as a docile disciple of Brahms, were not in sympathy with this new tendency, and these five works suffered neglect in consequence, though they were given in Bohemia by such conductors as Knittl, Adolphe Čech, and Janáček. Although the poetic basis may now seem ultra romantic and naïve, the musical content and treatment—above all the orchestration—of these programme works represent Dvořák at his maturest.

On his return he completed his last two chamber works, the Quartets in A flat, Op. 105, and in G major, Op. 106. Here he undoubtedly reaches the climax of his instrumental work, combining the strong national colouring and eternal freshness which pervade his work with complete command of classical form.

But opera still attracted Dvořák, and in his next work *The Devil and Kate* (1898) he deserts the grand manner for fantastic lyrical opera, although this is not so much music inspired by legend as a bright setting of a tale which gives him one or two new folk-types to work upon. The libretto, based upon a folk-tale, is by Adolf Wenig and offered a wonderful opportunity to Dvořák to produce a work intimately bound up with the folk-spirit and which would live in the people.

Marbuel, a minor devil, is sent by Lucifer to see whether the Princess who rules a certain district, and her minister, impersonations of tyranny, are not sufficiently qualified by their long list of misdoings to take up their abode in Inferno. Marbuel, having made his inquiries, finds himself with some time on his hands and makes love to the peasant girl Kate. Kate is a girl of character, something of a shrew, with plenty of rough and ready repartee at her command. The devil persuades her to elope with him, but repents when he gets her down below, because she sits tight on his shoulders and 'lets him have it' with the roughest side of her tongue; moreover he has unwittingly carried her off with a small gold cross hanging round her neck which weighs him down like tons of rock. A demon ballet is danced in the infernal regions, during which Jurka, a shepherd, carries off Kate to return her to her mother. There is a good deal in the subject which must have appealed to the primitive side of Dvořák's nature.

Following the success of *The Devil and Kate* at the National Theatre, Dvořák soon turned his attention to another fairy-tale opera, the setting of Josef Kvapil's lyrical legend *The Rusalka*. The first performance of *The Water-nymph*—perhaps the most popular and perfect of all the composer's operatic works—was given at the National Theatre, Prague, in 1901, under the conductorship of Karel Kovařovic.

The story is naïve: the water-nymph lives with the old water-sprite in a lake in the woods. She falls in love with a Prince and desires to become a mortal for his sake. The witch Jezababa changes her into a mortal on certain conditions: she will be dumb, and also if her lover fails her she will lose her mortal girlhood and be turned once again into a soulless water-nymph. She risks all. The Prince loves her and takes her to his palace, but tires of her dumb devotion and deserts her for a beautiful foreign princess. The Rusalka has to return once more to the watery haunts of the ugly old water-sprite, who, however, loves her too in a pathetic way. Afterwards the Prince in a fit of remorse comes back to Lakeside. It is too late, for the Rusalka can never become a mortal again. So the Prince implores her to stifle him with her ice-cold, unearthly kisses, since he can no longer live without her.

We should of course compare *Rusalka* with Humperdinck's charming fairy operas, so concrete, so German, so unmystical, in their content, rather to the disadvantage of the Slavonic setting of a folk-tale. It is perhaps an opera too sentimental, too old-fashioned for a generation whose taste in the fantastic is catered for by Stravinsky's *Nightingale* or Prokoviev's *Loves of the Three Oranges*; yet the music is attractive—both the love-music and the uncanny orchestration that accompanies the voice of the Vodnik or Water-King; while the poetic scenery, the dark forest, the moon gleaming on the haunted pool, all combine to make it one of the most delightful operas to see in the whole Czech repertory.

Whether Dvořák was a born dramatic composer or not is a fruitful subject of discussion among his compatriots. Certainly his subsequent influence has been in favour of lyric rather than dramatic music. He alternated, like Tchaikovsky, between dramatic and symphonic or chamber music; but if on the whole we have to rank him as a dramatic composer second to Smetana in imagination, psychological insight, and clear-cut characterization, especially of national types, we must concede that in absolute music he has no rival among Czech composers.

Finally Dvořák, following his usual procedure, doubled back upon his track and in his last opera, *Armida*, he seems to recall his early enthusiasm for Wagner, not in the naïve imitative fashion of *Alfred* or the first version of *King and Collier*, but as a man may do who, grown a little tired after innumerable mental excursions, turns his mind back to the ardours of his youth. The libretto by Vrchlický, based upon Tasso's *Jerusalem Delivered*, proved impossibly fantastic and unmanageable, though he struggled with it for more than a year. He finished the music, though not to his own satisfaction, in August 1903, and it was produced at the National Theatre on 26 March 1904. But it failed to find any general acceptance with his public, and it was thought that this failure, after long and almost unbroken success, hastened his end. He fell ill in April and died suddenly on 5 May in his sixty-fourth year. With other compatriots dear to the Czech people, he was buried in the national cemetery at Vyšehrad.

Common to the great bulk of Dvořák's music, with all its variety of form, is one arresting feature which points plainly to the composer as being Czech, or rather Slavonic. This strikes us at once in the character of his thought and invention.

Dvořák's musical ideas have an outline and character all their own. They are not merely echoes from a wide literary outlook, nor dim reflections from the past and the greatness of other lands; nor are his ideas laboriously and reflectively constructed. We may rather compare them with flashes of genius at dawn from which in due time will issue the golden glory of the sun. The charm of his musical thoughts lies in their melodic progressions, in their forceful rhythms. His melodies are always natural, and as free from all signs of effort as from blemishes of the commonplace. His rhythms are simple, varied, and clear. While finding one's way through the longest and most complex of his movements, the fundamental idea stands out distinctly, no matter how intricate may be the flow of his contrapuntal parts. He is a master of rhythm, and equally great and original as a melodist. The melodic or rhythmic element prevails according to the nature of his music. In his allegros—and particularly those in dance-measure—the rhythmic element predominates, while the chief interest of his slow movements is melody and the warm flow of his cantilenas.

The closest link between Dvořák's invention and the folk-art is seen in his rhythm rather than his melody. The rustic musician never quite died out in Dvořák. He could not forget the merry, pithy rhythms of the Czech folk-dances, heard in his childhood, and he played with them occasionally, cutting and polishing them till their facets sparkled like gems. As to melody, we feel at once that the spirit of Czech and Slavonic music sings to us here. In Dvořák's soft melodic line Slavonic tenderness is noticeable; so, too, is the melismatic richness of his examples of Slavonic tunes everywhere interwoven with new ornamentation. To search for any actual link between his art and the folk-music is, I think, a thankless and pedantic task. It is also a useless task because it is self-evident that Dvořák felt a joy in Czech and Slavonic melody just as any healthy Czech would delight in the sunshine.

Dvořák's methods of handling his musical thoughts and material is that of the classical masters, especially Beethoven. It is still our method of working, and is, to put it still better, the ideal way of composition. It consists in the organic development of the musical idea. The idea is the core round which the whole work is formed; the point of union between all those unknown or fortuitous atoms which go to the make-up of the living organism, in which each member is conditioned by the other, following each other, necessary to the logical result. We have seen—especially in Dvořák's symphonic and chamber works—how this fundamental principle of organic unity guides him throughout. The principle of organic development holds good, so far as the idea is concerned, only as regards the harmony. He has no wish to make harmony for harmony's sake; nor does he try to charm us with exotic and unusual combinations. He uses no harmonic coquetry. But he develops his harmony naturally and simply on lines of which the harmonic details grow richer and more interesting the farther he carries them along. And the chief charm of these harmonic lines lies in his modulations. Only a composer of genius would know how to carry on such a flow of harmony with such purity, spontaneity, and ease, yet at the same time with constantly new resources and a captivating roundness of tone. In Dvořák's harmony and modulation all rings true and beautiful as sterling silver for those who can appreciate what is unaffected and true. And the same applies to his counterpoint. It would be impossible to alter a note in any of his contrapuntal work. Though all is carefully thought out, it remains natural; a limpid stream throughout. And if counterpoint must conform to the demands of classical music, it does so in every note. Dvořák's counterpoint is pleasing, tender, warm, and gay as that of any contrapuntalist of the German polyphonic school. It is, as Knittl once remarked, genuinely Czech counterpoint.

With the principles of classical composition which he understood as including the post-classical masters, Mendelssohn and Schumann, and with his contemporary Brahms, he defended his faith in salvation through symphonic creation. He felt no need to seek out new forms. Yet at the same time he refused to accept any kind of worn-out conventions. He took over, however, those which after two centuries of development were sufficiently plastic to adapt themselves to the musical material which overflowed the master's heart. He accepted these, as we know, only after mature consideration, not from a blind confidence in their validity.

Classical sonata form, for instance—employed in trios, quartets, quintets, symphonies—prevails in all Dvořák's instrumental works. And the content of his work is the reason why Dvořák did not turn away in the least from sonata-form—enriched but entirely normal—even in the period of his fullest maturity. A further reason was Dvořák's extraordinarily delicate feeling for balanced structure, through the harmony of his lines. At the same time he succeeds, like Schubert, in preserving all his freshness and elasticity while keeping free from cold and superficial academicism.

Symmetry and proportion—these are qualities which Dvořák never fails to observe, even in such episodes in his music where the poetic basis plays the leading part. His symphonic poems upon Erben's ballads are far from being examples of unbridled licence and restlessness as regards form. We should rather take note that in this latest period of his music the master did not limit himself so exclusively to the very highest principles of form. Beside works firmly welded to the last touch stand others belonging to the period when fiery thoughts would bubble up and follow each other in a swift pulsation. This is not perhaps the lofty art which preceded it, but it is an art of variety and imagination, and of endless fascination.

Dvořák's clear sense for purity of construction leads us to the conclusion that at no period of his creative activity he turned away from classic form, even in his vocal works. He never was able to deny the musician within him so far as to sacrifice the musical lines, the form and symmetry, to the text.

He has been reproached because his culture was insufficient to allow him to do justice to a poetic text. In my opinion the reason for his failure must be sought elsewhere; in his exclusive musicality. It lies too in the generally conservative ideas of the master. To him the formation of a declamatory style appeared musically a poor thing in comparison with characteristic melody, therefore it could not continue regularly without contrast, which he used with the utmost economy. He is far more sparing than his classical models in the use of recitative. And even here we notice that he likes to sing softly. His own special sphere is music: full, warm lyricism, in a word—melody.

And again, Dvořák did not merely adhere to the word. He conceived the poem as a whole, in the same way as the classical composers, and achieved a great lucid and plastic form for it, just as they did. Apart from all other precedents, his choral works are models of beautifully constructed, plastic, and articulated form. In this respect he is at his highest in his oratorio St. Ludmilla, where he reverts to the grandeur and clear-cut simplicity of Handel.

As he is without rival among Czech composers in finish and ease of craftsmanship, especially where polished form is concerned, so too he stands alone in the matter of tone quality. Everything from his pen had sonority, colour, light, and shade. All his works sound full and fresh; varied and vigorous in colour, rich in the play of light and shade, yet harmonious and transparent. This splendour of colour is not far-fetched or overdone, but seems to be brought about quite naturally. Dvořák's colour is darkened by its Czech and Slovak features, and therefore in complete contrast to the dense, overcharged, and often muddy colouring of the German school, and the hypersensitive tenuity of the French. He never made colour an aim in itself. Just as he never isolated harmony from the rest of the work, so he never employs colour for its own value but purely for its effect. Also it is difficult to speak of colour effects in connexion with Dvořák. Colours flow out of the work and grow with the development of the themes, though they be simple in style. They are always new, in accordance with the character of the composition and the means which he employs. His colouring is equally rich in a simple Trio as in his symphonic works and operas. We need only recall the tone colour of the

'*Dumky*' *Trio*, with its endless wealth of half-tones, and again its moments of scintillation and glowing hues. The expressive power of his palette increased as the years went on. The American period and the years in Prague which followed it show how the master revelled in the intoxicating spell of harmonic colour. Nevertheless the outline, the structural design, do not suffer in the least. Only we regret that at a later time when his colour sense was most rich, the master surrendered it in favour of co-ordinate structure.

If we possessed all the musical details of Dvořák's works which I have mentioned here, it would still be necessary in order to arrive at a complete evaluation of them to point out how each individual composition was developed and perfected. His invention and basic idea, from the neo-romantic influence which first overshadowed his independence, matured with the consciousness of Czechoslavonic heritage, and gradually became more and more original and personal, taking on a definite colour of its own. At the close of his career American impressions brought new elements into his art, especially as regards rhythm. These elements Dvořák assimilated into himself; there was no loss of independence, but rather a widening of his ideas.

As Šourek has pointed out in his book, which is based on the study of all Dvořák's manuscripts, his sureness and clarity in the beginning resulted from his dependence on the classics. A lack of transparency, a narrow yet surcharged, formal outlook marks the period of his neo-romantic essays, which rested chiefly on Wagner. This mistaken excursion into paths which led nowhere was not, however, entirely unfavourable since it enlarged his harmonic views and enriched his work generally. In good time he reverted to classicism and classic forms, and regained a perspicuity and a power of organic construction which enabled him to compete not unsuccessfully with the distinguished heir of classical tradition—Brahms. Now he began to show in every direction a wealth and variety of invention, a clarity of thought, and at the same time a greater complexity in harmony and fullness of tone. In his eagerness he was never content with the *status quo*, but sought continually for every means of expressing himself still better. His art grew with astonishing and unerring certainty with each new work which he produced. We need only compare his Quartet in D minor, Op. 34, with the American Quartet, or his Symphony in F with the 'New World' Symphony. Or set the workmanship of *The Pig-headed Peasants* beside that of *The Jacobin.*

When we consider all this, it is impossible to accept unreservedly the current phrase as to Dvořák's conservative outlook. His art is conservative inasmuch as it originated in and remained in touch with classicism. But his methods of composing were entirely his own and new. Nor is his art conservative, because it opposes an obstinate resistance to advance, progress, and development.

To some extent the substance and psychology of Dvořák's music is the result of his origin, education, and surroundings. He was a simple and robust countryman without a trace of nervosity, a clean and unspoilt soul, and an equally sane and unaffected mentality. I often gathered in his society the impression that he was shy because he felt keenly his lack of schooling and general culture. But he strove assiduously to fill up the gaps in his intellectual equipment, and he probably succeeded in acquiring more than some who venture to criticize his lack of education. He had the gift of keen observation, and his judgement was clear and untroubled by prejudice and unclouded by sophistry. Apart from this his birthright was in itself a valuable education—of the heart. If externally he appeared somewhat rough, he was good and noble by nature, and his heart governed his actions. Those who were students at the Prague Conservatoire in his day relate instances of his vain attempts to keep the secrets of his benevolent impulses, which he always revealed in the end. But if his heart guided his actions, all his impulses were ruled by his moral and religious sentiments. His faith was profound and straightforward, and he drew from it the fervent devotion of Catholicism, both in external observances and inward piety. He loved his God with devout humility, and loved also his Church, and the rites by which it paid respect to his God. This piety had nothing in common with the religious emotion of some modern aesthetes who, satiated with worldly joys, seek late in the day for the ultra-refined sensations engendered by the dusk of the Cathedral, the perfumes of the censors swinging at the altar steps, the austere, harsh rhymes of the medieval Latin hymns and strange, ascetic melismata of Gregorian chants. The entire simplicity of the master's devotion was self-evident. He felt only that he was the blind and humble instrument of God's voice. He stood as it were apart from his work, and saw it all as a gift from God. Therefore he harboured not a shadow of pride or self-exaltation, only a profound gratitude to Him who stood above his work. Within the circle of other simple-minded souls he felt at his best. To the end of his days his home remained modest and unpretentious.

It was thus that he understood the genesis of his work, which, in truth, was something of a miracle. The whole current of his music flowed from the deep consciousness of a spirit above him which filled him with awe.

CHAPTER XI

SMETANA, partly because he was absorbed in the reconstruction and reorganization of musical life in Bohemia, and partly because of his encroaching deafness, which incapitated him comparatively early in middle life, took only a small part in the education of the younger generation. Upon Fibich, and more particularly upon Dvořák, first as Professor of Composition and later as Director of the Prague Conservatoire, devolved the task of instructing most of the promising talents who began their musical studies towards the close of last century.

Among Fibich's pupils for composition was Karel Kovařovic, born on 9 December 1862, in Prague. His early studies at the Conservatoire included the clarinet and harp, and on leaving the school he was engaged as harpist in the orchestra of the National Theatre until 1885. His proficiency as a pianist and accompanist recommended him to the violinist František Ondříček, who took him on tour to Russian Poland. He had some years' experience as orchestral and choral conductor before he got his chance of proving his remarkable talent in this branch of his art. This occurred in 1895, when Professor Hostinský suggested Kovařovic as the right man to organize a good orchestra and conduct the concerts of the Ethnographical Exhibition in Prague. His great popular success in this capacity seemed to point him out as the ideal conductor for the National Theatre. But here he met with a good deal of opposition and it was not until 1900 that a change of administration enabled his appointment as first conductor of the Opera. He held this position until his death, devoting his whole life to raising the standard of performance to a level with that of many better endowed and more famous continental opera houses. Under his exacting rule every production went with vigour and discipline in keeping with the spirit of a nation which had profited by the Sokol system. But Kovařovic was no mere drill sergeant. His aim was to blend his orchestra, chorus, and soloists into one finely balanced and highly temperamental instrument of expression, and this could only be effected by discipline; while discipline could only be maintained by a certain degree of aloofness and severity on his part, which was in reality alien to the indulgent tenderness of his inner nature. Like all men who carry

176

out a great task with singleness of purpose Kovařovic made enemies. They embittered his work but they did not alter the direction of it. He carried out his ideals with a firm hand. Some complained that he was too strict a janitor of the portals of the Národní Divadlo and that he stood in the way of modern, experimental music. It is true that he refused to regard the stage of the National Theatre as a trial ground for inexperienced musicians. He might have echoed Borodin's reproach to his students in chemistry: 'How can you make such evil smells in such a beautiful laboratory?' Kovařovic had his limitations. Although he was an eclectic, he drew the line at a great deal of modern music; and with the immense annual increase of works which just miss greatness, beauty, and originality, the ultimate destiny of which is becoming one of the problems of contemporary musical life, the Czechs have on the whole good reason to be grateful that the gods sent them a man of such fastidious discrimination. Very few failures were produced at the Národní Divadlo in his day. His name was a guarantee to the subscribers of the good quality of the music and the performances promised season by season. On one point there can be no question for dispute: his careful and polished production of Smetana's operas strengthened the confidence of the Czechs in their first messiah of music. A quarter of a century ago Smetana was still imperfectly appreciated, and Kovařovic's work in this direction was a revelation to the people. What he acquired from his study of Smetana he carried into his readings of other works, frequently to great advantage. Those who heard his production of *Meistersinger* in Prague were struck by its freshness and flow of humour. Unlike the specialist Wagnerian conductors, he lifted the work above the nebulous atmosphere of *The Ring* and all tragic memories of *Tristan* and set it in the wholesome sunshine of life. 'Could he', asks the Czech critic, Dr. J. Pihert, 'have arrived at this entrancing interpretation if he had not learnt to grasp such a simple, yet profound, philosophy of the human soul through the medium of Smetana's operas?'

In his early compositions Kovařovic suffered from the lack of a personal conviction. In his ears rang echoes of too many styles. As a conductor he heard too much of other people's music to find time to listen to the 'still small voice' of his own creative consciousness. He wrote, with facility and a sure instinct for stage effect, incidental music for several plays, the comic operas *Ženichove* ('The Bridegroom') produced in 1884, and *Cesta oknem*

N

('The Way through the Window'), 1886; also a successful ballet in the style of Délibes, *Hachich* (1881); a Symphonic Poem, *The Rape of Persephone*, and in 1892 an opera in four acts, *Noc Šimona a Judy* ('The Night of Simon and Jude'). There are indicatons in his Tragic Overture in C minor, in his brilliant Pianoforte Concerto in F minor, in the Romanza for Clarinet, and in the melodious String Quartets in A minor, G major, and E flat major, that he was seeking higher forms of self-expression. Several of his short melodramas were stepping-stones to a loftier dramatic style. His songs, delicate in melody and rhythm, though tending perhaps to excessive sentimentality, are still popular. An exception in its vigorous bravura style is the *Slovak Song* with which Destinova made a *succès fou* wherever she sang it. Meanwhile the public, accepting these lesser contributions to his art, had ceased to expect from Kovařovic anything deeper and more personal than 'conductor's music'. Then a new and bracing influence came into his life, the results of which proclaimed themselves in a work of real and enduring value. The success of his historical opera *Psohlavci* was almost sensational and has lasted over a quarter of a century. At the time of its production, 24 April 1898, it may well have seemed quite outside the conventional mould of opera. As in Moussorgsky's music-dramas, the women's roles are here secondary to the men's because there are no love scenes in the prescriptive sense of the words. The libretto, prepared by Šipek from a popular historical novel by a widely-read writer, Alois Jirásek, deals with an episode from the blackest days in the story of Bohemia. The Chods (pronounced Khods), a small rural population who in return for their vigilant guardianship of the south-west frontier had been granted many privileges by the earlier rulers of Bohemia, became suspect on account of their independence of spirit. Among the rights accorded to them was that of bearing their own banner with its effigy of a dog's head, symbolical of their loyalty and watchfulness.[1] The story is based on historic facts and the hero still lives in the popular memory. The period is 1695, when, following the overthrow of the Bohemian patriots at the Battle of the White Mountain, the Austrians, anxious to curtail the liberty of the Chods, appointed Laminger von Albenreuth governor of the district.

---

[1] The word *Psohlavci* means the 'Dog-heads'. A better substitute for this somewhat cryptic title which I have adopted for my unpublished translation of the libretto would be 'The Peasants' Charter'.

When the curtain rises, Kozina, a leading Chod farmer, is lamenting to his friend, Přibek the Piper, that the folk think him a half-
hearted supporter of their cause, and that even his own mother
does not trust him. Kozina appears at first in the light of a con-
ciliator rather than a hero; his love for his timid wife and his
young children tending to weaken his will. But when Laminger
—Slavonicized by the people into Lomikar—comes on the scene
with his soldiers and ransacks Kozina's house for documents, the
Chod, though anxious to avert bloodshed, shows that he is not
lacking in courage. The Austrians depart in triumph, carrying
with them a chest of papers, but ignorant of the fact that the most
important charter of all has been safely hidden on the person of
Kozina's intrepid old mother. Kozina and Přibek are arrested.
Later on they are released and summoned before the Court of
Appeal in Prague. Trustfully they bear with them the precious
charter, secure in the justice of their cause. But the judge, with
withering contempt, tears the document in two, tosses it back to
them, and pronounces it to be 'merely a scrap of paper'. Thus
does this opera of 1898 foreshadow the events of 1914. Lomikar,
entering the Court at this juncture, announces that the Chods
have risen in rebellion, and demands that Kozina, as the instigator
of the rising, shall be condemned to death. Kozina protests in
vain that he has done his best to avoid violence. In the next Act
we see him in prison, where the devoted Přibek comes to say farewell, and presently his mother, wife, and children take a heart-
rending leave of him. Lomikar offers at the last to pardon Kozina
if he will make a public recantation of his belief in the justice of
the peasants' claim. But Kozina, now risen to true heroism,
refuses. Proudly he turns from the entreaties of his family and
follows the priest to the scaffold. On the threshold of the cell he
warns Lomikar: 'A year to-day we shall meet before the judgement-seat of God'. The last Act shows a brilliant banquet scene
in Lomikar's house. It is the anniversary of Kozina's execution.
The haughty and sardonic Austrian recalls his victim's last words,
and sneers at him for a false prophet. Nevertheless his pallor and
agitation arouse his wife's anxiety. Laughingly he says that a
drink of wine will put him right. As he raises the cup to his lips
a mysterious gust of wind extinguishes the lights in the hall, and
Lomikar is dimly seen to stagger and fall dead, but not before he
has caught a flashing vision of Kozina reminding him of their
tryst.

Although the setting of this story is local, its psychology is universal. The exasperation of a deeply-injured people, the craftiness and political bias of the time-serving lawyers, the arrogance of the ruling race, embodied in the personality of Lomikar, the gradual bracing of a naturally easy-going temperament to a heroic resolution, maternal pride, the tenderness of a devoted husband and father—all these emotional elements belong not merely to the Chods but to humanity at large. At the same time the customs and quaint costumes of this conservative race add to the picturesqueness of the setting. The opera is frequently chosen for performance on special democratic celebrations and is loved by the working class.

In the music of *Psohlavci* Kovařovic strikes, for the first time, a clear note of nationality in the very opening number of the work, when the curtain rises on an empty stage and a woman is heard singing in the distance a song in the folk-style, lamenting the sorrows which have befallen the country. It was probably to the experience of the Exhibition of 1895, which brought him in contact with many sides of the folk spirit, that Kovařovic owed this impulse. The work, however, is far removed from the *naïveté* of folk-song opera. This would not have been possible for Kovařovic, versed by years of practice in the technique and requirements of the operatic stage. He uses the folk-colouring most effectively in the vigorous choral numbers and occasionally in the orchestration, where he echoes the bagpipes and other old-fashioned instruments in use among the people. Otherwise the music, which stands midway between the older style of Smetana and the most modern developments of Czech opera, follows in perfect freedom the powerful play of emotions, and colours the words so conformably that it becomes as it were the atmosphere in which the drama floats before our eyes and ears. The music of the two leading characters Kozina and Lomikar sets them in a clear and convincing contrast from beginning to end of the opera. The prison scene is, musically, so deeply affecting as to move the audience to tears, but in *Psohlavci* Kovařovic has laid aside all traces of the sentimentality which was the weakness of some of his earlier works. Its chief fault is an occasional tendency to sensationalism, hardly to be avoided by a composer who must have visualized his opera from the stage point of view almost from its inception.

Kovařovic's opera *Na stárem Bélidle* ('At the Old Bleaching-house') dates from 1901. It is as though the composer now resisted every temptation to write for effect and resolved to drop all theatrical gestures. Here he adopts no conscious style but keeps to the pure lyricism which was nearer to his spirit than the grand manner of *Psohlavci*. It is not strictly speaking an opera, but a series of scenes from national life linked up by music of great lyrical charm. The subject is adapted from a popular novel by Božena Němcová dealing with rural life. Babička (Grannie) is a lovable study of ideal old age. The years and sorrows that have passed over Grannie's head have left her sound and sweet and mellow as a winter-pippin. Life has taught her so much tact and sympathy that she simply and unconsciously pierces all barriers of class and age: a princess, the aristocratic landowners of the neighbourhood treat her as a friend. Babička reads the secrets of the younger generation, in the light of the one romance of her girlhood which remains embalmed in her heart as fresh and green at eighty as at eighteen. In each scene she is the fairy godmother, divining and smoothing away the troubles of rich and poor. She frustrates a plot against the humble lover, Mila, by which he would have been forcibly carried off as a recruit; and she comes to the aid of the princess's adopted daughter, betrothed to a rich aristocrat but pining for the love of a poor young artist, her drawing-master. The scenes reflect the country life of Bohemia as it was a century ago: a simple birthday party outside the picturesque old bleaching-house; the farewell of the conscripts dragged off to fight in the army of their conquerors; an attractive winter scene which shows the village girls at their spinning-wheels, busy by the light of the glowing fire, while Grannie tells them tales of her youth. All of which may sound tame to the votaries of *Salome* or *Tosca*, but for all its seeming homeliness it is packed with normal emotions and moves us to natural laughter and tears. The music woven round these idyllic scenes is in many respects of a higher quality than anything in *Psohlavci*. If it owes something to the composer's love of French music in its grace and restraint, it is free from the tricks and artificiality of much French opera in the 'nineties. There is a bloom upon it, as on much genuine Czech music, that needs delicate handling. *At the Old Bleaching-house* is a surprising work to have emanated from a man who spent his life as a professional conductor. Into this picture of a tranquil autumn declining to cheerful winter, he has infused a breath of spring. The libretto might have proved in sipid in the hands of a novice; but Kovařovic was a master in the art of colouring words.

Kovařovic visited England in May 1919, when he conducted the orchestra of the National Theatre at the Czechoslovak Musical Festival. He was then seriously out of health and his condition much aggravated by the lack of suitable food, Prague having endured many privations during the last years of the war. During the following summer he discussed with me the possibility of composing an opera on one of George Eliot's *Scenes from Clerical Life*: the delicate old-world atmosphere of Mr. Gilfil's love-story appealed to him and would have made a companion work to *The Old Bleaching-house*. But as the autumn advanced it was evident that he was failing rapidly, and he was released from his sufferings on 6 December 1920 and was buried on the anniversary of his birth.

Although they worked under the same master, it would be difficult to find two musical talents more dissimilar than those of Kovařovic and Foerster. Kovařovic, though by no means dry or pedantic, had the clear, alert, and somewhat objective view of his art that might be expected from an expert conductor. He was, *par excellence*, the professional musician, not unintelligent, but pre-occupied almost wholly with the practical problems of his art.

It would hardly be correct to describe Josef Bohuslav Foerster as a direct pupil of any master, for his musical education must have begun almost from the hour of his birth; nevertheless it is in the company of Fibich's disciples rather than those of Dvořák that it is customary to include him. He comes of a family which boasts more than one generation of musicians. His grandfather Josef Foerster of Osenice was a typical Czech Cantor—a village schoolmaster whose life was spent between the school-house and the organ gallery. In such families musicianship is an imperishable heritage. Grandfather Foerster's two sons Antonin (1837–1915) and Josef (1833–1907) both followed the musical profession. The former spent most of his life in Jugoslavia as organist and conductor; while Josef established himself in Prague, where he took an active part in the reform of Church music and eventually became Professor of Harmony at the Conservatoire, and organist and choirmaster of the Cathedral of St. Vitus. Josef Bohuslav was born at Prague, 30 December 1859. On leaving school he entered the Polytechnic Institute, but he was already marked out for a musical life and at the end of a year abandoned mechanics for the Organ School and the study of composition. He acted as assistant organist to his uncle Anton, to whose post at the church of St. Adalbert he succeeded. Work was not far to seek in Prague for the son of his father, and he became successively singing-master at two public schools, deputy professor at the Organ School, and director of the choir of the Church of Our Lady of the Snow. He started early in his career as musical critic, a branch of work in which he was actively engaged for many years.

From his father's side Foerster inherited musical ability, a certain level-headedness which always restrained him from excessive experimentalism in his creative art, the gift of stubborn perseverance, and a temperamental toughness of fibre, both moral and physical. From his mother he acquired quite contrasting qualities: a stillness of heart which resisted the mercurial tendencies of the time, a fervent love of poetry, an almost feminine sensibility, and a tendency to melancholy alternating with exaltation. The atmosphere of his early years was deeply religious, and although in course of time his creed outsoared conventional limitations he still remained devout. His admirers dwell frequently on the spirit of 'humility and love' expressed in his music. During the years of his tutelage, which lasted more or less until his thirtieth year, he ventured on no works on a large scale. The surroundings of his home life—he lived in his father's house even after his marriage—were doubtless restrictive. He seems to have been attracted by the composers who appealed most to the softer side of his nature—Schumann, Tchaikovsky, and Grieg—on whose work he wrote a thoughtful essay. Although he must have come into contact with the leading native musicians of the day, Smetana, Bendl, and the successful Dvořák of the 'eighties, it almost appears as though his literary development during this time far outdistanced his musical growth. It was risking contraction of spirit for a young man to live, as Bartoš tells us, shut away in his father's family, dwelling in himself apart, 'like an astronomer in his observatory', even though his vision was fixed on the beauty of the world. It was at this time that he formed those close relations with books and the intellectual movements of the day which continued in Hamburg and Vienna, and made him for good and for evil essentially a 'literary' musician.

In 1889 he set up an independent household. He had married in the previous year Berta Lauterer, a successful débutante at the Národní Divadlo, Prague, and his life henceforth was to some extent governed, and widened, by the exigencies of her career. In 1893 Pollini engaged the young prima donna for the Hamburg Municipal Opera, and Foerster, seeing the engagement was likely to become permanent, left Prague to found a new home in the northern city.

So far, Foerster's compositions did not show any marked personality. He began with choral works on a small scale: Five Part-songs in the national style (1882), Song of the Ukraine, and Slovak Songs (1885); a few settings for solo voices of lyrics by Heine, Lenau, and Goethe. But neither in these nor in his Pianoforte Trio, Op. 8 (1882), his String Quartet in E, Op. 15 (1888), nor even in his First Symphony in D minor, Op. 9 (1887–8), was there any positive promise of individuality. A more ambitious work, *The Angel's Hymn*, Op. 13, for chorus and orchestra (1889), is interesting as showing his early conception of God as a glorious and triumphant Deity, whereas, as life went on, it was God as the suffering Saviour of humanity that filled his vision. It needed some sharp emotional shock to bring out the deeper side of his nature.

One more important work dates from these early years in Prague —the opera *Deborah*. As I have already pointed out, melodrama was an accepted form in the traditions of Czech music. Preserving the example of Fibich, who turned to melodrama because he believed it to be the logical result of Wagnerian models but afterwards made his recantation in the operas *The Tempest* and *Šarka*, Foerster approached dramatic music by way of the short melodramas: *The Three Riders* (1887), *The Legend of St. Julia* (1891), and incidental music to Kvapil's *Princess Pampeliška* ('Princess Dandelion'). But with his literary interests, combined perhaps with the fact that opera was a practical proposition in Bohemia, it was inevitable that he should be attracted to the theatre early in his career.

Since naturalism was repugnant to Foerster, and he lacks the objective outlook which is almost indispensable to the making of an impressive opera, he has at least avoided Tchaikovsky's mistake of trying to graft his intrinsically lyrical music upon historical or legendary sensationally lurid subjects (such as *The Maid of Orleans* and *Mazeppa*) and uses texts that serve as vehicles for his individual standpoints, intellectual and emotional, and alas, also ethical. The first opera, *Deborah* (1890–1) is of this type: the story of a conflict between passion and compassion. The text is by Jaroslav Kvapil after Mosenthal. The scene opens upon the village green where the people are leaving the church after the Good Friday service. The pastor has been preaching on the duty of kindness to our neighbours, and his ward Hana wishes to carry out his precepts by befriending a poor family of Jews who have paused in their wanderings and are living in a hut outside the village. At this moment the beautiful Jewess Deborah comes upon the scene, and the people, their anti-semitic passion stirred by the approach of Easter, pay no heed to homilies but begin to revile her. Deborah seems in actual danger of further violence when the magistrate's son Josef steps in to defend her. Until this moment Hana has regarded herself as the woman of Josef's choice. Now he declares openly his passion for Deborah. His father is surprised and vexed; whereupon the pastor takes him aside and suggests that he should give some money to the Jews and bid them leave the district. But Josef's feelings are deeply involved. He has arranged to elope with Deborah that very evening.

In the second Act the magistrate's servant Jakub meets Deborah's mother in the churchyard and gives her the money and his master's message. The old woman takes it and departs. Jakub then reports his success to the magistrate, but their conversation is partly overheard by Josef, who believes that Deborah has deserted him for the sake of the money. In this despairing mood he falls in with Hana, who offers him her sisterly affection and comforts him. They follow their elders into church for the Easter Eve service. Deborah now comes upon the scene and awaits the coming of her lover. She is prepared to run away with him; but when Josef comes out of church he turns from her with bitter reproaches. Deborah, ignorant of his wrongs, thinks Josef is tired of her, and, full of hate, the passionate Jewess curses him and his whole family; then, snatching the rosary from his hands, she runs away.

The third Act shows us Josef and Hana happily married with a little daughter. Josef takes leave of his wife and goes to join his men at the harvest festival. After his departure a beggar-woman enters the farm buildings. It is Deborah watching for a moment in which to wreak her vengeance. Hana does not recognize Deborah, but her kindness prompts her to offer hospitality which the beggar refuses. When Josef returns, Hana relates the episode and he immediately suspects the intruder to be his old love. They talk of the past and of the unhappy young Jewess with kindness and compassion, and Deborah who is still hiding in the background is so touched by their conversation, in which she learns that their child has been named after her, that her heart is softened. She moves stealthily to the sleeping child, drops the rosary into the cradle, and after kissing the little Deborah gently and wishing her happiness, disappears into the night.

This opera embodies Foerster's conception of love, not merely as a physical passion but as a motive power in existence. Here as in all his later operas the heroine at any rate loves with unbroken constancy and fights to the last for a chaste ideal of love. Foerster's women are never allowed to be happy in the consummation of a sensuous passion. Deborah, Eve, Alba in *The Invincibles*, 'drown their eyes or break their hearts' less because their swains are weak of will than because of their obstinate love of love as a dream dreamt by Foerster.

In Hamburg, where his wife established her reputation especially as a Wagner singer, Foerster was well received. He obtained a professorship at the Conservatoire and became critic of the Hamburg *Freie Presse* while continuing to write for the Prague *Národní Listy*. He found himself in the full tide of a musical activity which embraced many interests old and new. Hamburg was proud of her own son, Brahms; proud too of Gustav Mahler, leading conductor at the Opera from 1891. Arthur Seidl, the writer on Wagner, Richard Strauss, and modern music in general, and the German poets Lilkienkron and Gustav Falke were among his friends in the wealthy and art-loving city. Foerster, thus stimulated, now entered upon a period of remarkable creative industry. He followed up his Second Symphony by a third, in D major, Op. 36, which is emotionally linked to its predecessor, the problem of a death reappearing, but the note of victory being more emphatic than before. Bartoš calls it a hymn of victory.

At this time he was greatly attracted to the verses of Sládek (*Village Songs and Czech Sonnets*), a poet to whom the Czech song-writers owe nearly as much as German musicians owe to Heine. The words cried for musical setting and were the inspiration of several among the Nine Male Voice Choruses, Op. 37, composed in Hamburg in 1894, which brought him such great popularity as to be almost detrimental to his work in other directions. It is regrettable that a nation of choral singers like ourselves should know so little of these remarkable works: *Vast, wide native fields*

('Velké, širé, rodné lany'), *The Skylark* ('Skřivánek'), *The Field Path* ('Polní cestou'), and the deeply religious song *The Plowman* ('Oráči') with words by the poet-priest Lutinov. They are not imitations of folk-song; they are by no means 'wild honey', but their substance could only have been gathered and hived in 'the fields and groves of Bohemia'.

His second opera *Eve*, a much more mature work than *Deborah*, originated in Hamburg in 1895–7. Here he was his own librettist basing his text on a popular drama, *The Maid of the Inn*, by Gabriella Preissova. The scene is laid in Slovakia, and the characters are drawn from peasant life.

A handsome well-off Slovak youth, Manek, somewhat volatile, loves the poor semptress Eve. Their temperaments are not really in agreement, for Eve has a dark intensely passionate nature. Manek is influenced by his mother, who wants him to marry the plain but well-dowered Maryša. Eve's suspicions are awakened. She distrusts her lover. Manek's ambitious mother affronts Eve by suggesting that her love for her son is interested. In her indignation the girl gets engaged to the lame furrier Samko, who has long been attached to her. Manek now returns to Eve, but too late. The marriage with Samko is not happy and the child which was her consolation dies. Manek's mother still cherishes her spite against Eve. She visits the cottage to boast of Manek's happiness with Maryša. The unhappy couple have the strength and dignity not to show their feelings before her. But afterwards the estrangement is more complete. Shortly afterwards Manek confesses to Eve that he still loves her and implores her to come away with him over the Austrian border. In a new country he says they can marry. Eve is honest, though passionate, and she refuses. But during the interval Samko arrives home unexpectedly and finds her with her old lover. He refuses to believe Eve's story and reviles and strikes her. Eve leaves him and follows Manek away. But his shifty and easy-going nature leads him to let the situation drift. Eve suffers shame and humiliation. When Manek's mother pursues him to bring him back to his wife and family, he at last bestirs himself to try to 'make an honest woman' of Eve. But now he finds that he cannot legally do so, and Eve, tossed hither and thither by fate, good at heart but forced by circumstances into a cruel situation, broken-hearted, finds release in the waters of the river.

The sombre, passionate temperament of the heroine Eve gives

Foerster a fine central figure on which to work. The lyrical warmth; the scenic unity and firm treatment of the whole musical structure; the intricate thematic development; the clever use of the orchestra to supplement and throw into relief the psychological movements of the characters in this tragic love-tale—all combine to make *Eve* the most popular of Foerster's operas.

In 1899 he passed his fortieth birthday in Hamburg, and marked the event by writing the Symphonic Poem *My Youth*, Op. 44, a work in which life in all its phases remains the subject of his inspiration: a 'hymn of life' in which, despite its greatest sorrows, a positive, yearning, and metaphysical note reigns. To this year belongs also the song-cycle *Love*, Op. 46, conceived in a vein of sweet and melancholy feeling, while *Songs of Longing*, Op. 53, perhaps mark the summit of his powers as a song writer. This Hamburg period might be called the 'time of yearning'; the two melodramas *Faustutas*, Op. 31 (1897), and *Amarus*, Op. 30 (1897), are portraits of two people deluded by life yet with a wealth of sensibility deep within their souls.

In 1903 Foerster moved to Vienna, where his wife had been engaged by Mahler for the Imperial Opera in the Austrian capital. Here he was appointed Professor at the new Conservatoire and musical critic of *Die Zeit*. About this time a new era began in Vienna in the cultural and political atmosphere of which the Czechs took a more active part; new currents were moving in European music, literature, art, and philosophy. Western Europe was under the influence of Mahler's symphonies, of Debussy's impressionism, of Reger's free polyphony. The new Czech generation reacted to all these influences, building at the same time, however, on Czech tradition and preserving Czech racial individuality in music. Foerster was a link between the romantic age and the modern generation, and did much valuable work in the cultural and literary circles in Vienna.

Foerster's music is inspired by his life; sorrow is for him an inseparable part of existence. The loss of his nearest kinsfolk has been one of the most important sources of his musical inspiration: his Second Symphony in F major, Op. 29, and his Cantata *Mortis Fratibus* were in memory of his sister and brother; while his Pianoforte Trio in A minor, Op. 105, is a lament for his son who died in the flower of his youth in 1921, aged fifteen. 'Foerster's work', says his devoted admirer, J. Bartoš, 'emerges from the dusky sea of his sorrow'; and elsewhere he says of him that his whole art might be described—as someone has described the entire work of Spohr—as 'elegiac lyricism'. Personal loss certainly counts for nearly as much in Foerster's music as in Tchaikovsky's, but the menacing gloom of the Russian is absent in the Czech, who has in his nature a tonic and buoyant quality inherited from his Foerster ancestors. Bartoš calls this power of lifting himself above the mists of mortal tears and despondency, this dash of gallantry which enables him to look fate in the face and still give thanks for life—'Foerster's spirit of *quand-même*'; at all costs life is still beautiful.

In 1905 came his Fourth Symphony in C minor, Op. 54. After his earlier Symphonic Poems, *Youth* and *Love*, he gives to this brilliantly orchestrated work the title *Easter*, and here seeks a deeper consciousness and communion with God's immeasurable love for suffering humanity. Foerster's fine lyrical style is most marked in his symphonies; in form, perhaps, he follows Mahler, with whom he was much in touch during his days in Hamburg, but he follows in the footsteps of Dvořák in his deep religious feeling and his conception of God, Love, and Charity as his highest source of inspiration. His five symphonies are a further contribution to the Czech symphonic tradition founded by Dvořák.

Works of this period in a lighter vein are a Symphonic Suite, *Cyrano de Bergerac*, Op. 55, in five movements full of warm melody and rich orchestration, and a third opera which originated about the same time, *Jessica*, a work in which a quality of temperate humour runs through its pleasant melodious music and freshness of orchestration, qualities which entitle it to its frequent place in the repertory of opera houses in Czechoslovakia. The libretto, based on Shakespeare's *Merchant of Venice*, was arranged by the Czech poet Vrchlický.

In 1918 Foerster's next opera, *The Invincibles* ('Nepremozeni'), Op. 100, was given at the National Theatre, Prague, though its composition dates from 1906. In the opinion of some of his friends, it assumed in his mind the significance of a jubilee work, in which he wished to summarize all his preceding development —all the articles of his aesthetic faith. He is the originator and author of the libretto, a good deal of which is written in rhymed verse. The diction is natural without dropping into triteness, the melodic outlines less generous and flowing than in *Eve*, and the harmony simple.

The love of a young musician, Victor, for Countess Alba, niece of Count Hrabe, is the motive of the plot. But Victor is the son of the Count's gardener; an emotional, moody, melancholy young man. The first Act of the opera contains a touching love-scene. Alba at first reciprocates Victor's passion. When she leaves him soliloquizing upon his short-lived happiness, the Count, who has overheard the lovers, breaks in and protests indignantly. At first Victor defends his position; but gradually gives way under the pessimistic and energetic arguments of the Count, and promises to go away. There is an interesting use of leading motives in this scene, as, one by one, we hear the love-themes of Victor extinguished by the sceptical, suggestive motive of the Count.

Six years elapse between the first and second Acts. An orchestral Prelude depicts Victor's continuous longing. The curtain rises upon a soirée given by the aristocratic Velvarsky, at which the Count and Alba are guests. Victor has just played a violin solo to the admiration of all present. The social scene is very cleverly portrayed by the accompanying music with its occasional references to Haydn and Mozart's *Figaro*, and the introduction of a new valse theme. In a long monologue Victor tells of the growth of his creative power, called forth and helped by love. The reminiscences of youth's dream, the renewed hopes of the moment, are chased away by a gay dance-tune. Victor betrays that in former years he left the castle under pressure, but in the firm hope that on his return he would find Alba free. He makes passionate love to her, but she from various motives refuses to listen to him. She remains unconquered, although she betrays at the fear of his death that her old love is still alive. Victor goes away for the second time.

Ten years elapse and at the opening of Act III Alba, seated at her piano, reviews her life and realizes that the one beautiful thing in it was her first love. Count Hrabe interrupts her reverie. He tells her that she must marry Prince Roji in order to save the family from ruin. Alba is unwilling to decide. Then George, a minor character, enters. He has just returned from Italy, and tells her that Victor is ill in Naples—perhaps dying. Alba is filled with remorse and resolves that she will go to him. The final scene takes place in a tavern in Naples where the artists' club is holding a revel. Victor, ill and weary, sits apart from them all. Alba suddenly appears. Victor greets her with tears of weakness. 'Give me death', he says. And Alba answers: 'No, life'. While the lovers are lost in rapture a mysterious light seems to rise from the sea, which grows in intensity until the fall of the curtain. Throughout the opera a complicated system of suggestion by means of leading motives and their modifications is pursued.

A very interesting work of this Viennese period is his Chorus for Mixed Choir and Orchestra, entitled *Four Heroes*. In this work the poet Sládek writes of four heroes who set out for foreign lands promising each other that after a year and a day they will return home again: a monk, a citizen, a nobleman—and Honza, a patriot with a deep and fervent love of his country. Adventures abroad seal the fate of the three 'problematic' heroes, but in Foerster's setting of the poem Honza is carried to great heights as the symbol of the eternal imperishable Czech sentiment.

So, with the freedom of the country and establishment of the Republic in 1918, came the longed-for return to Prague, and fresh successes for the sixty-year-old composer. In spite of his classical traditions he did not fail to assimilate new ideas brought by the post-war period. His later works—his Fifth Symphony, his opera *Srdce* ('The Heart') (1922), and a dramatic oratorio *St. Wences laus*—all show further development and fresh impulses. Foerster never attempts in his operas to depict the dramatic moments of human love, as with Janáček; rather does he dwell on the lyrical and psychological aspirations of the human soul. In his latest opera, *The Simpleton* (1934), it is by the strength of his pure faith that this simple-minded soul attains his ultimate happiness.

On his return to Prague he was appointed Professor at the newly organized Conservatoire of Music, of which he was also later Director. His immense creative output, especially in choral works, has had an extensive influence on the development of present-day music, since in his later years his work became more and more the common heritage of the Czech people.

Prominent among the pupils of Fibich is Otakar Ostrčil, who was born in Prague, 25 February 1879. Deterred by his parents from following a musical career, he first took his Degree of Philosophy at the Prague University, working privately in his spare time at the Conservatoire. In his early works, such as the Symphony in A major, Op. 7, and his first opera, *The Death of Vlasta*, Op. 6, he follows his master, from whom he acquired an early mastery of composition. He had, however, little of the romanticism of Fibich in his nature, but the latter soon awoke in him his dramatic gifts. *The Death of Vlasta*, based on a Czech mythical subject, belongs to the sphere of Smetana's *Libuše* and Fibich

Šarka, and won the composer his first success at the National Theatre in 1904.

But we soon find a more independent outlook in his work. His development stands somewhat apart from that of Suk and Novák, his contemporaries, on account of the strictly intellectual and logical tendency of his mind, which enabled him more easily than either of them to make a clear break with romanticism, and build up a style and method of his own. In search of this independent path, he met with a guide in the person of Gustav Mahler, who opened new horizons for him. If Novák reacted in his own way to the influence of French impressionism, Ostrčil reacted to that of Mahler, from whom he learnt especially the principle of free polyphony. This tendency to free construction is apparent in his later works, which show qualities of intellectualism and mysticism combined with a complete mastery of modern technique, and interest us mentally while rarely giving a sharp shock to the emotions. But in spite of this constructive, logical style, Ostrčil is of Moravian stock and has in his nature something of the gay and sympathetic temperament, together with his fellow-countrymen's love of melody and landscape.

In his next opera, *Kunala's Eyes*, Ostrčil has turned to a strange mystic Indian legend, treated by the Czech poet Zeyer, to which he gives a strong dramatic interest, but avoids any over-passionate exotic Eastern tendency. The music already shows new melodic and harmonic effects, and a concise polyphonic style.

Following Smetana's example, he turned from this tragic vein to a comedy in his next work for the stage. *The Bud*, a setting of Zvoboda's popular one-act play, is a delightful and charming picture of contemporary life, in the music of which Ostrčil combines traces of the romanticism of Fibich and the lyricism of Foerster, with his own independent method of rapid melodic changes particularly suited to the quick repartee of the humorous moments; and at the same time illustrates the firm and concise musical structure which he had achieved.

We find this also in another opera, *The Legend of Erin*, Op. 19, based on one of Zeyer's dramas, which reproduces much of the Celtic epic atmosphere, but seems out of place in the opera house, where, even in Czechoslovakia, people go not to muse on archaic civilizations but to be amused. The music certainly repays leisurely study in quiet hours.

The growing individuality is most characteristic in the composer's orchestral compositions, where his virtuosity is of the kind that is never futile: the *Impromptu*, the Suite in C minor (1912), and the *Symphonietta*, Op. 20, are some of the most interesting works to study from this point of view. Perhaps his most important addition to the modern orchestral works of his country is his Symphonic Variations, *The Stations of the Cross* (1928); in this work of broad, large structure, depicting in fine and lofty tones the human sufferings of Christ, the composer has attained the summit of his creative powers.

In his last work, *John's Kingdom*, an opera based on Tolstoi's fairy tale, Ostrčil combined both tragedy and comedy.

Ostrčil was also well known in his country as a talented conductor, for after many years at the Vinohrady Theatre in Prague, he succeeded Karel Kovařovic, in 1920, as Chief Conductor of the National Theatre, which position he held until his death in August 1935. As Kovařovic had done much to revive and establish national opera under difficult conditions, Ostrčil took over and carried on the development of this important work during the years of the First Republic. He included in the repertory many of the less known works of Smetana, Fibich, Foerster, and Dvořák, while those of his contemporaries, Novák, Karel, Zich, Jeremiaš, and many others were given a place in his ambitious and comprehensive programmes. Nor did he limit his attentions to native compositions, for his interest in modern music of other countries was very active, and many performances of Russian and German works were given. In this work of building up the activities of the National Theatre, he sought the collaboration of young Czech scenic artists and the talented producer Ferdinand Pojman, and though, like his predecessors Smetana and Kovařovic, he met with some opposition in his work, his success in carrying on their traditions will not be forgotten by his compatriots.

Another pupil of Fibich, who in his early years made some use of national subjects such as Procházka's folk-scene, *Prastky*, is Karel Weiss. But he soon sought operatic material outside his native country, and spent much of his life in Germany, where his operettas became well known on the German stage. Born in the same year as Kovařovic (1862), his first important opera, *The Twins*, was produced in Prague in 1892; the libretto is based on Shakespeare's *Twelfth Night*. But it was not until nine years later that the composer made a reputation for himself both in

O

Prague and abroad, particularly in Germany, with *The Polish Jew*. This opera, based on Erckmann-Chatrian's novel, was given its first performance at the German Theatre in Prague in 1901. In 1912 he composed *The Attack on the Mill*, venturing into competition with Alfred Bruneau, who had already utilized Zola's story for operatic purposes. He returned to a national subject, however, for his last opera, *The Blacksmith of Lesetinsk*, the libretto being taken from Svatopluk Čech's *Lesetinsky Kovar*. The work was produced in Prague in 1920. Weiss uses the orchestra with brilliant effect in his *Czech Dances*, and especially in his opera, *The Polish Jew*, but nowhere does his art reflect the essential qualities of a national style.

CHAPTER XII

FROM the time of Fibich and Dvořák, music in Bohemia diverged into two main currents: the pupils of the former pursued the dramatic path, while the followers of the latter tended towards absolute, or perhaps I should say symphonic, music. The two most distinguished disciples of Dvořák are Vítězslav Novák and Joseph Suk, born within a few years of each other. It is difficult to separate these two important and most harmonious influences in any study of contemporary Czech music. They afford indeed a delightful example of the truth that a complete contrast in temperament and achievement can be the surest foundation of friendship. No narrow-minded admiration united them, but the deep respect and affection which grows up between two artists who have lived and worked through the dark years and emerged together into the light of a more hopeful day.

Vítězslav Novák, born at Kamenice, 5 December 1870, was the son of a medical man. After a course at a Gymnasium, like many other musicians, he first entered the Prague University and there studied jurisprudence and philosophy. Later on, having chosen the musician's career, he worked at the Prague Conservatoire. Novák, Suk, and Nedbal were regarded as the most promising pupils in Dvořák's class, and each, after his own fashion, has fulfilled expectations. In 1909 Novák succeeded his master as Professor of Composition at the Conservatoire.

In the first thirty years of creative activity Novák passed through several well-defined phases. His early compositions were not unnaturally influenced by the men who were regarded as the 'moderns' of his youthful years: Brahms, Dvořák, Grieg, Tchaikovsky, the German romantics, more especially Schumann. From this interesting, but immature, stage he emerged suddenly. Slovakia the high, cloud-trapped Tatra, has been much the same source of refreshment and inspiration to the Czech poets and musicians as the Caucasus to the Russians. Foerster had already used the characteristics of Slovak folk-music in his opera *Eve*; Novák goes still further in his artistic exploitation of the folk-style of Slovakia and Moravia. Just as Smetana inclined to Czech melody and excelled in depicting Czech character, so Novák has been drawn to the wilder rhythms of Slovak folk-music. The

Slovak Suite, Op. 32, the Symphonic Poem, *In the Tatra*, as well as his popular national opera, *Lucerna* ('The Lantern'), are coloured by his impressions of Slovak scenery and temperament; while his *Wallachian Dances* (for piano) are a delightful series of pictures from national life, first devised as piano pieces, but afterwards brilliantly orchestrated by the composer.

The influence of Debussy and the French impressionists next showed itself in the music of Novák; but it is a fleeting phase. Having learnt from impressionism—all there is indeed to learn—a new method of working, Novák reached the only sure ground on which a composer can tread a progressive path of achievement: his own ideas and his own methods of expressing them have guided his musical advance since the composition of the Symphonic Poem, *Eternal Longing*, based on one of Hans Andersen's symbolical tales. The inspiration came to him while spending a holiday by the shores of the Adriatic, and, in spite of the less concrete and more psychological nature of the subject, the tendency to descriptive painting rather than symbolical suggestion still lingers in the work. The poem consists of two sections, one diatonic, the other chromatic, linked together by the theme of the moon with which the poem opens and closes.

In certain respects Novák's career has proceeded inversely to that of most artists in whom the lava-flow of sensuous passion comes early and the cooling and incrusting process follows with the growth of a more stoical and mature philosophy. There is a foreshadowing of the erotic phase in the cycle of songs called *Melancholy Songs of Love*, Op. 38; but its climax is reached in a Tone Poem of sensuous warmth and beauty, *Toman and the Wood-nymph*, Op. 40. This was followed by an Overture, in which the romantic eleventh-century love-story of Godiva, wife of Leofric, Earl of Mercia and Lord of Coventry, is the central theme. *Lady Godiva*, Op. 41, was first played at the inaugural performance, at the Municipal Theatre, Vinohrad, of Vrchlický's tragedy of the same name. This distinguished Czech poet, the author of much original lyric and dramatic verse, did a great service to his countrymen by his excellent translations from the French, Italian, German, Spanish, English, and other languages. The principal melody, first heard, expressive and entreating, in the clarinet as Lady Godiva pleads with her implacable husband, is finally worked up into a triumphant peroration.

To this period also belong the String Quartet in D, the Sere-

nade for Small Orchestra, Op. 36, and the Songs to German
Texts, Op. 39; also the Cycle of Poems for Piano entitled *Pan*,
Op. 43. This work seems to be the summing-up and close of this
middle period of Novák's activity; it may be described as an
intensive effort to embody in one work a complete expression of
all he has said or indicated in previous compositions. But here he
groups all preceding impressions and experiences according to
the primary forces which were their origin. Hence the reason for
the complicated form of the work which is in essence a drama in
four acts with a Prologue, the separate acts or movements being
entitled: The Mountains, The Sea, The Forest, The Woman.
In later years Novák orchestrated *Pan*, in which form it is really
more accessible.

The dramatic tendency of *Pan* is still further emphasized in
two remarkable Cantatas: *The Storm*, Op. 42, and *The Spectre's
Bride*. The former, described by the composer as a 'Sea Fantasy
for Soli, Chorus, and Orchestra', and dedicated to the Brno
Musical Society, is a setting of a poem by Svatopluk Čech which
offers fine emotional contrasts. Although Čech writes of the sea
with the inherent authority of one who has lived much by its
shores, yet his poem, which consists chiefly of lyrical numbers,
offers considerable dramatic and graphic variety for musical treatment. Its main psychological themes are the Passion of the Sea
and the Passion of Love: both are manifest in their many and
complex moods. Novák, in spite of his Central European origin,
is a sea-worshipper, and brings to his task impressions of visits to
many coasts: the changeful Adriatic, the cold, grey, shallow waters
of the Skagerrack, and the Atlantic rollers breaking on the shores
of Brittany. *Storm* is almost a sea symphony with chorus obli-
gato. The work is laid out for strings, three flutes, two oboes,
cor anglais, two clarinets, bass clarinet, two bassoons, double-
bassoon, six horns, three trumpets, three trombones, and tuba;
a full complement of percussion, harp, pianoforte, and organ;
solo soprano, tenor, baritone, bass, and chorus. The piano is
used as an orchestral instrument for many special and realistic
effects, such as the tossing spray showers, the cracking of the whip
in the slave's reminiscences, and so on.

The musical form of the work is only partly conditioned by the
requirements of the text, which contains a series of well-defined
episodes for musical setting, while leaving the composer free to
intersperse them with an equal number of symphonic interludes.

The chief poetic episodes begin with the prayer of a maiden on shore for the safe return of her lover on the sea; this is followed by the chorus of the ship's crew, telling of the familiar spirit who dwells in the ship's hold and quits the vessel only when some catastrophe is imminent. Then the look-out boy, perched aloft, sings a gay and reckless ditty of the joys of sea-life. The maiden's lover follows on with a song of yearning remembrance to his sweetheart ashore. And here the element of Love enters the drama. The youth's love is pure and loyal; but the poem contains another aspect of passion. An important episode which comes later deals with the unbridled desire of a black slave for his beautiful mistress. The approach of the storm—which affects the psychology of each individual in a different way—loosens the bonds of restraint. The slave sings deliriously of his love, and of a past in which he sat enthroned in purple in his far-off, desert kingdom. Amid this powerful but somewhat repulsive episode, the storm strikes the ship. The sailors, who believe her to be doomed because the familiar spirit has abandoned her, refuse to work the pumps. Now, amid the roaring of the elements, are heard snatches from all that has preceded in this climax; the despairing cry of the lady as she reads her doom in the eyes of her ruthless slave, the last piping phrase of the look-out boy before the lightning shatters the mast, the lover's prayer to the Virgin ('O Star of the Sea'), and the ribald chorus of the drunken sailors.

A long orchestral interlude separates the scene of anguish and destruction from the two final numbers. When the storm has abated, two longshore robbers, searching the beach for treasure, discover the lover's body and recognize him as the sweetheart of the girl whose cottage stands on the cliff above. The ruffians are not wholly evil and forbear to steal the betrothal ring from the lover's finger, but push the body back into the sea. At the same moment they see the girl emerge from the cottage and throw herself into the waves. The text ends with a kind of requiem hymn recalling the motive of 'O Star of the Sea'.

Storm belongs to Novák's full maturity, and is especially characteristic of certain aspects of his musical philosophy.

Needless to say that Novák's treatment of Erben's ballad, *The Spectre's Bride*, so modern in harmony, in orchestration, and in the subtle way in which he evokes the spirit of evil from obscure depths, has very little in common with Dvořák's setting. This work is really what the composer calls it: a Symphonic Poem of Horror.

From these cantatas it was but a short step to opera. Novák was forty-five when he produced his first work for the stage, *The Imp of Zvikov*, and surprised the musical world of Prague; for a comic opera—an old-fashioned *Lustspiel*—was the last thing the public expected from him. Laughter seemed alien to his nature, in spite of occasional touches of grim humour in his music. In *The Imp of Zvikov* Novák made the same daring experiment as Moussorgsky when he set to music Gogol's comedy *Marriage*, a prose libretto, without altering a single word of the original text. Novák has accomplished this *tour de force* successfully on the whole; but the fact remains that prose dialogue sometimes proves rebellious to musical setting even in skilful hands.

Novák called his second work for the stage a 'comic opera', but *A Night in Karlstein*, Op. 50, is something more than a *Lustspiel*. Every one who knows Prague and the vicinity knows also that superb and romantic pile which Charles IV erected as a place of retirement—the Montsalvat of Bohemia—from which the female sex was as rigorously excluded as from a monastery. But Charles, a man of matured philosophic wisdom, whose reason, however, is warmed by the glow of a great and benevolent heart, reckons without the uncontrolled love and jealousy of his romantic young Queen, who succeeds in forcing his stronghold. This time Novák started with an excellent lyrical libretto arranged by Otakar Fischer from Vrchlický's play, and he has drawn two fine musical portraits of these contrasting temperaments—clear, convincing dramatic figures. The love-duet between the King and Queen and the broad serene aria for Charles himself are favourite pages in the work. It was first produced at the Národní Divadlo, Prague, in 1916, under Karel Kovařovic. The tale undoubtedly appealed to two aspects of his temperament: the erotic and the patriotic.

In 1930 Novák celebrated his sixtieth birthday, and in the Ballet-Pantomime *Signorina Gioventu*, Op. 58, which he composed for the event, there is, as in so many of his compositions, an autobiographical significance. Here he takes leave of his youth, and maybe feels that he has left behind him some temperamental phases—the impressionism of *Pan*, the glowing eroticism of *Toman and the Wood-nymph*, the Slovak tendency which led him for a while to a more objective and national style; but the difference between fifty and sixty is a gradual one, and there are still no signs that the composer of the operas *The Lantern* and *Grand-*

father's Legacy has said farewell to his imagination, his satirical humour, or his extraordinary technical skill. If he has chosen temporarily to follow Stravinsky in the creation of his later ballets, it is because he wished to be entirely free from the restrictions which operatic singing impose upon a musician, and to utilize to the full all the symphonic resources which are his, essentially and by acquirement.

Signorina Gioventu is founded on a tale by Svatopluk Čech. 'The story', says Novák, 'remained in my mind from my student days; but only now, when my youth has gone beyond recall, do I fully understand and feel its meaning.' It is the pathetic story of a lawyer's clerk, 'neither young nor old', whose life has been spent in the dry-as-dust atmosphere of his office. One evening during the Carnival he asks leave to go home because he feels ill. Permission is grudgingly given him. Giddy and bewildered with fever, he makes his way through the Carnival crowd. Hardly conscious of what he is doing he is lured by a shopman into a store of costumes and masks. Out of a number of gaudy dresses, one attracts him especially—that of Helios the Sun-god. The enterprising representative of the firm of Sonnentrahl persuades him to try it on. The sick man makes but a faint resistance. Attendants from the shop help him into his chariot and accompany him to the ball. His entrance is impressive; but the admiration of the spectators is turned to derision when they see on the back of the chariot the blatant advertisement of the firm. Ashamed and shy, the unhappy clerk makes his escape and takes refuge among the palm-trees in a small ante-room. He takes off his false crown and sinks into a chair; no longer a sun-god, but a sad and weary mortal. Suddenly a lovely girl appears to him. 'Who are you?' he asks. 'I am Signorina Gioventu, your Youth, whom you deserted. What have you been doing all this time?' He confesses that he has wasted all the years in a lawyer's office. 'Now I am leaving you for ever,' she says, and flutters away to the ballroom like a bright butterfly. The sick man starts up and chases her in despair. Long she eludes him, but at last he catches her in his arms and they dance a wild measure. In the dawn a party of revellers find a man lying outside Sonnentrahl's shop. They think he is sleeping off the effects of the Carnival and try in vain to rouse him. The poor clerk is dead.

The Pantomime is in seven scenes, or tableaux, linked up by symphonic interludes. Novák uses about thirteen themes in the

course of the work which, however, teems with ingenious deriva-
tions, mostly employed in dance forms. The chief theme is that
of the clerk, which is touched with deep pathos and somewhat
Slovak in character. It is foreshadowed in the Prologue and runs
throughout the scenes in many metamorphoses. The Prologue is
an explanatory melodrama, and reminds us that this form has
never ceased to be cultivated in Bohemia since George Benda
composed his once famous *Ariadne in Naxos* (1774).

This was followed by another Ballet-Pantomime, entitled
Nicotin, Op. 59, also in seven scenes, on a tale by Sv. Čech.

As a pupil of Dvořák, Novák was attracted to all forms of
musical composition. We find chamber works of excellent design,
such as his Trio for Piano in D minor, two String Quartets, in
both of which Slovak popular melodies were a source of inspiration; many choruses and arrangements of Moravian and Slovak
folk-songs, which are often to be found in the repertory of the
Prague and other male-voice choirs of the country. His *Ballad
on the Vah* is but one example of dramatic choral writing, in
which psychological delineation and landscape painting are combined in a masterly way. A series of song-pieces for children
shows his educational interest in the rising generation, just as his
choruses in celebration of the Independence of the Republic and
of President Masaryk's election to the Presidency show him in
touch with the political and national movements of his day. But
it is in symphonic form that Novák's creative ability is best seen:
in such works as the Symphonic Poems already mentioned, the
orchestral interludes in his opera *Grandfather's Heritage*, and
more especially in his *Autumn* Symphony (1934). In 1919 Novák
was appointed Director of the Prague Conservatoire, which had
been newly organized after the establishment of the independent
Republic in 1918. Sociable, sincere, not in the least pedantic,
Director Novák, while always interested in the work of his pupils,
was at the same time naturally and keenly concerned with the
fate of his own works, some of which found their way to this
country.

Joseph Suk, born on 4 January 1874, at Křečovice, South
Bohemia, where his father was both schoolmaster and choirmaster, received a sound elementary musical education at home
before entering the Prague Conservatoire at the early age of
eleven. A pupil of Benevic, the predecessor of Sevčik at the
Prague Conservatoire, he passed his final examinations in 1891,

but stayed on for a year to become more proficient in chamber music under Wihan, and to work at composition under Dvořák. Before leaving the Conservatoire he founded the Bohemian String Quartet in co-operation with three fellow-students—Hoffmann, Nedbal, and Berger. He is perhaps best known in this country as a member of that organization, long the delight of all lovers of fine chamber music. English amateurs will most familiarly recall Suk's personality by his rugged head and sturdy figure as he sat alert at the second desk of the Quartet; but he pursued many other activities in the world of Czech music. He was one of the most efficient Rectors of the Prague Conservatoire (1924–6); but it is as a composer—the heir of Dvořák's art—that his compatriots will most permanently honour his memory.

Suk was Dvořák's favourite pupil at the Conservatoire, and in his early days the Master kept the youth's nose to the grindstone and was reticent in praising his works. This did not prevent the student from cherishing a real devotion to Dvořák, whose son-in-law he afterwards became. Suk's development was entirely different from that of Novák. It proceeded on quiet, almost wholly interior lines, very little affected by extraneous events. The adventures of the soul; the glorious quests of youth; the tender impassioned pursuit of ideal love; the mysterious and thrilling event of death; the satisfaction of overcoming sorrow and disillusionment; the rapture of making one's desert blossom like a rose—these are the things of which Suk speaks in his music. His quick emotionalism, his freshness and sanity, his complete lack of insincerity and pose are all in keeping with the Dvořák tradition.

In a study of Suk's development Richard Vesely says: 'He belonged to the favoured few who, as sons of musicians, had the opportunity in early youth to hear and perform music continually. In such cases the parents naturally give thought and care to the musical education of the child. Thus did old Antonín Suk, nurturing the recognized talent with a wise blend of love and severity. The boy was sensitive from the first to the due balance of technique and subject-matter.' Speaking of his childhood, Suk himself says: 'I was the darling of my parents and the youngest one. My father was very kind, serious, of a strong character, and an ardent musician; all he could give was devoted to the Church and "to the glory of God". I remember especially the Christmas-times, when my father played the organ there so beautifully, and sang with such enthusiasm that all the people listened spell-bound. I always loved to listen to music, and once I ran away from school to follow a player with a bass-viol to the neighbouring village. I stayed away from home all day till some one found me weeping outside the musician's cottage.'

Suk's youthful works are influenced by the later classical models of Schubert, Brahms, and Dvořák. The Quartet in A minor, Op. 1, a work of engaging freshness, and the Serenade for Strings, Op. 6, called attention to him while still a student. The idea of the latter work was suggested by Dvořák himself, who wished to persuade Suk to undertake a work of a lighter character than the earlier 'Dramatic' Overture, in which an austerely emotional tendency prevailed. Indeed already in this early work he foreshadows—perhaps unconsciously—his later character. 'We may find in it', writes Richard Vesely, 'a sort of summing-up of all the emotional changes of the growing period. It is rooted in a mood of pessimism, characteristic alike of the crises of youth and of the closing years of the nineteenth century. But it is typical of Suk that his suffering does not end in a desperate hopelessness. Though his life was full of struggle, he always answered misfortune with courage and self-reliance. In this Overture, pathos and deep passion are combined with immense energy, and the composition rises at the end to a mighty manifestation of disciplined will.' But the pupil did not disappoint his teacher, and produced a work pervaded with a certain romantic spirit, but maintaining a poetic serenity and a delicate humour peculiar to the style of a serenade.

Two years later the Pianoforte Quintet, Op. 8, confirmed the favourable opinion already formed of him. In spite of a naïve ebullience, which has its charm, for a youth still in his teens the work is surprisingly sure in form. But this did not suffice the composer. Writing to Otakar Šourek of his early works he says: 'I still like some of my early efforts and am touched when I hear them, but the Piano Quintet, the Fantastic Scherzo, and the Symphony in E major, Op. 14, are not my true self—of that I feel sure.' But such compositions serve to anticipate new ideas which lead to something better and more profound. A new source of inspiration was soon to come.

At the time of his courtship and marriage to Dvořák's daughter, Otilie, he fell under the spell of the romantic poet and novelist Julius Zeyer, and composed incidental music for his dramatic fairy-tale *Radůz and Mahulena*, a Suite from which Op. 13, became popular in the concert room. Zeyer pressed the young musician to supply music to his next play, *Pod Jabloní* ('Under the Apple-tree'), a love idyll permeated with mystical feeling. In these two works Suk shows his essentially lyrical gift, glowing and superabundantly vital.

The development of his gifts may be clearly followed in his numerous works for piano. From the *Liebestod*, Op. 7, through the cycles *Jaro* ('Spring') and *Léto* ('Summer'), and *O Matince* ('About the little Mother') we observe a steady ascent until we reach that fine collection of pieces, *Životem Snem* ('Things lived and dreamed'),[1] the very title of which is expressive of the whole aim and content of Suk's art.

Suk's musical evolution was as much the result of circumstances as of any sudden inward impulses. Every note he writes is part of his life, an experience or a dream. He does not need to search for sources of inspiration apart from his own rich subjectivity. Naturally the very quality of his art inclines him to programme music: not to a realistic, concrete programme, but to a suggestive, psychological one. His early orchestral works, the Fantasia in G minor for Violin and Orchestra (Op. 24), dedicated to Karel Hoffmann, leader of the Bohemian Quartet, and the Scherzo Fantastique (Op. 25), are exceptions in having no definite programmes.

A ripple of passionate restlessness in the Fantasia seems again to forebode the shadows lying ahead upon his life's path. But between this starting-point of great emotional depth and the trials which were to stamp Suk's work with a new image and super-scription, he completed his first Symphonic Poem. *Prague*, Op. 26, produced in March 1905, took rise in the heart and mind of the musician during a long tour which separated him from the beautiful city that dominates Vltava. It depicts, but not in the clear literal way that Smetana employs in his *Fatherland* cycle, the city's glorious past, the vicissitudes of triumph and bitterness which have been its lot, and refers to the prophecies of Libuše for a future greatness and happiness. The work coincides with the advent of Suk's 'impressionism' and lays the foundations for his later mature style.

In 1904 Fate struck a first blow at Suk in the death of Dvořák.

---

[1] These pieces were finely appreciated and delicately introduced to this country by the late Fanny Davies.

The Symphony *Asrael*, Op. 27 (1906), designed as a memorial to his friend and master, was before its completion to contain also a lament for a beloved wife, who died fourteen months after her father. This dual loss of the two best-loved presences, so swiftly and ruthlessly removed from his life, left him with an outlook on life too gloomy for so young a man and in a mood of sorrow and pensive melancholy. The composition was for awhile laid aside, and the Finale, which Suk had planned as an apotheosis to Dvořák, remained unfinished. 'The brooding presence of the Angel of Death', writes a Czech critic, 'hovers over the whole work; the composer has written this lament with his heart's blood. Utterances of heart-shaking intensity follow each other, which compel us to share his sorrow and realize his loss.'

The first movement of the Symphony *Andante sostenuto* is built up on the two leading themes: the Motive of Fate is given out by violins, violoncellos, and bass clarinet, and develops to a powerful and passionate climax. A short plaintive melody which recurs later in the work is heard from oboe. First indicated *pizzicato* in the double basses, the full orchestra finally introduces *molto marcato* the ominous motive of Death. In the masterly working-out section its triumphant, harsh, discordant notes are heard loudly in trumpets and trombones; while the movement ends with a return to the sad and tender oboe melody.

A mystical charm pervades the *Andante*, which opens with a long sustained note for flutes and trumpets; its very persistence suggests some forebodings of sorrow, in spite of the beautiful theme which develops in the strings. Here Suk has introduced a motive from Dvořák's own *Requiem*. After a short Fugue in which the motive of Fate and the motive of Death recur the movement dies away as mysteriously as it began with a long-held note.

The thematic material of the preceding movements is brilliantly developed in the *Vivace*, which serves as Scherzo. Here Suk rises to heights of thematic development and orchestration which prove him a true disciple of his master Dvořák. After an expressive middle section, *andante sostenuto*, in which there is a beautiful melody for violin interrupted by reminiscences of the motive of Fate, we return to the quick tempo of the opening. An intense and mighty struggle between the motive of Fate and the motive of Death ends the movement and Suk's original conclusion of the work.

When the composer took up the completion of the Symphony after a long pause he dedicated the *Adagio*, 4-4, to the memory of his wife Otilie. It contains none of the themes previously used. The warm and passionate love-song, a reflection of youth's joys which were destined to last so short a time, first given to violoncello and double bass, is afterwards heard in oboe, flute, and violins. A wonderful intensity and fervour pervades the movement, in the development of which the violins play an important part.

The beautiful love-song is rudely interrupted, and all the forebodings and dread of the earlier numbers return in the final movement. We hear again the motive of Fate, the motive of Death, with references to the plaintive melody: despair and despondency, pity and compassion combine till a turning-point is reached, *andante maestoso*. To the last and worst catastrophe finally succeeds a deep and tender feeling of resignation and the work ends on a note of reconciliation and comfort.

After these staggering blows of Fate, Suk was two or three years before he could again find consolation in composing. Later he realized that *Asrael* had been the turning-point in his inward evolution, teaching him that 'such work has only a right to exist if its author is in a position to give out comfort to humanity with convincing utterance, and this he cannot do unless he has experienced the full cost of a great sorrow'. Stunned for a time, Suk returned to creative activity with that renewed strength which sorrow gives to those who 'take life's woes full-breasted as they come'.

The Symphonic Poem *A Summer Tale* ('Pohádka Léta'), Op. 29, seeks and finds comfort in Nature. The work is in four movements entitled: Voices of Life and Consolation; Midday in Summer-time; The Blind Musician; and Phantoms of the Night —each one a mood picture expressed in music through which runs an ever-shifting play of light and colour.

Technically Suk had now reached his fullest independence and power, with harmonic and rhythmic means at his disposal, built upon polyphonic principles, and equipped with a wealth of melodic invention and a tone-colour indisputably original. Thus armed at all points with the complete accoutrement of a modern musician he approached his later very individual orchestral works of large design and difficult of execution: the Symphonic Poems *Maturity* (Zraní), Op. 34, and Epilogue, Op. 39.

The earlier work, produced in Prague in 1918, is based upon the beautiful poem by the Czech poet Antonín Sova in which the author seems to stand in contemplation before the broad, golden harvest fields, listening to the harmony of nature's calm, deep autumnal breath and seeing as in a vision the procession of life from its vernal promise to the rich fulfilment of harvest days. Suk's work has clearly a profound autobiographical significance. We recognize that it deals with an individual life: a life become affirmative and mature. It is a work in which energy and reflection are united in a remarkable degree. The titles of its three sections suggest its scope—*Life*, *Work*, and *Love*; but the word love has here a wider significance than in former works. It is the broad unselfish Shelleyan love of his fellows which desires above all the freedom and happiness of mankind. Here we may watch the transmutation of a blind cry of personal suffering into the expression of a deeper and more universal sympathy with mortal grief.

The work originated before the War of 1914–18, but its orchestration went slowly on account of the depression which the composer shared with so many of his compatriots, and it was only completed in 1918. The score shows daring technique and fascinating harmony.

The culminating work of this Symphonic Cycle, *Epilogue*, sets forth the ever-increasing conviction that only in love and renunciation lies the salvation of humanity. Though Suk probed the depths of suffering, these elegies are quite free from any touch of sensationalism or funeral pomp. *Epilogue*, a Symphonic Poem for mixed chorus, solo soprano, baritone, and bass, is dedicated to the conductor, Vaclav Talich, and the score is inscribed with the following words from Březina's *Myth of a Woman*: 'I taught the dumb lips to speak with the tenderness of my kisses, but my deepest words of hope I told not'. The text is taken from the First Book of Moses, the Psalms, and from Zeyer's *Under the Apple-tree*, and was arranged by Vycpálek.

The work falls into five sections. The first *Adagio* gives out the motive of Mankind in violoncellos and basses rising gradually to a fortissimo of human desire. A deep silence is then followed by the motive of Death. The solo bass asks the question: 'In the valley of the Shadow of Death shall I not fear Evil?' This is answered by a *Vivace* in the voice of the Furies—'Fly from the horror of Death!'—and the section ends in a terrible song without

words which dies away in a shuddering pianissimo. Then from
the violins comes the announcement of the second part which
may be called *The Mother's Lullaby*. All the joys and pains of
motherhood are suggested in the development of this motive,
blending finally with the motive of Death. The third part introduces a new theme, *The Prophet's Vision*, in which the motive of
birth and death is lifted into an apprehension of Eternity. The
fourth part suggests the stirring of divine discontent. After the
first glimpse of the heavenly vision, mankind can no longer rest
satisfied with the earthly joys which were enough for him before.
In the last section there enters a pilgrim consoler. The people are
perplexed as to what they should offer him, but he says: 'Bread
offered with love is never bitter'. The work culminates with the
answer of the choir to the previous question: 'Yea, though I pass
through the valley of the Shadow of Death I will fear no evil.'
An *Adagio molto sostenuto* changes into a final C major as in
Asrael.

Perhaps because Suk's imagination ran so easily riot in pure
musical tones, he did not need the stimulus of the written word,
for his vocal works are comparatively few. His two collections of
Choruses for Mixed Voices, Op. 19 and Op. 32, are, however,
much appreciated by Bohemian choral societies; and I distinctly
recall a picturesque arrangement of a Montenegrin cradle-song,
a tender and melancholy tenor solo which stands out against a
rather sombre and virile vocal accompaniment.

Joseph Suk died in his sixty-first year, on 29 May 1935, only
a few months after his old friend and colleague George Herold,
who was for thirty-four years the viola player of the Bohemian
Quartet. Of the Czech Quartet some pleasing reminiscences may
be quoted from a compatriot, Bohuslav Hostinský. 'The kernel
of the Quartet's repertoire', he writes, 'was Beethoven and
Dvořák, but they also played a good deal of Schubert, Schumann,
and Smetana. . . . I heard Maestro Suk only in the Quartet,
where he was second violin. He also played the piano as an accompaniment to songs. In 1903 I heard him play, with Hoffmann,
Bach's Concerto for Two Violins. They played like two brothers,
equal at their art. But Suk, though he had marvellous capacity
for solo music, never liked playing alone; and it was fortunate for
chamber music that he remained in the Quartet for forty years.'
Another characteristic tribute to Suk has been paid by Jaroslav
Mikan, a devoted listener to the Quartet for many years. He says:

'I always felt that Suk had all the necessary qualities for first violin. His technical power was well known to his teacher at the Conservatoire, Benevic, who regretted his sacrifice of a soloist's career for the greater pleasure of composing. But Suk showed himself a supreme artist in his treatment of the second violin. His instrument never sounded as second in the gamut of qualities, but as the equivalent of Hoffmann's; yet he never forgot that he was the second violin. The Quartet was as a democratic republic; but it was not for him to emphasize his own ideas—it was a joy to subordinate himself to the unity. This was the secret of their art as players. Moreover, Suk, as a composer himself, could often discern and interpret not only the written score, but the implicit meaning of the work he had to play.' But as his life-long friend Hoffmann says, 'This generous-hearted, gifted man, full of a deep knowledge of life and a great sense of humour, a devoted friend, will never be forgotten', and his creative works of exceptional sincerity and rare beauty will remain a precious possession to the Czechoslovak people.

Among the Czech composers of this period Rudolf Karel stands somewhat apart. He was born in 1880 in Plzen, where he attended the Gymnasium and later studied law at the Prague University, turning afterwards to music as a more congenial career. He then entered the Prague Conservatoire. The war overtook him in Russia where he was spending the summer of 1914. Here he was first interned as an Austrian subject, but later joined the Czechoslovak legionaries, with whom he managed eventually to return to his native country.

Though he is the last direct pupil of Dvořák, from whom he early acquired a thorough knowledge of musical construction and technique, he did not fit into any existing group representative of his tendency. The strong virile nature of his aspirations did not admit of feelings of sentiment. He is essentially an orchestral composer who builds his works on large lines and infuses into them an urgency of passion that concerns itself all the same very little with the sensuous side of his art. Endowed with a profusion of ideas and an elaborate technique he has been compared to Max Reger. His wealth of imagination does not admit of simple motives without recurrent changes; this power of constant variation is to him a source of creative joy. His themes, however, in their original form are of classic simplicity; his music epic rather than lyric. Thus his *adagios* are generally rather meditative,

P

perhaps even cold, rather than of fervent passion. At the same time his harmonic resources are uncommonly rich and interesting, giving a well-founded, logical directness to his art, in which there is nothing effeminate or impressionistic.

An early work, a Symphonic Poem, *The Ideals*, 1906–9, contains two Adagios and two Scherzos written without a break; a Symphony in E flat minor and a powerful Sonata for Violin and Piano are among other individual works of this period. In his Symphonic Poem *Daemon*, Op. 23, 1918–20, composed while a legionary in Russia, it is the conflict of the soul with the body rather than the desires and languor of the heart that attracts him.

Four Slavonic Dances, published by Simrock, show that this pupil of Dvořák knew how to free himself from his master's influence; they have not the lightness, the elasticity of the dances of either Smetana or Dvořák, nor the joy of folk-dances; rather are they pieces for musical epicures, elaborate in harmony and rhythm.

In 1909 he made one attempt at a lyric drama, *The Heart of Ilse*, and in his two male-voice choruses, *Zborov* (1922) and the Cantata *Resurrection*, composed for the tenth anniversary of the Independence of Czechoslovakia, he has adapted his technical problems to vocal uses. But in his latest works—a Cantata, *Ballad of Childhood*, Op. 29, to words by R. Medek, and the opera, *Godmother Death*, Op. 30, to a libretto by Mojžíš-Lom, which has been well received in many cities in Central Europe—it is interesting to observe that he has forsaken his complicated polyphonic style for much greater simplicity.

CHAPTER XIII

In Moravia, and in Slovakia, the ardour for the folk-art inspired a whole group of composers of whom Leoš Janáček is perhaps the most remarkable. The fresh, primitive bloom of the folk-music of these provinces had been utilized by many Czech composers—Dvořák, Novák, and others; while for men of less originality and resource it has been a treasury into which they could dip their fingers at will, in order to supply their own deficiencies of inventive power.

Leoš Janáček was born 3 June 1854, at Hukvaldy, a village in Northern Moravia, where his father, and his grandfather before him, had been village schoolmasters; which fact implies a certain degree of musical culture in the family. At nine Janáček became a chorister in the community church of the Austin Friars at Brno, where, while still in his teens, he was appointed choirmaster. Poverty was a drag upon his further career. By the time he had saved sufficient money to enter the Leipzig Conservatoire, he had passed the age to benefit from a state of pupilage. He went on to Vienna where he studied the piano with the idea of becoming a virtuoso. Fortunately circumstances were against this, and in 1882 he returned to Brno as conductor of the Philharmonic Society. He remained the greater part of his life in this town, where he founded the Organ School, started concerts for the working classes, made a systematic study of the folk-music and folk-speech, and composed, but without much hope of getting a hearing outside his immediate vicinity.

While the popular melody of Western Bohemia has passed under foreign influences and become more regular in its rhythms and more ordinary in its tonal system, the folk-music of Moravia and Slovakia retained its relations with the old Church modes, and showed structural peculiarities and a rhythmic pliancy not to be found in the Czech songs. And not only in music have the peasantry of these eastern provinces preserved their old-world characteristics; their ancient costumes, the sense of form and colour displayed in their embroideries, pottery, and peasant arts in general, vie with their songs and dances in giving expression to a strongly marked racial temperament. It will have been seen that many Czech composers introduced touches of the local colour of Slovakia into their works, while others made complex artistic settings of the folk-songs in order to supply the demands of such highly organized choirs as the Society of Moravian Teachers.

In 1904 Leoš Janáček made a more ambitious effort to interpret the soul of his race in music in his first opera *Její Pastorkýna* ('Her Foster-daughter'). This work was immediately given in Brno, but, though destined eventually to travel far afield under the more familiar title *Jenufa*, did not receive its first performance in Prague at the Národní Divadlo till 26 May 1916. Although produced then under war-time conditions and at a moment of great political tension, it became instantly the topic of the hour, and secured Janáček's position as the much-discussed and most prominent composer in Czechoslovakia.

The opera is based on a realistic tale of peasant life in Moravia by Gabriella Preissova, which is saved from being sordid by the element of an all-forgiving, generous love, exemplified in the hero Laca. Two young men love Jenufa, who lives with her stepmother, the caretaker of the village church. Jenufa is infatuated with Steva, a handsome ne'er-do-well. When the stepmother finds that Steva has ruined Jenufa's life, she implores him to marry her. He refuses, saying that he is engaged to another. The old woman, maddened by the idea of family disgrace, steals the unwanted baby and drowns it in the mill-stream. After a long and hard frost, the thawing of the stream reveals the crime, and an angry crowd of villagers attack the wretched Jenufa, while Laca, who loves her devotedly, defends her and keeps them at bay. At last the stepmother confesses her guilt. Jenufa is broken-hearted at her child's fate and the sorrow she has brought upon the faithful Laca, but her heart is infinitely good. 'God comfort you', she says to the criminal, who, forgiven, follows the Mayor to judgement. She then bids Laca leave her to face her tragedy alone; but he soon shows her that his only happiness lies in the sharing of her burden. So in an atmosphere of pity and reconciliation—as mellow as that which pervades the last act of a late Shakespearean drama—this remarkable opera comes to an end.

The music of *Její Pastorkýna*, though strongly tinctured with the folk-spirit, is in substance a very individual creation. The form of the opera is modern in the sense that it presents no set numbers, duets, trios, &c. It has an affinity with the realistic idiom of Moussorgsky's operas, in that the composer relies for his dramatic element upon the 'melody of the spoken word'.

But the more efficient musicianship of Janáček has produced in *Jeji Pastorkýna* a far less uneven work than the Russian composer's *Marriage*, for example. When produced in Vienna the work was compared, not inaptly, with Charpentier's *Louise*. The orchestration, generally speaking, has a colour and tang of its own. Occasionally there are effects which consciously aim at the imitation of local instruments used by the peasants—such as the *dudy*, a small bagpipe, the *fujara* or pastoral flute, or the cymbal. Each Act is preceded by a short orchestral introduction which prepares us for the special dramatic aspects of life to follow, and leaves us in the right frame of expectancy. In the opening pages, the clear dry tones of the xylophone give out a persistent figure against the pizzicato notes in the basses, suggesting the ceaseless, relentless click-clack of the mill-wheel, which turns stolidly on, through situations of extreme tension.

As Brno before 1914 was particularly influenced in musical matters by its German element it was not difficult for Janáček, a Moravian who made no propaganda for his compositions, to remain in obscurity. And even in Czech circles it was not until the production of *Her Foster-daughter* in Prague that public interest was awakened in this new genius in their midst. It was received with mingled feelings by the critics, for it broke down the long-cherished Smetana tradition—and other operatic traditions also. Its novelty, convincing sincerity, and human appeal carried it far afield. It is universally intelligible, since the manifestations of the broad emotions, love, hate, and merriment are much the same in all races.

When in 1916 *Jeji Pastorkýna* astonished and finally conquered the musical world of Czechoslovakia, Janáček had already finished the first part of *The Excursions of Mr. Brouček*. It was probably in the flush of his first success that he decided to set the second half of Svatopluk Čech's fantastic satire, and early in 1918 the whole work was completed and presented to the directorate of the National Theatre. The opera was dedicated to President Thomas Masaryk. This time there was no hesitation on the part of the directors of the National Opera, and *Brouček* was produced in the Bohemian capital on 23 April 1920. The conductor, Karel Kovařovic, was then incapacitated by illness, and the work was produced by Otakar Ostrčil.

In Mr. Brouček, proprietor, Čech conceived the portrait of an average Philistine of pre-war days; a superficial patriot, a materialistic opportunist, fond of his beer and his sausages; a character whom Janáček more than once compares with Goncharov's Oblomov. We first meet Mr. Brouček outside the ancient inn, called the Vikarka, in the precincts of the Hradčany, or Castle, of Prague. The orchestral Introduction is built on the theme of the old Inn; the slightly atmospheric and capricious motive of the Moon, and a calm broad *cantilena* depicting the earth lying in bright moonlight. These in their turn engender other well-defined themes; for in this opera Janáček not only weaves a tissue of short motives of melodic speech, but makes a more definite use of developed and extended motives, to recall certain places and incidents from time to time: 'leading motives' in fact, which stand out in relief upon this fabric of more thread-like, and shifting, ejaculatory themelets.

The curtain rises on the Inn, a favourite resort of the artists of the town, and we hear fragments of their songs through the open window. Brouček appears 'in a rosy mood'—full of beer and rather irritable. One of his pet theories is that the moon is inhabited, and that an innkeeper would soon be free of his daily worries if he could get there. Presently we see him staggering up the steps of the castle, where he falls into a doze. The potboy from the inn calls after him, 'Mr. Brouček, you've forgotten your sausages'—but already he has passed into a kind of trance, and the music indicates his transmigration to a new atmosphere. In the land of the Moon he meets again in a different guise all the neighbours he has known below. The themes used on earth reappear with skilful modifications, and the white, luminous atmosphere of the Moon is well suggested by the music.

While in Janáček's *Pastorkýna* the special melodic curves of speech which he uses are those of love, anguish, and tender reconciliation, in *The Excursion to the Moon* the curves most insisted upon are those of irony and sarcasm. It would be impossible to follow in detail all the intricate musical psychology of this part of Mr. Brouček's Excursions. There is a wide range of humour, from biting satire to broad farce. Some of it we can hardly appreciate without a very intimate knowledge of Czech history, literature, and social life. But any one who procures a pianoforte score of *Vylety Pané Broučekovy* (published by the Universal Edition, Vienna) will certainly get a good deal of fun for his money.

The second part of *The Excursions of Mr. Brouček*—his *Excur-*

sion to the Fifteenth Century—although it is linked psychologically, and here and there musically, with *The Excursion to the Moon*, is very different in feeling from the almost extravaganza nonsense of the first picture of this diptych. The light, if mordant, satire of the Moonland adventure becomes something altogether more weighty and logical from the first bars of the orchestral Prelude with its rather tempestuous evocation of a troublous past. The curtain rises upon the underground treasure-house of King Wenceslaus IV. Mr. Brouček forces his way into it, boasting of his knowledge of the secret passage leading thereto, and at the same moment steps into the fifteenth century. All the former characters again appear, changed for the second time, and take part in an historical scene, leading to an heroic climax—the victory of Žižka. Brouček protests that Sigmund and his Catholics, or Žižka and his Hussite warriors, are all the same to him, and when the news comes that Prague is attacked, he slinks away and avoids all active service. Afterwards, however, he boasts of his prowess in the deliverance of Prague, but his pretensions are quickly found out, and he is sentenced to be burnt at the stake. In vain he protests that he belongs to another century. With a wild crescendo of the 'traitor theme' in the music, he is driven to meet his doom. Here, as in the Moon, the translation from the dream world back to reality is contrived with amazing musical skill.

After hearing *Její Pastorkýna*, it seemed that it was impossible to go further in opera in the direction of organic unity and emotional concentration. But in *Kat'a Kabanova* Janáček has performed a miracle of dramatic and musical condensation. This is partly because the sombre, tragic lights in which the plot is enveloped are focussed almost entirely on the central figure of the work. The story of *Kat'a Kabanova*, familiar to all students of Russian literature who have read Ostrovsky's drama *Burya* ('The Storm'), is a tragedy of everyday life, played out amid the spacious scenery of the Volga.

In the narrow spiritual enclosure of her mother-in-law's house, Kate Kabanov dwells body and soul a prisoner; while, outside, the shimmering, shoreless waters of the Volga speak of unlimited freedom. The voice of the river, in eternal movement, deep, fateful, heedless of the petty human drama enacting on its banks, yet promising a refuge at the last, pervades the whole opera.

The period of the tale is the 'sixties of the last century, when in provincial Russian families there were many spiritual descendants of Ivan the Terrible, who 'knew how to rule'. Savjol Dikoj, a merchant, and Martha Kabanova, another merchant's widow, have each a particular victim of their tyranny. Dikoj's nephew Boris, a cultured aristocrat, is compelled to live with his low-bred uncle and endure his coarse abuse. He has fallen in love with Kat'a, who is still fond of her husband, and might have lived happily with him but for the poison of his mother's tongue. Her sole confidant is a merry girl named Vavara, who has a secret love-intrigue with Kudrjash, a young professor of chemistry. A crisis is reached when Widow Kabanov sends her son Tichon to Moscow on business, and Kat'a feels she cannot endure being left alone with the cruel old woman. She has a fearful presentiment of ill, and soon temptation comes to her through Vavara, who gives her the key of the garden where Boris is eagerly seeking to meet her by night. Yet she deceives her own heart when she takes up the challenge: What harm in a few words with a man as unhappy as herself?

The double love-scene—in the garden of the Kabanov house— is one of the least conventional and most convincing ever seen in opera. Two love-interests are carried on alternately offering the strongest possible psychological contrast. The love of Varvara and Kudrjash is full-blooded, gay, impermanent, conscienceless. In the green dusk of the evening, the young professor waits at the foot of the stone steps leading to the house. To pass the time away till Varvara comes he sings a Russian song, pointedly rhythmic, to a thrumming balalaika accompaniment. Boris comes in and speaks of his passion for Kat'a. In spite of his light-hearted philosophy of life and love, Kudrjash is alarmed for the young wife and warns Boris. Then Varvara's voice is heard in the distance. She and Kudrjash answer each other in a delightful duet in the Russian folk-style, and then trip off gaily to the riverside.

The poignant, yearning, apprehensive love-scene of Kat'a and Boris then follows. With her sensitive conscience she realizes her feelings as sinful. But passion, fatal and strong as the flow of the Volga, breaks down her resistance. She gives herself with complete abandonment, but without joy.

Act III, played on a terrace by the Volga, introduces a terrific thunderstorm which affects the destinies of the chief protagonists, each responding according to individual temperament. Kat'a is utterly unnerved by the old people's superstitious talk of the judgement of God upon sinners, and when her husband returns

she falls on her knees confessing her guilt aloud, and sinks uncon-
scious into his arms. Tichon is moved to pity rather than anger,
but Kat'a, recovering consciousness, breaks away from him and
rushes out into the night. When Tichon and the serving-maid go
out with lanterns to seek for her, Vavara and Kudrjash flit across
the stage. The storm means nothing to them; the girl only asks
how she shall live when she can no longer endure the old widow
who gives her a home. Kudrjash answers gaily, 'Why, come with
me, of course!' And with no pangs of conscience they make off
to 'Mother Moscow'.

Kat'a returns alone, and a wordless chorus of music is heard,
distant and unearthly. It is the voice of the Volga, so strangely
blended with her fate. Boris joins her for one poignant moment,
and the same voice accompanies their last agonies of farewell.
When he is gone she falls—or leaps—into the river. When Dikoj
at last recovers her body, Tichon flings himself upon it, and as the
curtain falls the wordless chorus swells to a majestic volume.
The Volga rolls on, unmoved, triumphant.

One dwells long—too long perhaps—upon the literary side of
Kat'a Kabanova, but Janáček's music is so integral a part of his
libretto that it is almost impossible to separate them for analytical
purposes. Here one can only say that the music is one with the
text, so perfectly does it fit the words.

Like *Jeji Pastorkýna* the opera opens with a Prelude, which
again is not so much a thematic exposition as preparation of the
mind and emotions for what is to follow. Early in this introduction there is a startling fateful drum-figure heard against the
muted trombones which sounds like a rhythm of destiny; and the
wood-wind give out melancholy wailing phrases between the two
repetitions of this figure; but we soon go on to a rushing *Allegro*
in which, however, the drum figure is not lost sight of. The
orchestral treatment is very original: the oboe and clarinet are
peculiarly well suited to express the kind of speaking, melodic
fragments which make up Janáček's musical fabric. He uses also
the *viola d'amore* with its 'sweet seraphic tones', as Berlioz
describes them. Another orchestral interlude precedes the love-
scene; its changes of measure are characteristically swift and
subtle, 9-8, 6-16 alternate; leading on to 6-8 in contrast with 2-4
in Kudrjash's serenade-like song, a forerunner of that unconven-
tional love-scene, in which Kudrjash and Varvara in light rhythmic music, in the Russian folk-style, express their careless philo-

sophy of life. This alternates with the passionate and poignant music of the love-duet between Kat'a and Boris.

As in *Její Pastorkýna* Janáček has caught the melodic accent of the Slovak tongue, so in *Kat'a Kabanova* he reproduces with extraordinary fidelity the lilt and inflections of the Russian speech. There are moments when he succeeds in evoking with magic realism the echoes of Russian life and the rhythm of the Russian language. But the real secret of this opera's greatness lies in its concentrated emotional power. Our eyes and ears are rivetted from first to last upon the suffering figure of Kat'a. If in *Její Pastorkýna* Janáček has found the motives and melodic curves of virile passion, pardon, unselfish love, egotistical respectability, and maternal tenderness, and given us an opera with much of the thrill and glow of Elizabethan tragedy, in *Kat'a Kabanova* he moulds the melodic curves of aspiration and spiritual exaltation, of fatal foreboding, of cruelty, dignity, and madness into a work the truthfulness of which is burnt into us as we listen. *Kat'a Kabanova* is as strong, as irreversible, as absolute in effect as an antique tragedy.

The three masterpieces which I have described, each so entirely different from the other, suggest three differently coloured and cut gems in one setting; *Její Pastorkýna*, that drama of peasant love and crime and false respectability, glows with passionate colour, deep, incarnadine as the heart of a fine Bohemian garnet; *The Excursions of Mr. Brouček*, by no means a transparent jewel, a little clouded and motley, may be compared to an opal in its harlequin display of many-tinted humour; *Kat'a Kabanova* is a dark, tragic, light-absorbing amethyst.

Janáček never repeats himself in his operatic works; yet it is not given to many composers to mix new colours on their orchestral palette after sixty, and to bring this feature of their art to its highest development at the age of seventy. But in *Lyška Bystrouška* ('The Cunning Little Vixen'), produced at the Národní Divadlo, Prague, on 18 May 1925, the power and freshness of Janáček's music has an added quality for which one was hardly prepared: the quality of a new style.

In the choice of an 'animal' subject Janáček has not been guided by the same motives which produced the *Insect Play* by the brothers Čapek, or Rostand's *Chanteclair*. Satire or caricature are not his aim. His animals are animals, his human beings remain human beings; each playing distinct parts. The opera is

based on a tale by the Moravian poet Tešnohlidek, of a vixen cub
caught by the forest ranger and given as a pet to two teasing
children. The clever little animal escapes, is wooed and married
by Goldbeck, Prince of Foxes, and with him brings up a happy
family of children. Parallel with their story runs a much slighter
tale of human characters. A somewhat mythical heroine (who
never appears on the stage) plays havoc with the hearts of three
men—the Ranger, the Parson, and the Schoolmaster. Perhaps
she is meant to represent the waywardness of 'the eternal feminine', since none of the three men wins her at the last. She
chooses instead a poaching and tippling lout who, with a random
shot, kills the little fox and brings the glad and free life of her
family to an end. In spite of flashes of pathos, Janáček sees the
animal world without any mawkish sentimentality, but rather
with the gentle humour of a St. Francis; and we shall look in vain
for a moral in the last act.

The music supplements and carries out the slight literary web,
filling in its blank spaces and lighting up its obscurities. The
myriad short themes, born of a close observation of melodic
speech and of nature's voices, are no longer scattered over the
music without apparent design, as in Janáček's earlier works, but
welded into a completely cohesive, expressive language. His use
of the whole tone scale is, for him, something new. The orchestration is brilliant and sure, and the colour effects infinitely varied.
The music answers in rhythm and sonority all the emotional
phrases in the opera. It is often mirthful, as in the amusing ballet
of hens, pathetic when it follows the unhappy love-affairs of mortals; full of mystery and foreboding in depicting the life of the
forest, when a specially constructed instrument, the ocarina, adds
to the strange unearthly quality of the woodland voices. In spite
of difficulties of transplantation, *The Cunning Little Vixen* may
well become a popular opera abroad.

All who were intimate with Janáček's music awaited his next
operatic work in the sure expectancy of something new and
unique. *The Makropulos Affair* had already made a thrilling
impression as a play before Janáček was drawn to it as material
for an opera. It was not, however, its sensationalism which
proved so immediately provocative to the composer. On the contrary, having obtained a free hand from the author, Janáček has
relieved the play of much of its grotesque and weird element; but
it was the seething, dramatic vitality of Čapek's play, welling up

like some of the hot, life-giving springs of Czechoslovakia, that appealed to the musician. Janáček has always tended towards the creation of a 'conversational' opera, as the vindication of his life-long theory of speech-melody. No wonder that he responded at once to the vibrations of life oscillating in this rapidly moving drama, conveyed in terse and vigorous dialogue.

The plot of *The Makropulos Affair* turns upon the elixir of life, and deals with the famous lawsuit of *Gregor* v. *Prus*, which has occupied the lawyers for generations, and the search for a lost will. The present client, whose fate depends on the will being found, is the hot-headed young spendthrift Gregor. A fascinating opera-singer, Emilia Marty, intervenes on his behalf, and surprises every one with her detailed knowledge of the past. Gregor falls violently in love with her; Prus pays dearly for a long-past liaison with her by a packet of letters found in his house; while the sentimental dotard Hauk claims her as the selfsame Spanish gipsy who once enslaved him in his youth. The mystery of her identity deepens, but her directions for finding the lost will prove perfectly correct.

In the first and second Acts Čapek's text is set verbatim, but the third Act has been condensed and modified by Janáček himself, who made it at once more dramatic and more human. Driven into a corner by Prus and the lawyers, Marty reveals the truth about the Makropulos affair. She is the daughter of Makropulos of Crete, Court Alchemist to the Emperor Rudolph II who, at his master's orders, prepared an elixir of life. But at the last moment the aged monarch shrank from the experiment and insisted on its being tried upon the alchemist's daughter Elina. Condemned to live three hundred years, she passes through a variety of experiences and under many names. As Ellen Macgregor she was the mistress of Joseph Prus; therefore, as she tells the disgusted Gregor, she is his great, great, great, great, grandmother. Externally she is still attractive, but she has outlived normal joys and ties; her soul has mummified in isolation. In the opera, the merciful hand of Janáček intervening, the woman 'weary of good and of evil, weary of earth and of heaven' is allowed the deliverance of death. 'I have felt the touch of death, it was not dreadful,' she sings at the end of the opera. Dying, she offers the document containing the secret of Makropulos to the young singer Christina as a compensation for the defection and suicide of her lover, Johnnie. 'Take it, child,' she says, 'be famous, and a greater artist than Emilia Marty.' Christina takes the paper, but only to burn it. As the last sparks die out Marty passes away.

Musically the opera does not reveal any fresh technical departure, except for a few instances of *parlando*, or, more accurately, the use of reciting-notes, which occur in some of the long and rather dry monologues of the lawyers, especially in Act I, and are an innovation in Janáček's operas. There are no extended dissertations, and *arioso* is too slow a method of procedure to suit the composer's precipitate eloquence. The musical language is the same speech-melody used in *Jenufa*, developed with greater logical freedom and conviction in *The Cunning Little Vixen*, and rising in *The Makropulos Affair* to the highest level yet attained in any of the composer's works. In the intricate network of themelets suggested by the words, each conveys its contribution to the emotional core of the matter as surely as the capillaries carry their minute contributions of blood to the physical heart. Janáček has the most complete and logical control of his melodic theory. It is the fashion to speak of him as a 'primitive'. But can we correctly so describe a man who has weighed the accumulated traditions of his art, and consciously simplified them for his own uses? He is less primitive than eliminative. The orchestration is original and masterly, each instrument has its own place and individuality; there are few moments in which he permits an outburst from the full orchestra. From this point of view the opening prelude is exceedingly interesting. The most striking moments in the work occur at the close of Act I (does the telephone here make its first appearance in opera?); the humorous dialogue between the charwoman and scene-shifter in Act II; and almost the whole of Act III. The dramatic intensity of the close is electrifying. A majestic motive is heard when Marty, touched by the hand of death, reappears on the scene like an apparition. And now occurs the only ensemble in the work, breaking first from the awe-stricken characters on the stage, and afterwards from a male-voice choir concealed in the orchestra, which reiterates the valedictory words of the dying woman. But the intense emotional pressure is not unduly prolonged; a few pages suffice for this impressive termination. The heroine dies, invoking some mysterious divinity— 'Pater hemon!' The abnormal composite personality of Emilia Marty, Ellen Macgregor, Elina Makropulos holds us spellbound to the end.

The Makropulos Affair was produced at the National Theatre,

Brno, during the last weeks of 1926, and met with an immediate success. The enthusiastic applause with which it was then received proved no mere local tribute to the veteran composer in his own city, for the work was soon to be heard in other cities throughout the Continent.

Generally speaking, Janáček was reserved on the subject of the genesis of his works, and we may receive with caution a statement made during an unusually gossipy interview, published in the *Lidove Noviny*, in which he said that while on a visit to the baths of Luhačovice the rainy weather recalled to his mind another downpour when, a few weeks previously, a tablet was fixed upon the house where he was born at Hukvaldy. Among those who took part in the ceremony, conducted under umbrellas, was Leopold Precan, Archbishop of Olomouc. Touched by this act of courtesy, Janáček conceived the idea of composing a Festival Mass and dedicating it to the prelate. Possibly a much deeper reason lay at the back of the composer's mind. The fundamental idea of his Mass, which dates from 1926–7, was as much patriotic as pious: something of the impulse which caused Brahms to write his *German Requiem*. The actual title of the work—a *Glagolitic Mass*—supports this view. But since the word *Glagolitic* conveys little to the general public, we may justifiably accept the title *Festival Mass*.

The origin of the Glagolitic alphabet may be told in a few words. When 'the twin stars of the East', SS. Cyril and Methodius, citizens of Solum, set forth on their mission to the Western Slavs (A.D. 862), they spoke the Slavonic of the Macedonians. St. Cyril had already translated most of the Bible into this tongue, having invented for the purpose a new alphabet known as the Cyrillic. But, on arrival in Moravia, they found this unsuitable for the needs of the Western Slavs and evolved a second alphabet, the Glagolitic, the credit of the invention being generally attributed to Methodius. While the Cyrillic became the ecclesiastical language of the Russians and Eastern Slavs, the Glagolitic spread westwards to Croatia and Dalmatia. The German ecclesiastic regarded it with suspicion, but the contemporary Pope, Adrian II, upheld its use on the grounds that 'all languages should praise God'. The *Glagolitic Mass* existed for some time side by side with the Latin liturgy; but Bohemia, as a Roman Catholic country, gradually accepted the Roman rite and after its revival, through the influence of Charles IV in 1347, the Slavonic liturgy

survived in only one monastery and became extinct in Bohemia
after the fifteenth century.

From time to time, however, the remembrance of the Slavonic
Mass and the desire for its revival return on a tide of patriotic
feeling, and for Janáček, a Moravian and a patriot, this ancient
form had a deeply national significance. Another reason may also
have influenced him; on the vocal score of the Mass is a picture
of St. Wenceslaus, the patron saint of Bohemia, whose millen-
nium was celebrated in Czechoslovakia in 1929. Possibly Janáček
had the coming Festival in mind when he wrote this work, for it
was on the *Glagolitic Mass* that Prince Wenceslaus was brought
up in youth.

Apart from patriotic feeling, the varied emotional content of
the Mass, dramatic and lyrical, must have offered a strong attraction to the composer. The element which struck him most forcibly was that of ecstatic joy. Had he attached a motto to his
score, it must have been some jubilant quotations from the Psalms
of David, such as: 'God is gone up with a shout', or 'Let him
praise His Name in the dance'. His Mass is something quite
dissociated from the mystical emotion induced by the 'dim religious light' of church interiors. It is intended to be joyful and
popular. Here, as Ludvik Kundera says in his analysis of the
work, 'the people praise their Redeemer in cheerful tunes and
folk-musicians accompany them with rich instrumentation'. It
cannot be compared with any other Mass; its gaiety is quite
a different thing from Haydn's cheerfulness—something more
approaching to animal spirits; its pathos is not the pathos of
Beethoven; there is none of Verdi's tone-painting; it is absolute
music; and although the national impulse shows in both works,
it does not pair with Kodaly's *Psalmus Hungaricus*, but contrasts
with it; nor has it anything of the asceticism of the Eastern
Church.

The thematic material with which Janáček works is purely his
own and might have been drawn from one of his later operas; he
generally makes use of two themes—one choral and one instrumental. From these he derives a few smaller figures employed
chiefly in the orchestral tissue of the music. When a theme has
served his purpose he does not attempt to put fresh life into it by
complicated developments, but lays it aside for some new invention. The construction of the Mass is on large and simple lines,
but shows one or two special features, such as the interpolation

of several brilliant organ solos and the linking of the Sanctus and Benedictus into one number. There are two instrumental intro-ductions to the Mass. This peculiarity is the outcome of Bohemian custom. In bygone years, and in country churches, the Mass was often preceded on festal days by an *intrada* which bore little or no musical relation to the Mass itself. It was simply a somewhat showy and dignified accompaniment to the entry of the officiating clergy. Janáček in his popular Mass has preserved this usage. The *Intrada* has a secular character and might have been designed as a movement of the composer's 'Military' Sin-fonietta.

Janáček needs the inspiration of the spoken word in order that his music may rise to its highest expression, for he is realistic and dramatic by temperament. He carries his vocal style, with its close-knit ejaculatory figuration, into his instrumental music. What he has to say is said tersely, swiftly, and directly, with no time lost upon extended developments. This is strongly marked in the Sinfonietta for Orchestra (1925), a work in five movements, each of which is scored for a different combination of instruments.

In an earlier orchestral work, the Rhapsody *Taras Bulba*, the literary idea of which is taken from Gogol's vigorous tale of Cossack life, Janáček sought inspiration in Russian literature, for which he had a great affection. The work was composed in 1915–16, during the War of 1914–18, and is dedicated to 'our Czecho-slovak troops'. Janáček himself explains his choice of subject as follows: 'I composed this Rhapsody not because Taras Bulba slew his own son for his treachery against his nation, but because, to use the words of the old Ataman, Taras, I feel that "nowhere on earth are there fires or torments capable of destroying the strength of the Russian people".' The work was first heard in Prague in 1924, under the conductorship of Vaclav Talich, and received its first performance in England at a Czechoslovak Con-cert at Queen's Hall, under the direction of Sir Henry Wood, in 1928.

Another work of Russian origin is the String Quartet, dedicated to the Czech (Bohemian) Quartet and inspired by Tolstoi's novel, *The Kreutzer Sonata*. It is full of sudden emotional changes, in which its short eloquent themes speak of furtive perturbation, of longing, of cruelty. The work does not follow the strict sonata form, though its free but perfectly logical design is clearly re-vealed. Remembering the atmosphere of sombre force and baneful passion which surrounds the personality of this Russian Othello, Pozdynchev, the music demands a strong and fervid interpretation.

Nature and early memories of the composer's own life, spent out of doors in the beautiful surroundings of his native village in Moravia, are characteristics of many of his later instrumental works. The freshness of thought, the suggestions of outdoor life, the happiness rarely overshadowed by a pensive memory, which we find in the Sextet for Wind Instruments entitled *Mlada* ('Youth'), may recall Dvořák; but the rhythmic subtlety, the original savour of the harmony, the unexpected developments of its thematic material, and the colour contrasts derived from his six instruments—these are peculiar to Janáček's genius. It was one of the composer's chamber works to be heard in England on the occasion of his visit to this country in 1926, when its interpretation by the London Wind Quintet delighted Janáček. Again, the Concertino for Piano, accompanied by Two Violins, Viola, Clarinet, Bassoon, and Horn, might well bear the sub-title 'Amid Nature'. 'It is as though mounting some steep, laborious path', writes Dr. J. Vogel, 'we suddenly heard the voices of the forest; as though we suddenly beheld, stark and unconcealed, the life of the wild creatures within it; as though suddenly we looked across a limitless expanse of country, steeped in hot sunshine.' Nor is the work less original in the way in which every problem of instrumentation is perfectly solved.

Of one of his last compositions—Six Lachian Dances for Orchestra—he warned me not long before his death: 'When you write about my Lachian Dances, do not describe them as "Wallachian"'; they have nothing to do with that province which once formed part of Rumania. They come from my own district in Moravia.' The score of the pianoforte arrangement contains a descriptive note by the composer himself which clearly indicates the source of his inspiration. It is written in his characteristically vivid and intimate style, and gives a clear picture of this beautiful district.

Although the *Glagolitic Mass* was finished first, and might have been the culmination of the composer's work, Janáček's last opera, *The House of the Dead,* is essentially a valedictory work and, like many testaments made at the eleventh hour, shows a few signs of haste and caducity. Not that it is a weak composition; but the hectic expansion of some of Janáček's tendencies makes us realize

Q

that even in the most vigorous natures old age will not be denied. It seems, however, neither good sense nor justice to attribute its occasional aberrations to the pricking of Janáček's moral conscience. Critics who heard the first performances of *The House of the Dead* wrote of it as reflecting the spiritual havoc following an intempestive passion which disturbed the last months of the musician's life. No one who knew Janáček towards the end of his career could fail to see that his belated successes, coupled with a feverish desire to follow them up, drove him to such excess of labour as strained his mental and physical powers to the utmost. Possibly he lost his head more completely than his heart, but he was too great a philosopher and too much occupied with human nature in its totality, to use his music as a medium of personal 'penitence and expiation'.

Janáček turned again to Russian literature for the libretto of *The House of the Dead*, composed in 1927 and first produced in Brno in December 1930, and in the following year in Prague. He liked difficult subjects, and it is easy to imagine him carried away by Dostoievsky's novel, less because of what Maurice Baring calls 'its radiant moral beauty' than because it offered many problems to be overcome.

In later years Janáček arranged his opera libretti in his own peculiarly self-willed fashion, tearing out of the original work just the pages that suited his requirements. But in *The House of the Dead* he does not treat the author so cavalierly as appears at first glance. 'In general, although his perspectives are different,' says F. Pala, 'he aimed at the same as Dostoievsky; that is, not an image, but at the dramatic expression of a specific milieu. He does this mainly by selecting typical figures which he models from the total material of the novel, while for the sake of scenic clarity he intensifies them by accumulating striking qualities and incidents around a few actual types.'

Opera, however, is surely a misnomer when applied to this work, which consists rather of a series of tableaux during which the convicts discuss their wretched existences.

The first Act deals with the arrival of convicts at the Siberian prison, the initiation into the atmosphere of crime and callous cruelty. In the second Act there are elements of yearning tenderness and human affection. A little light, a ray of sallow sunshine amid the storm, breaks through in the scene wherein the prisoners are allowed to get up a play at Christmas. The third Act—the most heart-rending of all—takes place in the hospital. Even the pardon and departure of Alexander Petrovich bring a shadowy gleam of consolation, since he has to tear himself away from his beloved friend, Aley. This Tartar lad, of whom Dostoievsky says 'he was always so delicate, so considerate, so full of the wisdom of the heart,' brings the nearest approach to feminine interest in the work.

The musical language in *The House of the Dead* is made to say and do terrible things; the orchestral texture is like a strange piece of tissue, dark on the one side and garish on the other, woven in violent contrast. This is the result of the composer's method of using his orchestra in two main groups, one containing all the basses and grave tonal instruments, pitted against the shrill and acid tones of the higher-pitched voices. In the Overture, or Prologue, Janáček has incorporated part of the material intended for a violin concerto which he had in mind during his visit to London in 1926.

Dostoievsky sets out to describe people who live in a world of slander, calumny, bickering—in a word, in hell. Janáček, who has made pity a central theme in every one of his operas, has here searched the human heart even more deeply than the author of *Despised and Rejected*. 'In every creature there is a spark of God' is written upon his score. This is his answer to the tragedy of life. Are we to believe he was thinking only of his own soul? Or even of the Russia he knew and loved in her continuous suffering and oppression? Those who knew Janáček will prefer to accept the widest possible application of the motto he inscribed upon his last creative effort.

Leoš Janáček remained all his life at Brno, where he was for many years Professor of Composition at the State Conservatoire, and in 1925 the Masaryk University of that city conferred upon him the honorary degree of Doctor of Philosophy, an honour which he greatly valued. He died on 12 August 1928, at the age of seventy-four, while on a summer holiday at his native village of Hukvaldy, in northern Bohemia, but was buried with civic honours in Brno.

Q*

CHAPTER XIV

IT is no easy task for an outsider, however sympathetic, to lead others through the ramifications of a national music, the voice of a nation which was something of a *terra incognita* to the world at large, and to state, if not with sure at least with unbiased judgement, what are the most significant features of its musical life. One embarrassment which inevitably besets the writer is the fact that during the early years of the First Republic, the art itself was in a condition of ferment and teeming over-production, and offered no static instant in which to secure an accurate snapshot, much less a reasoned survey of its revolving activities.

For some time before the War of 1914–18, every spiritual force in Bohemia—and particularly music—was yoked to the service of one supreme end: the attainment of political freedom. The achievement of political independence by the Czechoslovaks in 1918 stimulated the activities of a young generation of composers, the final importance and durability of whose works it has been as yet impossible fully to appreciate. Increased post-war musical activities both at home and abroad, the hitherto unknown possibility of material assistance offered by the liberated state, the extension of the work of the Prague Conservatoire, the foundation of a new Conservatoire in Brno, and enlarged musical centres throughout the country—all had a strong influence and stimulated the growth of modern Czech music. The clear, beaconing ideal of independence having been reached, a reaction was inevitable; some of the younger generation found themselves temporarily, if not in darkness, in a confusion of lights and shadows. Energies had to be detached from one single-minded effort and find their outlet in many directions. Men in all walks of life told me that they suffered because the bow-strings of the spirit were momentarily relaxed. This was particularly likely to apply to music, always so closely bound up with the aspirations of the race.

Smetana had endowed Czech music with the earnestness of a religious faith and the prestige of a patriotic mission. It became incumbent upon his immediate successors to keep the nation, its hopes and sufferings, continually in view. Its sorrowful image hung before the composer's eyes, like the crucifix which adorns the monk's cell, for a perpetual reminder of the faith that was in him. Even Dvořák, then less consciously absorbed in a vatical errand, flooded much of his music with a fervent patriotism. Not long had Bohemian music acquired, simultaneously with political freedom, the right to complete liberty of expression.

Impressionism, which found its way into Bohemia through the agency of Debussy, was a distinct feature of the pre-1914 music. It caught Vítězlav Novák in its fascinating but brittle web. In his later works it is evident that the recoil from it was complete. As with the master so also with the pupils. Impressionism is not the pabulum on which to feed the sons of a new and lusty republic. The slight influence of Richard Strauss's flamboyant realism vanished after 1914. Russian music, that had once held a captive here and there, had no longer the same significance for the composers of the years of the First Republic. A more radical change was a loss of faith in folk-lore as a basis for musical creation; nor is this to be regretted since it had been superseded by a more comprehensive conception of the national idea. What then are the controlling forces during these years? The principal events which modified the aesthetic outlook were: the War, which swept away so many small and affected tendencies, checked the excessive consideration of merely technical questions and left the slate clean, so to speak, for the working out of fresh ideas and problems; and secondly the constitution of the Czechoslovak Republic, which lifted a weight of sorrow and apprehension from the people and put the desire for a new song into their mouth.

The leading personal influences were centred in a few men, teachers in the higher as well as the practical sense of the word, to whom, individually and collectively, most of the Czech composers of this period owe some part of their professional training. These are: Vítězlav Novák, Josef B. Foerster, Josef Suk, and Leoš Janáček.

Because Novák himself is an eclectic who has experienced a variety of influences—classical-romanticism (Schumann, Brahms, Dvořák), the fascination of the Moravian-Slovak folk-music, a pantheistic joy in Nature, and an intensely individual and erotic phase; because he has handled every musical form and has passed from lyrical symphonic music by way of dramatic cantata to opera; because he has looked with clear and tolerant vision on all kinds of tendencies and paradoxes, and has never sought to marshal his pupils in a strict school, but left them liberty of conscience in their development; therefore, in the group with which I deal first, we shall find the widest dissimilarity of aims and tastes, and only a few unifying qualities by which we may identify its members. A serious view of their art, a lively interest in all contemporary manifestations of it, together with a sound selective principle and a strong distaste for all forms of bravado and charlatanism, are the hall-marks of his pupils. Some of them have passed under other influences while they developed.

In spite of his prolific creative output, much of Novák's early life had been spent in teaching; his high standard and his clear and liberal views on musical questions counted for much in the development of such gifted younger composers as Vycpálek, Jaroslav Křička, Vomačka, Tomašek, Novotny, and many others.

Perhaps the most remarkable of this group is Ladislav Vycpálek, who, on account of his ethical outlook and uncompromising polyphonic style, stands out from the rest. He was born at Vrsovice (Moravia) in 1882, and after studying at the grammar school of his native town, entered the Prague University and took the degree of Doctor of Philosophy, working at the same time at music under Novák. In 1907 he was appointed Librarian in the University of Prague.

Vycpálek's first appearance as a composer was made at a concert of Novák's pupils in his twenty-eighth year; consequently his musical convictions were more or less formed and permanent from the beginning of his public career. From the first he endeavoured to penetrate the mystical texture of things. The influence of the older Czech composers, Smetana and Dvořák, is not strongly perceptible in his music; it is more likely that his deep researches into medieval music have left traces upon his development. His first opus, a set of four songs, *Ticha Usmireni* ('Calm Reconcilement') shows a thoughtful and individual tendency; a distinctive personality striving from the beginning to follow its own artistic dictates. Admitting that even in later compositions, such as the interesting song-cycle *Tuchy Vidiny* ('Visions'), Op. 5, we sometimes find traces of the school in which he studied—for here and in his Pianoforte Pieces, Op. 9, Novák's influence crops up occasionally—in the works that follow, not so numerous but covering a wide range of psychological experience, Vycpálek steadily builds up the central principles of his art.

The subtle subjectivity of his early songs underwent a sharp reaction during the War of 1914–18, when the struggles and sufferings of his own and other nations caused him to look outward and upward rather than within. The most notable of the compositions published between 1916 and 1922 are the settings of the Russian poet Valery Brussov's *V Boži Dlani* ('In God's Hand'), four songs, Op. 14; the choruses inspired by the stirring days through which his country had passed, *Naše Járo* ('Our Springtide'), Op. 15, and *Boj Nynejši* ('The Conflict of To-day'), Op. 15; the Five Moravian Ballads for Voice and Pianoforte, Op. 12, dedicated to Emil Burian; and the collection of Ten Moravian Folksongs, Op. 13, in which he gives a touching picture of the soldier's fate by means of a happy choice of texts culled from the folkpoetry and framed in very individual settings.

With time his music showed itself clearer and more virile, and his religious sentiment more definite. His mysticism, which seemed to be an inheritance from the days of the Bohemian Brethren, is, however, quite detached from militant Protestantism or credal conflicts of any kind, and reveals itself rather in a grave meditative attitude to life, a resigned acceptance of destiny, and a deep sympathy with his fellow men. At the moment when poets and composers were engaged in hiding the scars and losses of war under songs of hate or victory, and in obscuring the true meaning of death by pompous requiems, Vycpálek wrote the Cantata *Of the Last Things of Man*, Op. 16. It came as a protest against the grasping post-war spirit of nations great and small; 'thou hast too much and I too little'. The two old Moravian folk-songs selected as the text of the Cantata have the directness of primitive folk-poetry. The cadaverous imagery of the first indicates its probable survival from Gothic medievalism. The work falls into three sections, described by the composer as the Triumph of Materialism, the Triumph of Death, and the Triumph of Faith.[1]

It was in 1915 that the composer came upon the poems, but it was not until December 1920 that he set to work upon the task, without any pre-arranged programme: 'I must say', he wrote himself of the work, 'that it did not seem to chime with the hour. In the year which saw the birth of our state I was writing of death and the Four Last Things. And yet, when later I came to reflect upon it, I saw that the work was directly evoked by the times, and that I could not have written anything different. In that year all

[1] The work was first heard in England in 1928, at a Liverpool Philharmonic Society Concert, under the direction of Sir Henry J. Wood.

the seeds of war were still putting out strong growths: the greed of humanity for money, the inconsiderate impatience for the fulfilment of individual interests, all the brutal materialism born of war, still threatened to smother everything higher and less aggressive. The Cantata originated like a secret thing, but came forth as a glowing and poignant protest against materialism. It is meant to give a glimpse of death and its nothingness, and to emphasize only the spiritual side of man.' In many respects this work stands outside the main current, lyric and dramatic, of contemporary Czech music. Its originality, simplicity, and seriousness of purpose, and the interior piety which it reflects, seem to affiliate it to the fifteenth century and the spirit which inspired the Unity of the Bohemian Brethren. Only in its insistence on the ultimate equality of all humanity, and the futility of all values but those of the spirit, it is manifestly in keeping with the democratic ideals of the new social order of the Republic of Czechoslovakia.

The chief values in Vycpálek's music are purely spiritual, and his art eschews the sensuous and merely enjoyable qualities and makes no compromise with the popular taste. But though it is veined by streaks of austerity and asceticism, the substance of his music does not lack passion and vitality. It is, however, the passion of the mystic rather than of the materialist. This outlook upon his art has led him to seek an equivalent idiom for its expression, since it does not bend easily to the yoke of ready-made forms and fluent phrases. Vycpálek makes no compromise in his polyphonic methods. His diatonicism is austere in its logical procedure. The individual parts move independently, each on its own melodic line, and there is no shirking of harsh and archaic results. The texture of his music is frugal, his rhythms are even, and his music in general free from spasmodic emotional breaks and changes. He moves clearly and with measured steps to the attainment of his ends, and occasionally reaches lofty lyrical climaxes.

The breadth of Vycpálek's human and political sympathies brings him into touch with the national spirit, which he assimilates not with the superficial idea of spinning thematic material out of the folk-melodies, but because in the poetry of the people he finds the most varied aspects of the inner life: an intimate reflection of the order of things most precious to him—sincerity, homeliness, love, suffering, and the sole remedy for human suffering, faith.

In an appreciation of Vycpálek František Bartoš says: 'His art is deeply and typically Czech. He has much to say, and knows how to say it in an urgent and convincing manner. In him the younger generation found the values they were seeking. Is not the simple abstemiousness of his method one of those ideals for which the age was striving when it tried—and failed—to return to Bach? And is not his entire simplicity a clear protest against the lyrical prolixity of his predecessors?'

A sharp contrast to the stern philosophical Vycpálek is Jaroslav Křička, one of the most representative of the middle generation of Czech composers. He is a Moravian, born at Kelci in 1882. He studied for a time in Berlin and attracted the attention of Humperdinck, who offered to take him on in a subordinate capacity in his Master-School; but Křička, who had in the meantime visited Russia and felt the attraction of Slav to Slav, accepted a post as teacher of composition in the music school at Yekaterino-slav, where he remained for three years. He was deeply influenced by Russian culture in general, and in music by the Russian 'mighty band'—especially Rimsky-Korsakov. On his return to Prague, he entered the circle of which Vítěslav Novák was the leading spirit. Excessive Russian influences were now moderated, and he acquired a stable and personal style in which a deeply religious sense, a charming and simple humour which puts him in happy touch with child life, and lingering, sometimes tragic, memories of his Russian years combine to give distinction. As a composer he has made a reputation by his interesting lyrics, his pianoforte pieces, and his music for children. His tendency is lyrical rather than dramatic, and his songs well repay study, such as *Northern Night*, Op. 14, settings of four texts by the Russian poet Balmont, which won a prize offered by the Vienna Society of Arts in 1910; the delicately descriptive picture, *The Albatross*, the Three Legends, Op. 21, which have charm and character, and *Four Songs of Farewell*.

His work tells nothing of fierce conflict—rather it converses animatedly and pleasantly. Hence his preference for small forms as in his *Fables*, for Voice and Pianoforte, in which he shows his humorous qualities. His first opera, *Hippolyte* (1916), the libretto arranged from Maurice Hewlett's novel, was followed by a charming children's opera; while in his comedy *The Ghost in the Castle*, his witty and amusing style won for this work much popularity in his own country and abroad. The subject was suggested by

Oscar Wilde's *The Canterville Ghost* and the libretto arranged by Jan Lowenbach.

It was perhaps in his many years as choirmaster of the Prague Choral Society *Hlahol* that Křička acquired his wide knowledge of the requirements of modern choral technique, for it is in his choral works that he has achieved great success. Some of his most interesting choruses are settings of poems by his brother, Petr Křička, a distinguished poet of the younger school. The composer's deep religious sense finds expression in the Cantata for Chorus, Soli, and Orchestra, *The Temptation in the Wilderness*.

Among other distinguished pupils of Novák was Jaroslav Novotny, who unfortunately perished in the last war, after writing a number of songs full of promise in their freshness of melody and lyrical charm. He also wrote a String Quartet, Op. 7, which was often in the repertoire of the Czech Quartet. Of the two brothers Jeremiaš, the elder, Jaroslav, did not live to hear the performance of his first works—an opera *The Old King* and an oratorio *John Hus*. He had assimilated much of the technique of composition from the school of Novák, but, influenced also by Mahler, his works were conceived and planned on a large and ambitious scale. The younger brother, Otakar, developed more slowly under Novák's teaching, but afterwards came under the spell of Wagner and aimed at large dramatic and choral works, which he achieved in *Zborov* and in the opera *The Brothers Karamazov*, adapted from Dostoievsky's novel. His music is powerful but often enigmatic, suggesting depths of passion under a surface of idyllic peace.

Of quite a different character is Vacláv Stepan (1889); an accomplished musician, he is perhaps best known as an interpreter of modern music. Among his most successful compositions are a Pianoforte Trio, a String Quartet, and many works for piano.

Karel Jirák (1891) gravitated from the circle of Novák to that of Foerster, to whom he owes a great deal. He has a strong sense of form, deals with his material in a deft and clean-cut style, and is at times a clever musical satirist, as in his *Tragi-comedy*, a song-cycle with orchestral accompaniment to words by Heine. His popular *Suite in the Olden Style* for Pianoforte does not show the deeper side of his nature, but he reveals this in his two Symphonies and some interesting chamber music. His fertile and creative brain revels in wit and irony, sometimes at the expense of sentiment; but the vigour and brilliance of his early opera *Appolonius of Tyana* carries the story well and incidentally discloses an influence from Strauss. He also came under the spell of Mahler, and in general developed great instrumental technique and a superfluity of brilliant ideas in modern orchestration, and in later years took an active part, not only in musical life in Prague, but in international musical circles. He was conductor at the Prague Radio and Professor at the Conservatoire, where he had much influence with the younger generation, as illustrated in Jaroslav Rídký and Anton Modr.

Boleslav Vomáčka (1887) has unfortunately composed little, but has always shown the careful nicety of workmanship and earnest purpose that stamp the true disciple of Novák. He was late in attracting notice by his Song Cycle with orchestral accompaniment ' 1914 ', while his Pianoforte Sonata, introduced to Paris by Mme Blanche Selva, became well known on the Continent. Later he devoted himself to musical criticism and has done much valuable work during his years as editor of the monthly journal of the musical section of *Umělecka Beseda*.

All the representative pupils of Novák illustrate his insistence on sound structure and the wise use of traditional forms; but no less marked is their courage in pioneer work and in new and well-considered experiments in technique. The school of Foerster on the other hand is more firmly planted in the traditions of Smetana and Dvořák, and his pupils strive chiefly for deeper lyrical and philosophical thought. This group includes some who are not directly his pupils, but have sought and welcomed his influence on their work. One of the best of these is Vaclav Kalik (1891), who reveals great lyrical and melodic resource in compositions for the piano and violin, and also in choral and orchestral works such as the Symphony entitled *The Adriatic* and *Peace*.

A link between the younger generation of Prague and the school of Janáček, which constitutes a special group of Moravian composers, is found in Emil Axman (1887), whose steady progress in composition assures him an important place in contemporary Czech music. The buoyant emotionalism which he brings from the Moravian side has been tempered by the dicipline he learnt from Novák. Thus from the rhapsodic fervour of Janáček he passes to more orderly forms, and in his later symphonies and cantatas he combines a wealth of melody with sound structure and dramatic power.

In the Moravian Conservatoire at Brno Janáček had many

pupils, though few who show it directly in their music. The compositions of Jan Kunc (1883), who as mentioned elsewhere has devoted much time and work to the collection of national folk-songs, are considerably coloured by the folk-material; but his creative output has been restricted by his activities in musical educational work, since in 1920 he was appointed Director of the Brno Conservatoire. Others who studied with Leoš Janáček are Jaroslav Kvapil, Oswald Chlubna, Bakala, and Vílem Petrželka. The last-named has written many charming songs and pianoforte pieces, but reflects in his construction the influence of Novák. His chorus *Ostrava*, the *Song of the Silesian Coal-miner*, the text by the workman-poet Petr Bezruč, with its brooding sense of rebellion against injustice, its strange subterranean rumblings and passionate outcries, bristles with technical difficulties, such as the modern choral societies of Czechoslovakia are happy to study and surmount with consummate ease. In the Cantata *Nicolas the Sailor* (1929) he has attempted a work on a larger scale and in a more developed style, into which he has introduced the ultra-modern elements of jazz, quarter-tones, &c.

In addition to these younger composers whose musical interests have been centred within the country, there is a group that has gravitated abroad. Among them is Bohuslav Martinů (1890), who settled in Paris in 1923 and in his early ballets and such works as *Half-time* (1925) betrays the influence of Stravinsky and Honegger. In his later works, however, he is definitely reverting to a more national style, a deeper emotionalism combined with greater simplicity of technique. Alois Haba is well known in international musical circles as the exponent of the 'quarter-tone' system; and another notable member of this group is Jaromir Weinberger, whose opera *Svanda the Bagpipe-player* has attained considerable success on the Continent. He has undoubtedly assimilated the national characteristics of his Czech predecessors.

The progress of modern music in Slovakia has been slower than in Bohemia and Moravia. Though the natural sense of the Slovaks for music is apparent from their great wealth of folk-songs, till recent years there was no definite encouragement and few musical centres in the country. But such composers as V. Figuš-Byštry, N. Schneider-Trnavsky, and M. Lichard, who had perforce to make their studies at foreign conservatoires, did much to preserve the folk-music; while after the political independence of 1918, a new cultural centre was established at Bratislava which produced

a younger generation of artists including Frico Kafenda and
A. Moyzes.

It is a fact—indicative of the mental indolence of the multitude
—that only the few will trouble to climb the hills of knowledge to
drink at the authentic sources of movements in art and literature.
The majority will linger on the plains, involving themselves in as
little effort as possible, and content to accept what the streams of
fashion and opportunity may bring to their feet. This is why the
initiators of certain tendencies are frequently only recognized
after their continuators have won worldwide appreciation. Such
pioneers as Smetana and Glinka in music, Signorelli in painting,
Christopher Marlowe and Griboyedov in literature, have waited
on their successors for their fame—on Dvořák, Tchaikovsky,
Michael Angelo, Shakespeare, and Gogol. And if this is true in a
general way, it is particularly true of ourselves. It is a feature of
English mentality that we are usually satisfied to plunge *in medias
res* without showing much curiosity as to the origins of what
pleases us in art. Here is at least a partial explanation of our
enthusiasm for Moussorgsky while Glinka was unknown to us,
and of the fact that we took Dvořák to our hearts when we were
content to remain ignorant of all but a fraction of Smetana's work.

But there is another and perhaps more cogent reason for our
neglect of the pioneers of Czech national music: our restricted
interest in the wider fields of opera in which many have accomplished their finest work. We have never had in this country the
kind of permanent repertory opera-house which ventures to experiment with public taste. With us, one exclusive school of
opera has merely made room for another; for years we rang the
changes upon Italian grand opera and Wagnerian music-drama,
until private enterprise brought a Russian opera company to our
doors. Before the war of 1914–18, when there was a large public
for comic opera in England, it is true that we unconsciously
absorbed something of Smetana in the music of Oscar Straus and
Lehar. But these sparks from the glitter and gaiety of *The
Bartered Bride* which reached us through Vienna were not the
real Smetana. The essential Smetana is to be found in the more
delicate Mozartian humour of *Hubička* and the dignified, epic
romanticism of *Libuše*. How should we have accepted these operas
in days when *Cavalleria Rusticana* and *Madame Butterfly* were
practically the sole rivals to Wagnerian music-drama? I believe
that had it been possible to give a selection of Czech operas in

London during the last twenty years, sung by a company from the National Theatre of Prague, adequately staged and in the spirited interpretation of such a conductor as Karel Kovařovic or Otakar Ostrčil, they would have been welcomed as warmly as was the Russian opera in 1913–14. Our appreciation might indeed have been even more unanimous; for, as operas, Smetana's works are more compact and coherent, and wrought out with greater technical efficiency. The Czech composer was a trained musician, with several years of experience as a conductor when he wrote his first opera. The reproach which we so frequently heard levelled against the Russian school, of amateur inefficiency, could not possibly be brought against Smetana or his successors.

The question that concerns us most is—what chance would Smetana's, and indeed other Czech, operas have in England? It may seem ungracious to cast any doubt at all on the question of their success; yet—greatly as I have enjoyed performances of many in Czechoslovakia—I feel that only one or two of Smetana's are suitable for production in this country: *The Kiss*, *The Bartered Bride* (which, as mentioned, has found its way to our operatic stage), and perhaps *Libuše*. The rest, even including the popular *Dalibor*, can never be to any other people what they are to the Czechs. The essential condition of their first performance would be a native cast. From this proviso it need not be deduced that the works are too restrictedly national ever to take a place in a general operatic repertory. But the first outset is all-important. What would have come of the Wagnerian tradition if the first performance of *The Ring* in the 'eighties of the last century had been left in the hands of an all-British opera company? How long would it have taken Italian opera to cast its spell upon the whole world if fate had ordained that it should be disseminated by German singers in the German tongue? With opera the value of music as a means of expression is not everything; if victory is to be won, a clear interpretation of the spirit of the work is half the battle.

The celebration of the first centenary of Smetana's birth was something more than an honour paid to the memory of an interesting composer. Never, since Tyrtaeus rallied the courage of the Spartans and launched them to victory with his songs, has any musician been so closely identified with the griefs and hopes of his race as the author of *Ma Vlast* ('My Country') and *Dalibor*. To recall the picture given by Athenaeus of the Spartan soldiers in camp ending the day by singing in turn the songs of Tyrtaeus, is to visualize immediately the Czech legionaries on many fronts during the last war—and now—gathering to sing the songs of their homeland; not merely the folk-melodies of Moravia and Slovakia, but doubtless remembering too the soul-stirring prophesies of Libuše as embodied in Smetana's operas, and the heroic theme of Dalibor, the personification of the unconquerable and music-loving spirit of Bohemia. Smetana was the consoler and uplifter of men's hearts in the dark uncertain hours of his people's history; and the Czechs, who so recently won through three centuries of oppression and stepped over the threshold of a promising future, did well to emphasize this centenary, even in the darker days now fallen upon them.

Smetana's heart responded as readily to the comic as to the tragic tone of his race. His imagination, steeped in the past history of Bohemia, enabled him to reproduce in music such typical heroes and heroines as the peasant King Přemysl, Dalibor, Libuše, and Milada; his unaffected delight in everyday human nature served him even better in depicting such purely Czech types as the stuttering yokel Vašek, in *The Bartered Bride*, and the obstinate lovers Lukas and Vendulka in *The Kiss*; while his profound love of the fields and forests of Bohemia peeps out from the bedrock of his music at every turn. This spirit, compounded of passionate patriotism and a wholesome realistic attitude towards humanity at large, lives on in Smetana's descendants, as I have attempted to show in this volume, in more varied, complex, and enlarged aspects. If in the past we have unjustly neglected Smetana's music, we may yet honour his memory by knowing more of the works of those musicians who have carried on his traditions in Czechoslovakia: Foerster, Fibich, Janáček, Ostrčil, Novák, Suk, and many others have all received Smetana's message, although each interprets it in a spirit of complete individual liberty. The time for imitation has happily passed. In their progressive methods, in the elasticity of their nationalism, which no longer seeks to impose a yoke upon their own inspiration or that of their younger disciples, the Czech composers have on the whole remained true to Smetana's ideals. These may be summed up in a few maxims: seek your subjects in the literature and the features of nature which are most familiar to you; avoid artistic pose and all that is based on mere catchwords; keep your hearts fresh and your aesthetic outlook clear. To these principles Czech music owes its vivid and spontaneous quality, and the kind of vernal bloom—derided as excessive *naïveté*—that is so easily spoilt by unsympathetic interpretation. Those who care for the music of Czechoslovakia are willing to concede its occasional *naïveté*, but recognize it as the essential emanation of a certain simplicity of soul, not as a result of technical inefficiency or lack of self-criticism. In the school of musical experience the Czechs have sat on the same bench as ourselves, and have long been lectured on their inferiority to the Germans. But for Smetana they might have accepted the verdict with apathetic resignation. Although in the post-war crisis of feverish over-activity in musical creation the Czechs, like every one else, showed signs of a tendency to fabricate trifles and call them by grandiloquent names, yet on the whole the rising generation kept sound, largely through the traditions of Smetana, whose influence has always been opposed to aesthetic grimaces and affectations. It is greatly to be wished that we may find our way back to Smetana through the medium of contemporary Bohemian music.

Though in this outline of the music of Czechoslovakia I have only been able to indicate some of the later developments, the nations which are still ignorant of such operas as Foerster's *The Unconquered*, Janáček's *Her Foster-daughter*, Kovařovic's *The Peasants' Charter*, and Novák's *The Lantern*, and many orchestral works, such as Suk's Symphonic Poems *Asrael* and *Maturity*—to mention but a few—have some leeway to make up in the progress of their musical culture. Meanwhile we salute Smetana, in Browning's words:

That was music! good alike at grave and gay!

INDEX

Adalbert, Bishop, 4.
Ambros, A., 4, 46, 63.
Apt, Anton, 45.
Arnestus, Archbishop, 4, 5.
Axman, E., 235.

Bach, 132.
Bakala, 236.
Barnby, Joseph, 135.
Bartoš, F., 133, 141, 186, 188, 232.
Bax, A., 94.
Becker, Jean, 138.
Beethoven, 43, 44, 71, 76, 107, 135, 144, 147, 150.
Benda, Carl, 21.
   František, 17, 18, 21, 22, 23.
   Friedrich, 21.
   Jan Jiři, 21.
   Jiři, 21, 22–6, 57, 201.
   Johann, 21.
   Joseph, 21.
Bendl, K., 127, 128, 130, 183.
Benevic, 201, 209.
Berlioz, 47, 62, 64, 94.
Bezruč, P., 236.
Blahoslav, Brother, 8.
Blažek, 126.
Borecky, 49.
Brahms, 107, 138–40, 143–4, 147–50, 156, 159, 164, 167, 173, 203.
Branberger, Dr., 8, 9, 13, 28.
Brandes, J. C., 23, 24.
Březina, 207.
Brixi, Fr., 17, 31.
Bruneau, A., 194.

Bülow, Hans von, 146.
Burian, E., 231.
Burney, 12, 30.

Cagliostro, 30.
Čapek, K., 218, 219, 220.
Čech, A., 74, 85, 96, 99, 129, 130, 143, 145, 167, 201, 213.
   Svatopluk, 194, 197, 200, 201, 213.
Čermáková, A (see Dvořák), 128.
Černohorsky, 17, 27.
Červinkova-Riegrova, M., 153.
Charles IV, 3, 6, 7, 108, 199.
Chmelensky, J., 48.
Chvala, E., 111, 128.
Chrysostom, John, 17.
Čížek, Dr., 81, 82.
Colles, H. C., 151.
Cyril, St., 4, 6, 16, 51, 222.
Czernin, Count, 54.
Czerny, Charles, 29.

Debussy, 94, 196, 229.
Dobrata, 5.
Dobrovsky, 66.
Dreyschock, A., 43, 59.
   R., 104.
Dušek (Dussek), Fr., 30, 41.
   Jan, 29.
Dvořák, A., 40, 73, 104, 110, 117, 124–51, 152–75, 183, 189, 193, 195, 198, 202, 205, 225.

Ehlert, Louis, 144, 156.
Eliot, George, 182.
Erben, K., 112, 159, 167, 171, 198.

Fasch, J. F., 14.
Ferdinand II, 10, 17.
Ferdinandi, Barbara (*see* Smetana), 61.
Fibich, Z., 40, 89, 104–24, 176, 182, 184, 191–3, 239.
Figuš-Byštry, V., 236.
Foerster, Josef, 126, 182.
  Josef B., 111, 182–93, 195, 229, 235, 239, 240.
Franck, César, 132.

Gabrielli, Cattarina, 26.
Gluck, 27.
Grieg, 183.

Haba, A., 236.
Habermann, Fr., 28, 29.
Hadow, Sir Henry, 31.
Halek, V., 46, 145, 154.
Hantich, 8.
Hanslick, E., 43, 105, 154, 156, 167.
Handel, 28, 161, 171, 155.
Harant, Christopher, 13.
Hartig, Baron, 14, 15, 28.
Haydn, 14, 20, 26, 31, 59, 147.
Herold, G., 208.
Hostinsky, O., 69, 100, 111, 143, 176.
Hůlka, Karel, 21.
Hus, J., 7, 160.

Janáček, L., 40, 51, 117, 167, 191, 211–27, 229, 235, 239, 240.
Jeremiaš, 193, 234.
Jirák, K., 234, 235.
Joachim, 139.
Jungman, J., 55, 66.

Kafenda, F., 237.
Kalik, V., 235.

Kalivoda, G. A., 13, 14.
Karel, R., 193, 209, 210.
Kittl, J. B., 46, 57.
Knize, F. M., 44.
Kollar, 48, 74.
  K. O. (*see* Smetana), 56–8, 61.
Komensky, J. (Comenius), 2, 108.
Kott, F. B., 45.
Kovařovic, K., 40, 69, 80, 89, 97, 109, 111, 117, 124, 130, 152, 166, 168, 176–82, 193, 199, 240.
Krásnohorská, E., 83, 85, 87, 89, 111.
Krejči, Josef, 44, 126, 140.
Kreutzberger, P. F., 13.
Křička, J., 230, 233–4.
Križkovsky, K., 49, 50, 51.
Kuhe, W., 43.
Kunc, J., 39, 40, 236.
Kvapil, J., 168, 185, 236.

Lauterer, Berta (*see* J. B. Foerster), 183, 186, 188.
Lichard, M., 33, 34, 236.
Lichtenstein-Kastelkorn, Prince-Bishop, 15.
Liszt, 47, 58–60, 62, 64, 91, 94, 102, 105, 108, 129, 135, 142, 150.
Logi, Count, 14.
Lobkovic, 125.
Lowenbach, Jan, 234.
Ludvik, Knight of Dietrich, 45.

Macha, Hynek, 46.
Machaček, 48.
Machaut, G., 6.
Mahler, 186, 188, 192, 235.
Manns, August, 144.
Martinů, B., 236.

Masaryk, President, 55, 81, 201, 213.

Methodius, St., 4, 6, 16, 36, 51, 222.

Mendelssohn, 127, 171.

Meyerbeer, 64, 65.

Modr, Anton, 235.

Mojžiš-Lom, 210.

Moscheles, I., 44, 104.

Moussorgsky, 64, 78, 153, 178, 199, 212.

Moyzes, A., 237.

Mozart, 26, 30, 41, 42, 47, 91, 110, 119, 132, 144, 147.

Mysliveček, 17, 22, 26.

Nedbal, 195, 202.

Nejedlý, Zd., 41, 64, 69.

Němcová, Božena, 181.

Neruda, Jan, 17, 46.

Mme Norman-, 105.

Nešvera, 111.

Nostic, Count Jan, 44, 45.

Novák, 40, 192, 193, 195–201, 229, 230, 235, 239, 240.

Novello, 159.

Novotny, V. J., 97.

J., 230, 234.

Ondříček, Fr., 176.

Ostrčil, O., 191–3, 213, 238, 239.

Palacky, 55, 160.

Petrželka, V., 236.

Piatti, 105.

Pichl, Wenzel, 30.

Pihert, J., 177.

Pitsch, Karel, 126.

Pojman, F., 193.

Pollini, 79, 184.

Preissova, Gabriella, 187, 212.

Procházka, L., 41, 63, 89, 136, 149, 193.

Proksch, J., 44, 56, 57, 58.

Reger, Max, 188, 209.

Reicha, A. J., 30, 31.

Reichardt, 25.

Richter, C. L., 104, 108–10, 112–14, 119.

Hans, 108, 141, 143, 149, 152, 161.

Rídký, J., 235.

Rieger, B., 44, 50.

Rimsky-Korsakov, 73, 94, 97, 233.

Ritter, W., 67, 72, 78, 86.

Ryba, J. J., 48.

Sabina, K., 63, 69, 111.

Samberk, 154.

Schulhoff, J., 43.

Seidl, A., 186.

Schneider-Trnavsky, 236.

Schubert, 128, 150.

Schumann, 105–7, 127, 150, 171, 183.

Shakespeare, 25, 189, 193.

Sibelius, J., 32, 35, 94.

Simrock, 136, 157, 160.

Škroup, 52, 53, 54, 58, 65.

Sladek, 63, 191.

Smetana, 31, 40, 44, 49, 54–80, 81–103, 110, 117, 124, 127, 129, 131, 141–3, 160, 183, 191, 193, 195, 204, 228, 238–40.

Šourek, O., 128, 129, 132, 133, 142–6, 148, 163, 173, 203.

Sova, A., 207.

Srb, J., 59, 74, 88–90, 101, 102.

Stamitz, J., 20.

K., 20.

Stainer, J., 16.

Stepan, V., 234.
Stern, Leo, 166.
Stoltzel, G. H., 14, 15.
Suk, J., 40, 192, 195, 201–9, 229, 239, 240.
Sušil, F., 50.

Talich, V., 207, 224.
Tchaikovsky, 71, 139, 183, 184.
Teige, K., 90, 98.
Thun, Count Leopold, 57.
Tomášek, V. J., 30, 42, 43, 45, 47,
Tomášek, J., 230.
Tovacovsky, A. F., 49.
Tůma, Fr., 17, 28.
Turk, 139.
Turnovský, J. T., 8, 9.
Tyrš, Dr. M., 37.

Vaclav I (Saint), 2, 4, 160, 220.
Vaclav II, 5.
Veit, V., 47.
Vesely, R., 202, 203.
Vitašek, J. A., 42, 44.
Vojaček, J., 51.
Vomačka, B., 230, 235.

Vrchlicky, 108, 112, 113, 118, 160, 169, 189, 196, 199.
Vycpálek, L., 207, 230–3.

Wagner, 44, 47, 64, 65, 71, 81, 110, 112, 115, 117, 128, 150, 169.
Waldenstein, Count, 54.
Weber, C. M. von, 43, 45, 46, 110.
Dionys, 42, 43, 44.
Weigl, 52.
Weinberger, J., 236.
Weiss, K., 124, 193.
Wenig, A., 167.
Wihan, 166, 202.
Wood, Sir Henry, 100, 224, 231.

Zach, J., 27.
Záviš, 5, 7.
Zelený, Dr. V., 91, 98.
Zelenka, J. D., 28.
Zeyer, J., 192, 203, 204, 207.
Zich, 193.
Živný, J., 13.
Žižka, J., 7, 215.
Zvoboda, 192.
Zvonař, 126.

PRINTED BY THE WESTERN PRINTING SERVICES LTD.,
BRISTOL